CAMPER'S DIGEST

3rd Edition

Edited by Erwin and Peggy Bauer

DBI BOOKS, INC., NORTHFIELD, ILL.

CAMPER'S DIGEST STAFF
Erwin and Peggy Bauer
Editors
Pamela J. Johnson
Production Manager
Sheldon L. Factor
Associate Publisher
Milton P. Klein
Publisher

ISBN 0-910676-06-2   Library of Congress Catalog Card Number 73-83467

CONTENTS

BACKPACKING:

by ERWIN A. BAUER

the Best Way to Camp Any Wilderness

LATE ON A clear, cool evening in June, my wife, Peggy, and I reached a fork in the narrow trail we had climbed most of the day. We paused there to study the weather-beaten U.S. Forest Service trail marker. In one direction the arrow pointed to "Green River Lakes .7 miles." The other fork led to "Trout Lake 1.1 miles." After consulting a topo map for several moments to make certain of our location, we turned toward Trout Lake and here the trail took a steep upward turn.

Now the going became really tough; the muscles in my shoulders and legs began to nag me. And my heart was pumping in low gear to match the thin atmosphere well above 9,000 feet. Even so sweat rolled down my body; I tried to adjust the load on my back for greater comfort, but the straps only seemed to bite deeper into my shoulders. Slowly we struggled, almost staggered to finally reach the crest of a thin ridge.

But once we gained the top, all of the soreness and the misery were forgotten. Well . . . *almost* forgotten anyway . . . because spread out beneath the opposite side of the Continental Divide was an alpine scene as magnificent and as awesome as a man is ever likely to see. Just below us was Trout Lake, a dark green emerald in evening shadows, but only one of a necklace of small mountain lakes. For a few moments we simply enjoyed that splendid scene before scrambling down to the shore of Trout Lake where we would pitch camp for the night. During a career spent largely in vagabonding around the American wilderness, I've seen few if any more spectacular campsites.

"All at once," Peggy said, throwing off her pack, "I'm not beat anymore."

Leisurely we pitched our two-person tent, unrolled and zipped together matching sleeping bags and set up a light cook stove with cookware designed for mountain trekking. Then in the gathering dusk we quickly prepared the dinner which we carried, freeze-dried and weighing very little, in individual sealed packets. I suppose it is hard to believe but the menu included beef

---

Basic Backpacking Hints

Start out slowly, modestly. Take short trips first, say maybe just a weekender during which you cover only a short distance, say 10 to 15 miles, mostly to field-test all of your equipment. Set up any tent first at home and douse it with a garden hose to look for leaky spots. In dry areas (especially in the Southwest) you may not need a tent at all; a waterproof cloth to cover your sleeping bag may be sufficient.

Keep in mind that much backpacking gear, especially tents and packs, can be rented inexpensively and this may be the best way to go. You can try out several sizes and models that way before making an investment. In many mountain or sporting goods shops, the rental you pay on a pack or tent can be deducted from the purchase price of the item. Also (in these same shops) check out the kits now available with which you can make your own tents, pack, even a light sleeping bag at home for a fraction of what the finished product would cost.

Backpacking equipment improves every year. This nylon tent for two, the sleeping bag, stove, food and sundries weighs less than 12 pounds altogether.

Tiny mountaineering stoves slide easily into a backpack compartment.

stroganoff, peas, pineapple cheesecake and coffee. It was so delicious that we wolfed it down like starving survivors of an Everest climb might have done. Sleep came instantly that night, and I only recall waking up because golden cutthroats were rising all over the surface of Trout Lake.

With five thumbs on each hand, I managed to set up the pack flyrod I'd carried in my pack and somehow knotted a fly onto my leader. Five minutes later and before Peggy had both eyes open, I had a pair of foot-long trout filleted for breakfast. But I could just as easily have caught a dozen because the trout were rising all over the lake's mirror surface.

Maybe all of the above reads like some fictional Heavenly Acres, but the place is really in the Rocky Mountains of western Wyoming. It is a region of lofty peaks and snowfields, of mountain meadows knee-deep in summer wildflowers, abundant with wildlife from tiny pikas to giant bull moose, punctuated with hundreds of jewel lakes, most of which contain trout. The highest peak in Wyoming lies in the middle of the Wind River range and another great waterway, the Green

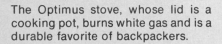

The Optimus stove, whose lid is a cooking pot, burns white gas and is a durable favorite of backpackers.

River, originates with the melting snow.

Still the Wind River Mountains are only typical of countless other, similar, high country regions which extend from New Mexico northward to Alberta, from South Dakota's Black Hills westward to the Cascades and High Sierra. All of these mountain masses have one thing in common—trail systems which vary from fair to extremely good, where travel is possible only on foot —your horse's or your own. Nowhere else on earth are there so many great opportunities for high adventure and all of it free than in western North America. All you need to enjoy it is a backpack, perhaps a tent, and some other light camping gear.

Not too long ago, backpacking was pretty much a game of the really determined outdoorsman, of the unusual guy who didn't mind suffering and lugging a 50-pound-plus pack to the most isolated places he could find. You had to be young, have a linebacker's legs and, many claimed, be not too bright. But all that has changed radically in the past couple of decades.

A well designed backpack, properly loaded can carry everything the early spring angler needs.

Hiking Boots

When buying backpacking boots, be sure to wear the same two pairs of heavy socks you will (or should) wear when hiking. Insist on a snug, but comfortable fit, with no rubbing or pinching anywhere. Walk around in the new shoes with a weighted pack on your back before deciding. If possible, try several pairs for comparison. No matter what shoes you select, they should be thoroughly, completely broken in before starting out on an overnight or difficult trip. That's a cardinal rule.

Besides all of those hiking trails (mentioned above) in the national parks, national forests and other public lands, to make the going easier, there has been an extraordinary revolution in backpacking equipment. All of the necessary gear, food and shelter included, weighs only a fraction of what it did two decades ago. Nowadays when you go backpacking, the other backpackers you will meet (and they will be numerous) will include all kinds of people from tiny tots to senior citizens. Almost half of all backpackers today (according to recent surveys) are the healthiest looking females you are likely to encounter anywhere. If you happen to be an unattached male, that alone is incentive enough to consider trying the sport. But even without the gals, it's among the richest, most rewarding experiences possible today. Backpacking simply feels good.

But let's go back to the beginning, keeping in mind that (as with everything else) there are problems and headaches as well as pleasures and pure adventure. Often the first headache is the bewildering variety and

amount of camping and packing equipment for sale today; a beginner has a hard time deciding which is best and selecting what he needs. It is important to have proper, although not necessarily very expensive gear to start out.

Consider footwear first because nothing else, not even the pack is more important when pounding steep, rocky trails. Any serviceable boots which you have used and which remained comfortable on long, hard hikes are satisfactory. Don't switch. But if starting from scratch, think most seriously about a pair of the now standard, waffle-stomper hiking boots. Developed originally in Europe for alpine hiking and climbing, this shoe is meant to give maximum support to ankle and arch. These lace from toes to ankle-high (about 8-inch) top boots have fairly stiff, lugged Vibram soles. The sole leaves an impression like a waffle pattern on the ground. The leather, which may be padded, is shaped to hold the foot snugly and should be heavy enough to protect the entire foot when traveling over rough, un-

Freeze-dried foods need the addition of hot water and this tiny snub-nosed tea kettle is well designed to do the job.

even ground. A hiking boot superficially resembles a mountain climber's boot, but it is neither as heavy nor as stiff. An excellent example of the hiking shoe is the Danner 6490 which is manufactured in Portland, Oregon, retails for about $70 a pair and which will last for many years of the hardest use.

Next in importance to footwear is choosing the pack. We should go into some detail here. First consider your own planned personal needs. Are you going to overnight on the trail? One night only or (eventually) several? Are you planning any really long wilderness trips? Will you go alone, with friends or your wife to share whatever the load?

For hiking only (no overnights), a nylon or waterproofed cotton-synthetic bag known as a daypack is carrier enough. Daypacks provide enough space to tote a rain parka, lunch, knife, matches, suntan lotion, insect repellent, camera, and so on. Daypacks can be multi-purpose, being used also for biking, fishing, hunting, or cross-country skiing. They vary in price from about $12 for the simplest to about $30 for those with zippered side pockets and large capacity. Beltpacks—light carriers that fit around the waist—are also adequate for day hikes. Some have compartments and adjustable waistbands and can carry lots of gear.

Backpacks differ from daypacks in that their great capacity is to carry enough supplies which will enable you to be self-sufficient for one or more nights. That means that backpacks can hold all essential gear—food, stove, mess kit, tent, sleeping bag, first-aid kit, survival kit, toilet items, knife, map and compass, extra clothing, raincoat—and some non-essential items such as camera and field guides.

Backpacks have become fairly standardized, with two choices: the more popular external aluminum tube

frame with the carrier bag that fits onto it, and the internal frame pack in which the frame, usually flat, fits inside the bag. The latter packs are called body packs and are more popular with mountaineers and cross-country skiers than with backpackers.

The pack itself—the nylon, water-repellant bag that attaches to the aluminum pack frame—often comes in

The Optimus 323 is lightweight and has a wind screen to protect the flame. The tea kettle's shape packs easily when not in use.

two styles: packs that have a single, large compartment and those that are divided into two or more internal compartments.

During the past few years backpackers have started carrying more weight on the hips where, for many (perhaps most) of us, it is much easier to tolerate. A wraparound hip belt transfers weight from the back and shoulders to the legs, which usually are stronger than the back and shoulders. Most of the better pack frames are now built with padded waist bands. A good pack frame will also be adjustable to better fit an individual's body.

Assume you are buying your first pack. If you plan only normal summertime camping trips of a week or less—and will be carrying less than 30 pounds—a frame

---

Backpacking-Camping Etiquette

In the past, before so many backpackers used the public trails, a hiker could plan to live off the land, at least to some extent. He could cut and burn firewood for fuel. He could trim enough evergreen boughs to make a soft trail bed. He could trap game, take a bath or wash a pile of dirty dishes in any stream. But no longer. The destruction to the wilderness became too great.

Now a new outdoor ethic is being observed. Carry a mini-camp stove and fuel instead of building an open fire. A foam mattress is better than pine boughs anyway. Always pitch a tent on rocky or hard ground, away from busy trails, rather than disturb the existing vegetation. Garbage and litter should be carried out, never buried, because animals will easily find and dig it up. Garbage should also never be burned. Carry a vial of bio-degradable soap (readily available) and use even that sparingly. Summed up: Leave behind no trace of your presence except your footprints on the trails.

---

that puts most of the load on the hips is almost certainly preferable. Carrying heavier loads than that on the hips will probably cause undue fatigue.

Load the pack with heavy items handy in the store, say 20 to 25 pounds worth, because any sack can feel good empty. Wear it full for awhile, walking around. If possible, climb some stairs. Granted, that does not duplicate how a pack feels after a few hours on an uphill trail, but it does provide a basis for comparison with other packs similarly loaded.

A brief word about beds because you need a good night's sleep after every day of trekking. Mattresses come in foam pads or inflatables, which one to pick being a matter of personal choice. I'll take foam every

time because it doesn't deflate during the night. Your choice in bags for summer backpacking is between down-filled or one of the synthetic fiber fills on the market today. Down is lighter and warmer for the weight, but is much more expensive, and once wet, no longer insulates. My vote is for less costly synthetic filled bag for summertime camping alone. But be sure to actually get inside *any* bag before you pay for it. Make sure you have plenty of room and do not feel "trapped" inside. A too-small bag is not a pleasure to use.

Exactly where to go backpacking depends on where you're located, on the time to spare and your reasons for wandering. Do you just like to explore a lot of magnificent real estate on top of America? Is your main goal photography, to watch wildlife or to try some of the trout fishing which ranks with the best anywhere? Maybe you want to try climbing a few peaks along the way. Fortunately, as I said before, there are plenty of choices and all very good.

Most veteran backpackers agree that California offers the most and the best. But California trails are also the busiest; you are least likely to escape here, especially in the popular Sierra backcountry of Yosemite and Sequoia National Parks.

But the high country of Lassen Volcanic National Park in northern California is not so crowded. Because of convenient access roads, distances are not great and hikes to lakes are comparatively short, making this an ideal place for the inexperienced backpacker to gain experience and test equipment. There are convenient campgrounds and trailheads near Summit Lake on Lassen Peak Highway (Route 89), at Horseshoe Lake via Warner Valley Road from Chester, and at Bathtub Lake south of Route 44 north of the park. A booklet, *Fish and Fishing in Lassen Park,* can be obtained at Park Headquarters, Mineral, CA 96063.

Almost the entire High Sierra of central California is punctuated with alpine lakes for a fishing backpacker. Many of the best, and most scenic are along or within reach of the John Muir Trail and its connecting links. This great trail roughly follows the Sierra Divide from Yosemite National Park, a distance of about 350 miles. From the north end, either near Hetch Hetchy Reservoir or in Yosemite Valley, to near Mt. Whitney and the trailhead at Whitney Portal near Lone Pine (on Route 395), a hiker would travel within a mile or so of 500-odd lakes of one to about 15 acres. Mt. Whitney can be climbed by strong hikers without technical climbing ability.

There is access to the John Muir Trail from the following popular trailheads: Grays Meadow from Independence; Glacier Lodge from Big Pine; Lake Sabrina from Bishop (junction of Route 395 and U.S. 6); Rock Creek Lake, Convict Lake, and Mammoth Lakes from near Casa Diablo; several points along the trans-Sierra Tioga Road (Route 120); near Giant Forest (Sequoia); South Fork of the Kings River Road (Route 180); and the Fresno Road to Lake Edison.

There are numerous guides to exploring the High Sierra, but the best is a Sierra Club Totebook, *Starr's Guide to the John Muir Trail and the High Sierra Region,* available with map for about $4 from the Sierra Club, 1050 Mills Tower, San Francisco, CA 94104. It is designed to fit in a jacket or backpack pocket.

Montana offers more high country opportunities for backpackers than any other state except California. And in Montana a hiker will meet fewer kindred spirits. In Glacier National Park alone, there are more lonely lakes than an outdoorsman might fish in a lifetime of summers. Most are interconnected by a splendid 1,100-mile trail network, possibly the finest in any single national park. At times bears have been troublesome in Glacier.

Hikers can reach the backcountry via numerous

Coleman's Peak 1 backpack and mountaineering stove makes camping, even in a snow storm, a pleasure.

Beware of Bears

In some scattered regions, bears have become a nuisance, if not actually dangerous, to backpackers. Normally the trails in problem bear areas will be closed until the animals are eliminated. Just the same, careless campers rather than bears are usually responsible for the conflict. Every backpacker should keep a meticulously clean camp. Keep foods in sealed, odor-free packages and cache or hang all food in trees far from the tent site when not in use. Never feed bears or any other animals. Especially in the grizzly bear country of Montana and Wyoming, always watch for bruins, especially females with cubs on the landscape ahead and give them a wide berth. Grizzlies are not ordinarily aggressive animals, but can be terrible if tormented or crowded too closely.

trailheads, all well marked, along the Going-to-the-Sun highway, especially those at McDonald Falls and Logan Pass, from Many Glacier via Babb (U.S. 89), at Kintla Lake Campground, and from Two Medicine via East Glacier (U.S. 2 and 49). The most magnificent mountains and much of the best fishing are in the northern half of Glacier Park, and in Canada's adjoining Waterton Lakes National Park. A "Hiking Trail Map of Glacier National Park" by Gingery and Wilhelm can be obtained at Park Headquarters (West Glacier, MT 59936) or any roadside ranger station.

Generally north of the Cooke City to Red Lodge highway (U.S. 212) is the Beartooth Primitive Area, covering parts of the Custer and Gallatin National Forests. Amid awesome upside-down landscapes are some 300 lakes that contain trout. Some trails to major

lake areas are very well marked but others are so little used as to be faint.

There is a lot of backpacking potential in Wyoming, and I have already mentioned the Wind River Mountains, which is the state's best area. Access is from Pinedale on the west side of the range, or from Riverton or Lander on the east. A splendid guide, *Wind River Trails* by Finis Mitchell is available for around $3 from Wasatch Publishers, 336 P St., Rock Springs, WY 82901. The Teton Mountains are well-known, in fact too well-known, for backpacking, and during midsummer the trails are too crowded to be enjoyable. But there is much less congestion in the Bighorn Mountains of north central Wyoming.

Arizona's best backpacking adventure is the trip down into Grand Canyon from North to South Rim, or vice versa, over the Colorado River and back again. But like all summer backpacking in similar hot, arid places, including New Mexico and the five national parks of Utah, there is the special problem of carrying enough water to last at least one day on the trail. Utah's Bryce and Zion Parks, plus Dinosaur National Monument, have excellent trail networks which are well marked. Utah's Uinta Primitive Area north of Duchesne and Roosevelt is top backpacking country. The same is true of the entire, super-scenic Sawtooth National Recreation Area north of famous Sun Valley in central Idaho.

Olympic National Park in the extreme northwest corner of Washington boasts a fine system of tracks through lofty, misty backcountry, but the one drawback here is damp weather during mid-summer and early fall. Also very cool and moist, but incredibly beautiful on sunny days is North Cascades National Park, also in the state of Washington. Always carry foul weather gear and a no-leak tent in these two places.

Summed up: Nowhere else on earth has a hiker and backpacker ever had it so good. So why not make the most of it?

Camping With Baby

by KATHLEEN FARMER

RELATIVES rejoice when a child is born and at the same time assume that the parents' fancy-free days are over. A really good mother, it is understood, puts her child first and subjugates her own desires to second, third, sometimes last place. Selflessness characterizes successful motherhood. Unfortunately this often results in a cranky baby and a tense and tearful mother.

The mistake occurs when family tradition locks the nursery behind four walls of a house. The best nursery of all is the whole outdoors. An infant surrounded by the same stuffed animals and a set routine is often bored and irritable. Mothers feel sorry for themselves and count the days until the offspring can begin kindergarten.

The salve for a troubled maternal instinct or a fussy infant is often the warmth of the sun, the caress of the breeze and the ever-changing scenery of nature. Leave the diapers in the pail, the dishes in the sink and get away from it all with the little tyke.

For first forays plan short outings close to home. You will soon become convinced that your offspring will get as much of a kick out of an outdoor adventure as you do. A change of scene and brisk exercise is the "upper" everyone needs.

Visit the zoo or a city park or walk around a farm. Introduce your child to other children. Let him hear their contagious laughter and see their madcap antics. Youngsters celebrate their existence by climbing the ladder to a slide, jumping rope or chasing a ball—all vigorous actions with lots of noise to entertain the tot still too young to join in the fun. A brighter outlook is infectious, and the brightest ones are beneath the expanse of the horizon.

After a few introductory sightseeing trips to gain confidence in the soothing and regenerating power of the outdoors, advance to activities like hiking and camping. Hiking offers the most exhilaration with the least amount of preparation and equipment. A hiking mother needs two things: a good baby backpack and a pair of sturdy, comfortable hiking boots. The backpack must feel comfortable and ride easily. With wide, padded straps that do not bind the shoulders, the frame should be wide and long enough to distribute the weight of the baby evenly. What may be satisfactory when the baby is still very small may not do with the larger, heavier burden. Think ahead and get a single backpack which will serve until the child walks.

Anyone can support more weight on the hips than on the shoulders. For this reason an elongated frame with a "belly band" is ideal. Attached to the frame and worn around the hips, this belt-like feature keeps the pack close to the back and passes much of the weight to the hips.

Some outdoor mothers remove the baby carrier pouch from its original frame and attach it to an ordinary backpacking frame. Designed to carry 35 to 40 pounds of gear, these frames are sturdier, better fitting and more comfortable. They are also more expensive than those built into a baby backpack, but by insuring a strain-free back they are well worth their price. You may already have one which can be converted to carry the baby.

From a backpack perch the baby is part of camping activities.

Dress both yourself and the baby for comfort during the day. Sun hats are especially important for babies with scant hair.

A portable bassinet also used at home is familiar and easily carried along.

Depending on the model, the baby can face toward the mother's back or away, riding backwards. Our baby has both types and does not seem to prefer one over the other. However, she is able to stand up on the foot bar and exercise her legs in the forward facing pack. A child who is active can usually be carried more easily in a front-riding model since a sudden lurch backwards can endanger the mother's balance.

Rocky, creviced trails can tire the ankles and the whole balancing system of the baby-toting mama especially as the child grows older and heavier. Sturdy hiking boots with Vibram soles and padded ankle supports transforms drudgery into pleasure. The added weight of the baby makes such boots indispensable.

Hiking at the correct speed is vital. The hiker *cum* baby must find the pace which enables her to walk long distances easily. That means a speed leisurely enough not to bring on early fatigue, yet fast enough to cover a reasonable amount of ground. A usual hiking speed for the ordinary outdoorsman over even ground is about 3 miles per hour. Your own pace will be faster or slower depending on physical conditioning, the weight of the infant, the difficulty of the trail and mental attitude.

The way a person perceives a challenge determines how well she will weather its trials. For example, on a hot day with a crying baby on your back, you reach a point on the trail that seems to ascend vertically. The hiker can either say, "I can't make it," or "Look where we're going next, baby. Up to the sky."

Of course there are ways to maintain a good outlook longer and to bolster a sagging attitude. First, dress properly. If your path traverses heavy brush or intrudes on populations of flies, ticks or mosquitoes, wear cotton slacks, a long-sleeved shirt and a wide brimmed hat for protection. Bring a lubricant for dry lips, an insect repellent to ward off pests, a canteen of water. Dress the baby likewise and don't forget the hat. Sunburn on an infant's sensitive scalp can haunt a mother long after it's past. Apply insect repellent at the beginning of the trip. (Concentrated lotion is more effective than spray or foam. However, spray is good for insect-proofing clothes.) Bring along baby's favorite drink (not milk) and raingear. While you hike, talk to your little papoose. Point out the sights, flowers, insects, the view, clouds, rocks and butterflies. Both of you then become more concerned with the surroundings than your personal comfort.

Back and leg muscles require conditioning to carry even a small infant easily. Unaccustomed to backpacking, begin with short walks. Start with 30-minute jaunts and work up from there. Soon your muscles will be in shape to tackle a mile or two of unpaved hilly terrain.

Walking with 10 or 20 pounds on your back forces you to breathe deeply and slowly. Unconsciously you take long strides and breathe in time with your pace. You stand straighter and seem to walk more easily than you did before. Suddenly you develop a purpose to hiking. Reaching a destination is secondary to feeling the movement of your own body propelling you and your baby toward new and interesting sights.

No matter how well conditioned you become you will find you reach a point where a break is needed. Then rest and munch a snack. Trail goodies provide quick energy and give you the perfect opportunity to eat sweets without feeling guilty about gaining weight.

13

With the exercise of hiking, calorie intake is being rapidly converted into energy. Candy bars, breakfast bars, beef jerky or gorp (a mixture of shredded coconut, M&M candies, Spanish nuts and raisins) are ideal. Salt lost through perspiration should be replaced by eating salty food like peanuts.

All babies love the closeness and motion of riding on mother's back. Many fall asleep and awake only when mother stops for a rest. Even at home the baby may seek the solace of being carried on mother's back during fussy periods. Primitive culture babies have always had this comfort.

Camping is another fun but simple outdoor activity to attempt with baby. The sleeping arrangement is the most important aspect. To fall asleep he needs to feel comfortable, secure and warm. At our home our daughter Brittany napped daily in a portable bassinet that could be folded and stored in a car. At 5 months of age when she accompanied her parents on a 10-day camping trip along the California coast, we packed the bassinet along as her sleeping bunk. Even on damp chilly nights in March in the brisk ocean breeze she slept warm in a polyester sleeping bag (it measured 24 inches x 36 inches) purchased from a discount store. It would be easy to sew one at home from an old blanket. For cold nights she wore a blanket sleeper and a hooded sweater too. To our surprise she slept warm and comfortable when we felt the cold permeating our Fiberfill II sleeping bags. A catalytic heater can warm a tent during a really cold night.

Polyester sleeping bags keep inactive tots warm on brisk camping days.

The secret to fun outdoors with a young child is simplicity. Simple food, disposable diapers and plenty of time to explore nature together. Brittany Farmer plays in the sand on the James River.

Food on an outdoor excursion should be simple to prepare yet nutritious. Use instant and dehydrated food as much as possible. Instant cereal, disposable bottles and fresh fruit like bananas cut cooking time to a minimum. When venturing outdoors leave the home routine behind, especially the chore of preparing formulas and sterilizing bottles. Purchase canned or bottled formula and try it out at home to be sure it agrees with your baby. If it does, bring a supply on the camping trip. Of course the nursing mother can just skip this altogether. Pre plan each meal and make a checklist of these foods as well as other items. Then the baby's cup, pacifier, or apple juice won't be forgotten.

Camping should be living outdoors comfortably. With a baby along there is extra work and there should be a specific division of labor between husband and wife. If the mother will take over chores relating to the baby, the father should use that time to help set up camp. While one parent feeds the infant the other could be making a cup of instant coffee. Only by working as a team can both husband and wife enjoy the threesome on a camping trip. If the wife/mother is burdened with *all* the chores, she rightly feels resentful.

Cleanliness is a major concern of all mothers and can be difficult without running water, a sink or bathtub. In terms of the camping spirit, she should relax the high standards upheld at home.

A baby need not be bathed daily. By using pre-moistened towelettes (such as Wet Ones) hands, face and diaper area can be thoroughly cleaned. The bath can wait for a warm day or a heated bathhouse. Because most babies dislike showers, a large plastic basin can be packed and used as a tub as well as a sink for the outdoor kitchen. It can even be a crib for a really tiny babe. Baby oil conditions dry skin and zinc oxide ointment guards against diaper rash. Raw little bottoms are helped by a little sunshine to the area.

Some women associate the outdoors with danger. Most potential perils are blown out of proporation. Perhaps the biggest hazard to personal safety is the

Instead of a daily bath, a dip in the lake will do on an outing.

possibility of getting lost. However this should not discourage campers from venturing afield. Prevention is the key here. Constant attention should be directed toward the whereabouts of children. Hikers should not attempt a short-cut across-country unless expert with map and compass. By following a trail or stream the fear of getting lost can be alleviated. Always bring the tot with you (into the tent, the outhouse, boat, garbage can, water spigot), and he cannot wander away unnoticed.

Preparing a very young child for the panic he'll feel when lost is a near impossibility. Survival experts recommend that children (and adults, too) wear a shrill whistle on a string around the neck. Because the shriek a whistle emits can be heard better than the loudest human voice rescuers can find the lost child more easily. A few "getting lost" drills at home in the backyard might be a good idea.

Our Brittany is now 19 months old and is fascinated by nature. She entertains herself as well as me by collecting rocks, sniffing wildflowers, watching birds and digging for worms. Even though she likes the feel of fish she does not yet appreciate fishing. Boating, on the other hand, thrills her. But once the boat stops she wants to get out. Sitting patiently inside a canoe waiting for a fish to hit a lure is not yet her idea of fun. So for now I find little time for fishing and concentrate most of my day outdoors observing the entrancing world of nature through her. While I am not as free outdoors as I once was, I profit from seeing a worn world afresh through the wondering eyes of a youngster.

Our outdoor experiences with Brittany have been mostly positive. On one occasion however, we camped at a waterfowl refuge in Missouri during September. We came to photograph ducks, geese, herons and egrets. After a night full of Canada goose serenades we woke to find our daughter's tiny face a mat of welts. Mosquitoes had found her a sweet morsel. I still wince from abdominal pangs of guilt although there was no lasting damage to the baby.

As Brittany grows up we change our routine for a smooth running camp. She is too big for the bassinet now and sleeps in a sleeping bag on a foam pad next to us. She stays awake until we slide in our bag. This, obviously, encourages us toward "early to bed and early to rise," but the early mornings are the best hours of the day anyway.

The food regimen is simpler, she eats adult meals at regular hours. Once in awhile though she tries to sneak a sand pie or rock sandwich just to remind us she's not entirely grown up quite yet.

Having introduced our little girl to the outdoors, she is more of a companion to me than a burden. I look forward to a new outing just to witness Brittany's reaction. Camping with baby offers a break from routine for all three of us. Charlie, her dad, also shares in her awakening awareness and fascination with the wild world around her.

Which Are America's Most

1. **Canyonlands National Park.** Anyone who loves the desert could hardly find a better place to camp than Canyonlands National Park. Two wild rivers, the Green and the Colorado, have eroded and carved the landscape until it resembles the surface of another planet. Campers can explore this awesome country by land, or they can take a powerboat-camping trip from the town of Green River down the Green to its junction with the Colorado, then up the Colorado to take-out at Moab. This 200-mile journey can be made in 3 days, but this leaves little time for enjoying the many attractions of the river. For instance, the channel cat fishing is very productive here, and there are old mines and abandoned Moki cliff dwellings to explore. Ancient Indian paintings decorate many cliffs. For those without their own boat, river tours are run frequently. The campground at Dead Horse Point, accessible from Moab, offers a magnificent view of the park. The temperatures here are most pleasant in spring and autumn, but generally this park can be considered an all-year possibility for campers.

2. **Tongass National Forest.** To me, Tongass National Forest in Alaska may offer the best camping adventure of all. To get there, you go to Juneau by daily Alaska car ferry from either Prince Rupert, British Columbia, or from Haines or Skagway, Alaska. About 10 miles from Juneau is a main campground at Mendenhall Glacier. From here the excellent king and coho salmon fishing out of Auke Bay is easily accessible, and during the runs there is also other

Exciting Campgrounds?

Here are my lucky seven!

(Opposite page) Camping in Canyonlands in Utah, is a memorable experience for the backpacking tent camper. This lightweight nylon shelter with its huge zippered windows lets cooling breezes waft through while the separate fly on top traps an insulating layer of air for comfort. This tent could hold four.

by

CHARLES NANSEN

The angling camper proudly poses with this beautiful, big brown trout.

fishing in such streams as Montana Creek. Rangers at a nearby visitor center lead tours around the blue ice of Mendenhall.

But that is barely a beginning. The Forest Service has built a system of about 50 camps consisting of a cabin or shelter and a boat on remote and scenic lakes and streams all around. Access is by charter float plane flight of 5 to 30 minutes at a cost of $50 to $100 depending on distance. A few camps can be reached by hiking. Camp rental is $5 per day per party, or a Golden Eagle Passport. Dolly Varden, rainbow, searun cutthroat, grayling and salmon fishing is good-to-sensational. Hunting for goats, blacktail deer, and bears is possible in season. Be sure to take your raingear. It can be very damp here, so go prepared.

3. **Farragut State Park** Once a U.S. Naval Training Station, Farragut State Park in Idaho, is large enough and has enough facilities to entertain the World Boy Scout Jamboree, which it did in August 1967. Family campers will enjoy a visit to the area; there's plenty of space in which to roam. Located at the south end of Lake Pend Oreille, the park is 4,566 acres in size, and has 50 campsites for tent trailers or pickup campers. There is even an outdoor amphitheatre that seats 50,000 people. Most visitors, however, come here for the fishing, which is famous. Kamloop and Dolly Varden trout are the species you'll catch in the lake. In fact, the world record for both species was taken here. The park operates a boat dock and launching ramp, and there are numerous bays ideal for safe boating with craft of any size.

Montana campgrounds beside famous trout waters offer angling for beautiful brown trout like this.

In addition to the angling attractions, there is an improved swimming area with a capacity of 2,500, and for hikers, trails lead to many high points and scenic outlooks. Wildlife watchers will also find this park a hotspot, for the area is loaded with whitetail deer. Altogether, Farragut State Park is one to watch; it may soon be the showplace of the Gem State.

4. **Helena National Forest.** Montana is full of excellent camping places, but Helena National Forest is one of the most unusual. The mountains here are studded with the ruins of long-forgotten gold and silver mining camps, where more and more campers are discovering the excitement of poking about in ghost towns. Elkhorn is one of the most interesting. Marysville and Granite are others. A whole summer can be spent visiting these historic spots.

Varmint hunting for marmots is productive and non-residents do not need a license for it. There are rainbow trout in Canyon Ferry Reservoir and jumbo brown trout in the Missouri River near Helena late in the summer. Montana Fish and Game Commission officials believe that the Missouri hereabouts is the best place for an angler to catch a bragging-size trout. Creel censuses annually bear this out.

One particular campsite at Gates of the Mountains on the Missouri River is accessible only by boat. Lewis and Clark camped on this exact spot a century and a half ago. It is still one of the most spectacular campsites anywhere—at least anywhere that I have ever seen.

5. **Myakka River State Park.** Luckily, this piece of real estate just east of Sarasota, Florida, was spared the logger's ax and the "development" that has drained the life and beauty out of so much of the state. Now set aside as Myakka River State Park are 29,000 acres along the Myakka River and its backwater pools. Fishing for bass and panfish here is extremely good, as is small-craft boating. But the main attraction is native wildlife in its natural habitat. Alligators, so rare elsewhere, are easy to see here close up. More than 200 different species of birds have been observed in the park, and upwards of 3,500 different kinds of plants, trees, and flowers have been cataloged.

To see the wildlife, which also includes deer, turkey, armadillos, and raccoons, there is a daily safari via a 60-passenger trackless train that winds through the sub-tropical forests, hammocks, and marshlands. Even more exciting is the nightly tour, when the small wildlife can be seen nearby with powerful

A stringer of delicious bass rewards this fishing camper who pursues his sport in a tube rather than a boat. With special foot paddles he can maneuver himself into tight shallow places where lunkers hide.

7. Rosebud Sioux Indian Campground. History surrounds you at the camping area owned and maintained by the Rosebud Sioux Indians, located beside the White River in the heart of the Great Plains. One feature sure to delight the youngsters (a lot of adults too) is the fact that if you wish you can rent a genuine Sioux tepee for $5 per night. There is a spring-fed swimming pool near the campground, and Indian ponies can be rented at low rates for rides into the surrounding South Dakota hills. Sioux boys will lead you over the same trails where once their ancestors stalked U.S. Cavalry patrols.

This is an excellent place to learn about the Plains Indians and their history at first hand. Close to camp nightly tribal dances are held, and a fine Indian museum is located at adjacent St. Francis Mission. Actually, this whole area is of interest. To the west is the Wounded Knee Battleground, and not far to the north is the Badlands National Monument (with another campground), a unique area of eroding cliffs and pinnacles, the site of some tremendous fossil finds. Noted for its beauty on moonlit nights.

Seeing real Indians while on a camping trip is a thrill for the children—and many adults as well.

spotlights. And at sundown there is an excursion to a 40-foot tower in a remote marsh farm from which you watch thousands of birds—herons, egrets, ibises—return to a treetop rookery.

6. Quetico-Superior Canoe Country. Canoes or light boats are the only means of transportation in Minnesota's Quetico-Superior Canoe Country, a roadless region made up more of water than of land. All food and equipment for your stay is loaded into your craft, and then you're on your own, free to stop wherever your mood dictates or nightfall finds you. Fishing for walleyes, smallmouth bass, perch, and northern pike is good throughout the area, and it improves in direct proportion to the remoteness of the water.

To enjoy a camping trip into this truly wilderness country, you don't even have to own any gear. Outfitters in Ely, Minnesota will rent you everything from the canoe and tent to sleeping bags, utensils and a waterproof map of the region. They will also work out your food needs for you and supply you with the provisions. Of course, if you wish to keep costs down, you can bring part of the gear yourself. All you need, though, is a knowledge of canoeing— and in some cases you don't even need that. Guides can be obtained if you wish. This "campground" offers a rare opportunity to really get away from today's world.

National Seashores: Our Newest

(Above) Some of the most beautiful rocky seashores in public ownership are along Route 101 in Oregon. Cape Perpetua can be seen in the background. (Opposite page) Skinny-dipping on deserted beaches is a delicious treat as the sun goes down.

PERHAPS the island received its name from colonial whalers who built huge bonfires on the beaches. And there is evidence that marauding islanders once lit fires to lure passing ships aground for looting. But more likely Fire Island was "named" by a myopic tax clerk who incorrectly copied "Five Islands" into the records. But no matter, because today, as Fire Island National Seashore, it is among the most valuable bits of real estate in public ownership anywhere on earth. It is also the most recent addition to a recreation system unique to America.

Americans have always felt an affinity for ocean beaches—for the magic mixture of sand, sun and surf in summertime. So it came as a shock for many, not too long ago, to discover that nearly all of these lonely saltwater shores had vanished. Of the 60,000 miles of

shoreline in the United States, excluding Alaska and Hawaii, only 21,000 miles of these are considered suitable for recreation and only a fraction remain in public ownership—some 366 miles on the Atlantic coast and 296 miles on the Pacific. Of course, that wasn't enough for the millions whose greatest pleasure was an escape to the beaches. Not too late, hopefully, a system of National Seashores (or National Seashore Recreational Areas) was established in 1953 by the Federal government to be administered by the National Park Service. Fire Island, only a few miles from Manhattan, was one of the most recent of seven acquisitions. Unlike the national parks where the major aim is complete protection of natural values, the main goal of the National Seashores is for recreation such as camping. They are vast, sandy playgrounds where Americans

National Treasures by ERWIN A. BAUER

can go tenting, swimming, fishing, beachcombing, boating, bird-watching, scuba diving, dune-climbing, hiking, horseback riding and exploring.

Take Hatteras National Seashore for example. No one really knows how many ships have been wrecked upon the treacherous shoals. But the ships' skeletons can now be examined by the passerby when they are exposed by shifting sands. The region was declared the first of the National Seashores in 1953. It is a thin 70-mile long stretch of shoreline from Nags Head to Ocracoke Island, North Carolina.

The Hatteras surf fishing is world famous and it deserves to be. Every year, large schools of channel bass, rockfish and bluefish migrate just offshore. Splendid fishing is also found in sheltered Pamlico Sound just west of the Seashore. Hatteras is naturally a favorite with campers and seven manicured campgrounds have been provided for them.

Another beautiful shore which has somehow escaped exploitation, even though only 30 miles north of San Francisco's Golden Gate Bridge, is Point Reyes. It became a National Seashore in 1962. Not many shorelines anywhere are as picturesque as the mixed, high coastal bluffs, offshore rock islands and watery caves of this California park. Colonies of sea lions clamber out onto exposed rocks to sunbathe. Saltwater ponds and marshes attract other birds and wildlife. Some villages and ranches still remain within the area, but there is talk that eventually all of the land may be purchased for recreational use.

Padre Island, Texas, is a ribbon of white sand from ½-mile to 3 miles wide extending for 80 miles along the Gulf Coast from Corpus Christi to Port Isabel. A good part of it is pure wilderness without dwellings or development. It is a rare place where a family with a 4-wheel-drive vehicle can have a chunk of seashore all to themselves, where the fishing is great and where coyotes serenade at night. The beach here is the loneliest in the National Seashore system. For some, that alone is the greatest recommendation.

Cape Cod National Seashore offers the other extreme. The Pilgrims—America's first campers—found shelter from the wild Atlantic behind the Cape's protective barrier. But they couldn't possibly believe the busy scene they would find on any summer's day 3½ centuries later. One third of all American citizens live within a day's drive of Cape Cod and a good many of them go to see it, if only briefly. Fishing is excellent, but mostly in autumn—after the crowds go home. Most summertime visitors are satisfied with the antique shops, whaling museums, seafood restaurants and art studios in Provincetown and thereabouts. Trails lead hikers over the dunes and along low cliffs above a noisy surf. In midsummer, campgrounds are crowded and gay. Away from the campgrounds, escape is possible, but just barely. Still, this is an immense national treasure of 44,600 acres and 46 miles of shoreline.

Owners of 4-wheel-drive vehicles and beach buggies are allowed by special permit onto certain, more isolated portions of Cape Cod. Here they can camp and fish somewhat away from the crowds. However, it is first necessary to meet certain insurance requirements and to carry along emergency equipment to obtain the permit.

Assateague is a 33-mile-long sandy barrier reef—the largest undeveloped seashore remaining between Massachusetts and the Carolinas. The only permanent residents are wild ponies which survived the wreck of a Spanish cargo ship long ago. Fishing and swimming are especially good during the summer.

Fire Island, New York, and Cape Lookout, North Carolina, are the newest seashores. Fire Island was established only 3 years ago, and although Cape Lookout was authorized by Congress at the same time, it is still waiting for the state of North Carolina to donate the required land. Few facilities yet exist at Lookout and none at Fire Island. Nor has all the land been acquired. To date, Fire Island is roadless between isolated communities, making 4-wheel drive by far the best means of transportation.

The National Seashores have matchless appeal for the vacationer, no matter whether the holiday is leisurely or vigorous. No one ever forgets the sound of the surf and screaming birds, nor the sight of breakers rolling in and washing the beach clean. Morning and evenings are the greatest time of all here in the yellow light of summer.

(Above) Fishermen at our national seashores hook into an endless number of species. This is a nice dolphin taken in Florida waters.

(Right) A moveable summer cottage like this fold-out camper trailer makes a fine dwelling for seaside campers who swim, fish or snorkel like this couple.

CAMPING SAFETY

THERE'S NOTHING like a camping trip to help you relax. To wake up to the clear morning air, spend a day in the outdoors, hiking, fishing, canoeing or relaxing by the water's edge, and then to turn in for a good night's sleep in your airy tent and warm sleeping bag—that's what camping is all about.

You can help to insure a fine experience by taking a few precautions. The secret to camping safety involves one basic principle—common sense. You're careful at home; you should also take care in the wilderness.

Be Prepared

Do a little research beforehand about the area you'll be visiting on your trip. Knowing the wild flowers and the wildlife in the vicinity will enrich your stay, and also prevent poison ivy or ground squirrels in your food locker. Follow the weather reports and survey the climate some too. Make sure your gear: tent, sleeping bags, and outerwear are adequate for the weather you'll be experiencing.

A good first-aid manual is a must. The reference information a manual like this provides is invaluable in many circumstances, from treating bug bites to soothing the sunburn you picked up this afternoon.

Choosing a Campsite

When camping today it's easy to find a comfortable site to pitch your tent. And you can choose the amenities you want to have close at hand. Fresh water is provided by most established campgrounds. But if you are really going to "rough it," carry an adequate supply of your own water with you or be prepared to purify natural water supplies.

You can camp out in the open if you like that spacious feeling, or pick a spot under strong trees for a more secluded view of things. When surveying the ground where you'll pitch your tent, take a look upward too because dead limbs could cause concern in unexpected high winds.

If camping by water, watch the high water line. Set your campsite well above it to insure a dry spot for your entire stay. Be careful in areas prone to flash flooding.

Fire

Since campfires are often part of the fun of camping, fire safety is important. Unwatched campfires can spread and cause unnecessary damage and injury. It's easy to prevent even minor accidents if you pay attention to a few simple rules.

First and foremost, obey the law. Build campfires only in areas where they are allowed. If you are truly in the wild, use your common sense and basic boy or girl scout rules. Build your fire well away and downwind from your tent on bare ground. Choose an area protected from wind and breezes and clear it of small twigs, leaves and other flammable materials.

Keep your fire small and controllable. Never leave a fire thinking that it'll go out by itself—regardless of how late it is when your evening songs and marshmallows are finished. Break up coals and spread them. Then give them a good soaking. Turn over branches to make sure that they're not still burning, then soak the site again. When all the ashes are floating where the campfire used to be, you're finished.

Even if you're cooking on a stove, do it outside and well away from your tent. One important *don't* is the use of candles, matches, kerosene lanterns or other flame sources in or near your tent.

At the Campsite

There's really nothing unusual you have to do to guarantee that your trip will be a safe one—again, it's

No matter how benign the weather looks, a boater should wear a P.F.D. (personal flotation device). It could just save a life.

merely a matter of common sense. If you canoe, you and everyone else should wear a life jacket. When swimming, use the buddy system—never swim alone or dive into unknown waters. Make sure that an adult is present whenever children are in the water.

When cooking over a campfire directly on a homemade grill, make sure that what you're using is not a shelf from an old refrigerator—many were coated with cadmium, which is poisonous.

Hiking alone is breathtaking. The sound of the trees in the wind, and the bird calls all seem magnified. But take a map and compass—it's still possible to get lost and wind up walking in circles. Also arrange a signal of sorts—such as three blasts on a whistle—which your family or group can use if someone gets lost or has an accident. And don't forget to take the whistle!

While camping, watch the weather for early signs of storms and be prepared. Keep a flashlight available in a convenient place, and know where it is at all times. (See *Predicting the Weather* elsewhere in this book)

Naturally, you'll want to know ahead of time what kind of climate you'll be camping in and select your equipment accordingly—or make sure that what you already have is adequate. A three-season sleeping bag will do in almost any kind of weather, as will a tent that keeps you reasonably cozy.

Even when you're well-prepared, the weather may surprise you. In that case, when temperatures are dropping far below what you originally expected, pitch your tent out of the wind and place sleepers close together for added warmth. Wear several layers of lighter clothing, instead of one heavy outer garment. The layers can be removed or added as needed.

If you'll be spending several consecutive days in cold weather, you'll want to make sure that you eat enough to keep your body well-fueled. Hypothermia—the reduction of body temperature—can be fatal. It can be caused by getting wet, the lack of food, harsh winds, or a sudden drop in air temperature. Symptoms include shivering, loss of appetite, uncoordinated movements, loss of contact with reality, and/or hallucinations. Someone experiencing any of the symptoms should stop all activity, get into dry clothes, drink warm liquids and cuddle or snuggle up next to another person to get warm again.

A Few Last Words

Your camping trip this summer can prove to be a success with a bit of foresight and day-to-day thoughtful behavior. In fact, it will probably be one of the best and easiest vacations you've ever had—one that you'll repeat again and again.

Note: Some of the above material is released through the courtesy of the Coleman Company.

summer in Montana's Glacier National Park.

We selected Glacier because it is immensely scenic, the wildlife is abundant and wonderfully available for photography. We met our guides at St. Mary early one morning, with only our cameras and personal gear; the outfitter furnished everything else as packers always do. There was a riding horse and one pack horse per person, but we did not have to do the packing. Then from a trailhead along Going-to-the-Sun Highway, we rode northward in single file through some of the most stupendous real estate on the face of the earth.

During the week's wandering, we covered about 5 miles of the park's more than 1,000 miles of marked trails, pausing in a new and idyllic campsite each night. The trails traversed lofty ridges and meadows so lush with mountain wildflowers as to resemble bright oriental tapestries. Herds of white mountain goats stared down dully at us from dizzying cliffs. One morning, we aimed cameras at a moose strolling through camp as breakfast cooked, paying no attention to us or the aroma of our coffee and bacon. Marmots always whistled from rock slides at our passing pack string and, late on in the afternoon, we had a rare glimpse of a grizzly

Cast iron skillets and smoke-blackened coffee pots are part of every camp kitchen.

A cluster of tents beside a mountain lake will be the campsite tonight.

Nightly camps in awesome scenery are part of the lure of a pack trip.

bear crossing a purple field of lupine. But it was too far away (somebody said fortunately) to film, even with a telephoto lens.

We seemed to live at least 14 days during that week-long Glacier trip, always amid scenes of extraordinary beauty. The trout fishing was fast, and we encountered only 15 other humans along the trails. Three of these were youthful backpackers, and the others were also having the holiday of their lives pack tripping.

Pack tripping is not inexpensive, and there is a good explanation for it. The average outfitter must maintain and feed a string of horses all year for a season which lasts 4 or 5 months at the most. In 1979 presently pack trips are costing about $65-75, per person per day, for groups of four or five. The rate was lower for larger parties and especially for any who were willing to help with such chores as pitching camp and cooking meals. For many these chores are only part of the game. It is also possible to negotiate a reasonable family rate with many of the best outfitters.

Most outfitters carry a bow saw for larger cutting jobs. This old sheepherder's stove will soon be warm enough to heat water for washing and later to fry steaks and sizzle hash browns.

Perhaps the best advice for a first-time pack tripper is to join one of the numerous trips which are organized and sponsored every year by such groups as the National Wildlife Federation, The Wilderness Society, American Forestry Association or Trail Riders of the Canadian Rockies. These are made annually with starting points ranging from Arizona and New Mexico to Alaska, at whatever time is ideal in any given area. With a capable naturalist assisting the outfitter, these are also outstanding bargains, most costing $50 to $65 per day.

Recently a new kind of mountain adventure has evolved—called the pack hike, or hiking trip with pack stock. It is really a compromise between backpacking, which requires top physical condition, and pack tripping, which can be expensive.

On a pack hike, each traveler walks rather than rides,

Pristine scenery and crisp clean air far from daily cares make pack trippers return year after year to refresh their minds and bodies.

but carries only a lunch, camera and whatever else he may need during the day. He uses a small rucksack. Meanwhile, the outfitter moves the camp and all gear ahead to the next overnight stop where all is waiting at the end of the day. These trips are made in easy stages, particularly at first, so that hikers of only modest stamina can participate. Costs run as low as $25 to $35 per day because no saddle horses are required. The Wilderness Society alone sponsors about 20 separate pack hikes annually. We made one of these across Wyoming's Gros Ventre Mountains, which was fairly typical. It spanned 10 days, cost $400 per person and was a high point last summer.

Pack trips may not be for all. Sudden summer squalls are are inevitable in those cool altitudes on top of America, and they can temporarily dampen a person's spirits. There may be times and places where mosquitoes are a nuisance but never so much that a good repellent will not discourage them. At times, horses may be balky and campfires smoky. Maybe ice will form on the water bucket at night, and the closest thing to a hot shower will be a sponge bath in a cold brook. But real hazards are few, and we have never known a serious accident to occur. Most suffer at least some knee stiffness or a charley horse in the thighs, but this becomes bittersweet at the end of the day around a campfire. Campfire sessions seldom last very long, however, because sitting astride a horse all day at high altitudes has a narcotic effect. Invariably all hands turn in early. In one way that's a shame, because they miss hearing the soft night sounds peculiar to that lofty portion of the world.

Children—whole families—probably love pack trips best. But we have met grandparents, "young" men and women well past 70, who were having a whale of a time. Here also is that rare opportunity to eat ravenously, shamefully, and never (well, maybe never) gain a pound of weight during the whole trip. He is a rare pack trip cook who does not ply his customers with wholesome, robust and at times even gourmet fare. If riders do not actually lose weight, claims one of our outfitting friends, then the riding redistributes weight to where it looks much better. Or so he convinces the ladies.

It is difficult for us to write about pack trips without sounding like paid publicity agents; we have seen too many salmon-colored sunsets, deer staring at us along the trails and have caught too many rainbow trout in virgin lakes. So let a Maryland mother speak for her whole family (and us) after a ride over the top of Wyoming last August.

"It's the best way we've ever found," she beamed, "to make the most of our summer holiday together."

But the best thing about any pack trip anywhere is that you're a better, wiser, healthier person when you finish than when you began. The memories will be even more indelible than the pictures in your camera. You're ready for the treadmill once again.

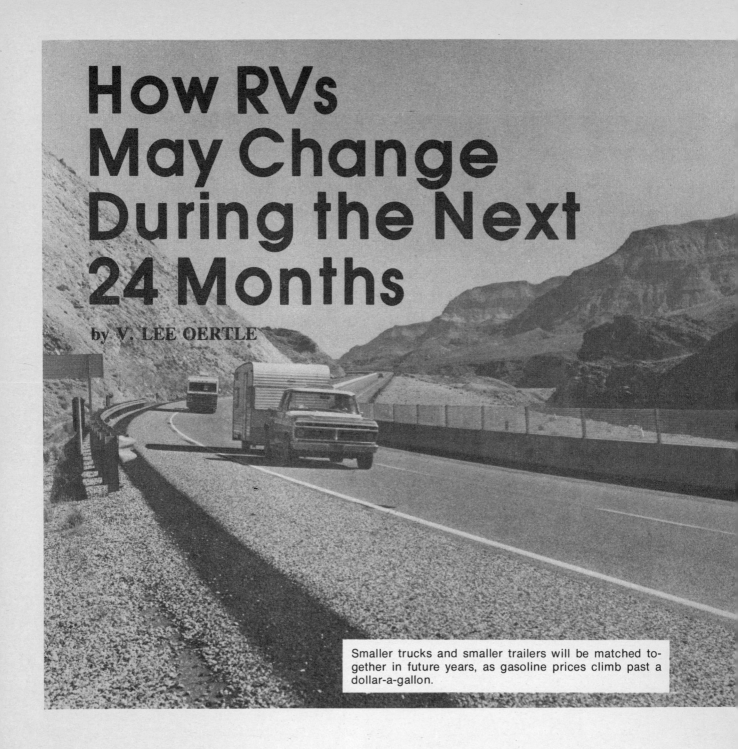

How RVs May Change During the Next 24 Months

by V. LEE OERTLE

Smaller trucks and smaller trailers will be matched together in future years, as gasoline prices climb past a dollar-a-gallon.

COMFORT HAS its price. In an RV, comfort is usually defined as extra floor space, wider aisles, longer bodies, taller ceilings, more closets and drawers—in short, everything we can do *without* when gasoline prices skyrocket. Cruising the freeways, it's difficult not to notice other drawbacks to over-weight over-long, over-tall coaches. Changing lanes amid busy traffic requires greater space and tighter control. Panic stops to avoid lousy drivers creates greater strain on brakes when 10,000 pounds is riding the wheels, to say nothing of the coronary squeeze such stops produce on the driver.

Many national parks, and some private campgrounds, limit the size of RV's to 26 feet in length, sometimes even shorter. That means more difficulty locating scenic camping sites. Lost time seeking turnaround space. Precious vacation time wasted searching for adequate large parking spots around restaurants, city parks, and rest areas.

On the open road, jumbo-sized RV's are first to suffer when hard winds blow, and last to reach the top on steep grades. Faced with detours around highway construction, some RV's require help to negotiate a sandy wash or a rocky road. Occasionally one is blocked by tunnels, overhanging trees and similar obstacles.

Off-road vacations, where many of us drift to find quiet campgrounds, are more difficult for owners of RV's that exceed 25 to 28 feet in length. It's a simple matter of arithmetic. Thirty feet is more difficult to turn around than 18 feet. Jumbo-sized models must sometimes be laboriously backed down narrow mountain roads while their drivers search for adequate turnout space. It's no laughing matter when you're high on a rainy mountainside, perhaps towing a small boat that's nearly invisible behind the gargantuan contours of a deluxe motorhome. Bad moments, all. No exaggeration is intended here. The larger the RV, the more problems a vacationer will face.

As if that wasn't enough trouble, the final insult is faced at the gasoline pump. At over a dollar a gallon, new priorities are being thrust upon American consumers. Budgets already strained by inflation and high taxes have to bend somewhere, or break. That means cutting down on unnecessary operating expenses, for one thing. The deck seems stacked against large RV's no matter how current sales figures support them. The fact remains—big RV's must go. In the natural scheme of things, facing new realities dawning with the 1980's, it's logical to expect the following changes in RV's during the coming decade.

One of the big reasons pickups will dominate the trailer-towing scene is shown here: the ability to ford streams, climb hills off road, get over large rocks is much superior. Fifth-wheel trailers will also emerge as the top seller, numerically, one day.

Folding tent-trailers can be towed by almost any car, offer little wind resistance, and provide a large amount of sleeping space.

31

Some sportsmen consider this combination ideal—4X4 station wagon towing compact trailer. Advantage of a trailer allows parking and leaving it at the end of the road while occupants hike or drive away where trailers could not be towed.

Loss of size. This need not mean loss of comfort. Only faulty reasoning presumes that large enclosures of space indicates quality. The truth is that the larger the RV, the more physical strain is eventually dumped onto the driver. The tension of gripping the steering wheel during a storm, high winds, or driving over icy roads has to be experienced to be understood. In the future manufacturers will offer medium-sized RV's with luxury equipment that has been scaled down and trimmed down to manageable proportions. Up to one-fifth the weight of current RV's will be lopped off during the next 24 months as manufacturers get serious about previous promises. Beyond 1982 models, and certainly by 1985, at least one-third the gross weight of motorhomes will have to be shaved to maintain a decent position in the marketplace. It's not just a matter of taste, but of waste. Our country simply cannot afford the unconscionable consumption of metals, plastics, and steel that over-sized models demand. Raw materials shortages are looming in some industries already. Cost-factors may force some RV makers to a choice: either scale down in size and weight, or increase prices so high that fewer consumers can afford their products.

Facing those inevitable events, RV manufacturers will be dragged (kicking and screaming, perhaps) into this realization: reduce sheer size, but compensate with new luxury and comfort packed into downsized RV's. What does that mean? Try some of these possibilities:

Interiors will be customized to individual taste. Virtually every model will be available with special upholstery, thicker mattresses, better carpets, improved no-squeak hardware, better vision, and extensive use of convenience options.

*Self-propelled models (motorhomes, mini-homes, truck campers) will ride on *improved suspension systems* that provide a sports-car feel to units two or three times heavier than compact cars. Leveling devices already available for static (parked) camping will be designed for RV's underway. That is, engineering will make every effort to remove road-sway, wobble, pitch and yaw from bothering RV occupants. Air-hydraulic systems may take much of the tilt out of RV travel, in coming years.

Lighting will be added around the exterior to provide safer camping. Examples: undercarriage lights near tire wells. Lights near the holding-tank drain. Mercury-switch lights to operate when outside access bins open to reach water heater, cargo storage, trunk, propane cylinders, and so on. All these areas have been dark spots. Lighting a gas water heater while holding a flashlight, perhaps with a fierce wind howling, is no easy task. Any hardware that frees one hand is worthwhile. Yard lights around the RV, too, are useful— perhaps operated by a photo-electric cell (when activated at the campsite) so that no one need step outside in complete darkness. Such ideas will one day occur to RV makers, and we can hope for them by the mid-1980's.

The range of all internal tanks and reserve storage will be *increased,* at least optionally. Gasoline tanks

It's expensive to lug around all that weight, thus motorhome manufacturers will scale them down in size, weight, and engine power. Despite their thirsty habits, motorhomes are popular.

will be doubled in size on models able to carry the extra weight. Optional extra tanks will be available on most all self-propelled RV's. Propane cylinders of larger capacity, water tanks with greater volume, 12-volt storage batteries of longer ampere-hours duration—steps in this direction will conserve fuel by requiring fewer trips out of a backcountry campsite to obtain a fresh supply.

The above options will of course add some weight, if utilized, but the owners of such special models can exercise discretion in useage. Over the highway, for example, they might carry only the minimum amount of fuel, water, and propane. At the edge of backcountry, fill such tanks to increase the range afield. It makes sense.

The useage of new RV's will become *more functional.* Sportsmen will benefit directly by such optional features as fish-cutting boards, hanger-hooks at all outside corners, slide-out dining tables built into exterior walls, insulated storage bins, and outside access ice chests.

New softer paint tones that blend with outdoor surroundings will come into favor. Influence of van-campers may create scenic mural paintings on the side of trailers and motorhomes, as well.

RV construction will steadily evolve toward tighter, draft-free, more heavily insulated coaches. Double-pane and even triple-pane storm windows, thicker floors, better door and window seals will stabilize interior temperatures and reduce the cost of heating and air conditioning. Smaller appliances can do such work in that improved environment, thus reducing both the overall weight and the fuel consumption of such appliances.

Electronic monitors will do a much better job of advising RV campers when batteries are low, water tanks are depleted, holding tank is full, propane supply is dwindling, and even tire inflation pressure needs attention. It presently requires several minutes to determine all those readings, and none too accurately at that. Such devices will be well worth their cost and weight by eliminating such problems as running out of water in the middle of a shower, or losing fire on range burners because the LP-gas suddenly ran out.

Which categories of RV's will be the hot sellers of the next decade? We predict that the following trends will soon develop:

Fifth-wheelers, already booming, will continue their strong surge because pickup trucks will replace family cars for heavy-duty towing jobs. American cars have already become so small that suspension systems will not handle the increasing hitch-weights of jumbo-sized RV's.

Travel trailers will remain the top seller during the next couple of years, numerically, but fifth-wheelers may overtake them by 1982.

Folding tent-trailers (which the industry calls camping trailers) will enjoy a new surge of popularity because they can be towed by much smaller cars. They also offer the most amount of sleeping space per RV dollar invested. The price of RV's will be as great a selling factor as compactness, however. The plain fact is, RV prices and gasoline prices have both reached painful levels at the luxury end of the scale. Bargains can still be found, will continue to be found, however, in modest-sized units. Surprisingly, there is no rush to build smaller RV's. Most manufacturers seem inclined to wait and watch, hoping for a return of the dinosaurs so recently in disfavor during the fuel pinch of early 1979.

Truck campers, after a near 10-year downtrend, may again achieve the popularity they once enjoyed. As larger, heavier mini-homes and motorhomes offered greater space enclosures, truck campers lost favor, unfortunately. No other RV can match a truck-camper for certain types of vacation travel. Off-road, sportsmen find them unbeatable. Pickups with 4-wheel drive offer that added advantage, too. (Although a few vans are now available with the 4X4 option, production levels are so low that there can be no comparison with pickups fitted with this option.) The smaller cars become, the more likely it is that American consumers will find a pickup truck and camper coach a sensible alternative to towing large trailers. (Fifth-wheelers are

Here's another reason that tall RV's get into trouble: Entrance to west Yellowstone area is blocked by low archway that some RV's cannot get under. Roof-mounted air conditioners, bicycles, and other gear carried on roof pushes them over the limit.

expected to defy this trend, because a certain segment of the buying public will always insist on larger models. Retirees and full-time RV travelers fall into this class.)

Fishermen, backcountry campers, hunters, and other adventurous types have a tendency to pay more attention to the rigging of special options on RV's. These trends may develop, too:

Wide tires may be displaced by high-pressure radials, more use of duals, and other tires that get better fuel mileage and longer life both on and off pavement. Low-pressure tires ordinarily do not enjoy the long life of conventional tires, but much depends on the driver's habits, the terrain, and the load endured.

Stick-shift transmissions will *not* recover the lost market they once enjoyed. New automatic transmissions are so efficient that only an expert driver could extract much of a fuel advantage by using a manual model. Automatics are too firmly entrenched.

Powerplants will not change drastically for several years. And contrary to some reports on this matter, diesels will not earn a large share of the RV market. Price differences between gasoline and diesel fuel shrink each year. During the recent pinch, diesel reached a plateau only a few cents per gallon below

gasoline in some areas. The availability of diesel fuel is also in question, at times, and of course, diesel engines cost much more to buy and to repair. Their defenders point out that diesels usually provide longer service and more miles before replacement is needed, and the point is granted. However, federal agencies have announced that diesel emissions may contain exhaust pollutants that are suspected of causing cancer in laboratory animals. If that proves true, diesels will be a long time winning large-scale followers in RV's.

The RV within the next 2 years will begin to display a new concern for weight and outside dimensions, but don't expect anything drastic to take place. We are entering a phase of gradual replacement, not of radical departure. RV makers are too much aware of consumer habits to rush into anything too different, too fast. But change is definitely in the wind, and we fervently hope nothing interferes with the long-needed transformation of the American RV. Making a good product less fuel thirsty and more cost-conscious will be a refreshing reward.

Taking a big rig off-road? You'll need extra ground clearance, tight turning circle and good traction, to reach the end of the trail. Motorhomes penetrate a surprising way, but other RV's pass them.

BOOKS FOR THE LIBRARY

by MARGARET REID

Shelters, Shacks and Shanties, by D. C. Beard, Charles Scribner's Sons. This small paperback, originally published in 1914 will be as necessary as the axe to the outdoorsman who wants to build any sort of temporary or permanent dwelling from materials at hand in the wilderness. Only that axe, a crosscut saw, mason's hammer and rope must be transported to the site. While some of the materials mentioned will not be used in these modern times (it is an easy matter to substitute polyethylene sheets for tar paper and foam mattresses for balsam boughs) the majority of the information in this how-to manual is as applicable today as it ever was. Beard, one of the founders of the Boy Scouts, was an early conservationist, advising against cutting more than was necessary and wanting any dwelling to be a part of nature. The chapter headings include "How to Build Elevated Shacks, Shanties, and Shelters," "The Adirondack Open Log Camp and a One-Room Cabin," "Cabin Doors and Door-Latches," and a very useful triad of chapters on building a fireplace and chimney, building the fire itself and tending the hearth. The illustrations are original line drawings, many showing better than a photograph could, the proper way to perform the particular job required.

Health Plants of the World Atlas of Medicinal Plants, by Bianchini and Corbetta, Newsweek book. A large, handsome volume with exquisite full page paintings by Marilena Pistoia of each plant. There are several paragraphs on each plant giving the geographical origin and where it is found today. Medicinal properties are listed in rather scientific language but there is a complete glossary for the lay reader. Also included is an appendix giving the particular plants which cure ills in categories such as the digestive system, cardiovascular system, skin, genitourinary system, etc. Properties attributed to the plant from mythological to modern times are described, too. Some "defend the heart," while others are a cure for warts or a poltice for the removal of freckles. In modern times many of these benefits have been found to be quite real.

Back to Nature in Canoes, A Guide to American Waters, by Rainer Esslen, Columbia Publishing Company, Inc., Frenchtown, N.J. 08825. Every vehicle on the road with a canoe strapped on its top should have this guide in the glove compartment. After a brief opening statement the book takes each of the lower 48 states (and a bit of Canada too) in turn listing all canoeing waters which are shown on an accompanying map. It describes each trip in the area, the scenery or lack of it, the trip's length, what you will need and where it can be secured locally as well as canoe rental agencies. In all it describes over 1,000 rivers, tributaries, ponds and lakes. In case anything necessary has been omitted, the book also lists with each state available literature with even more information.

The Official Boy Scout Handbook, by William "Green Bar Bill" Hillcourt, Simon & Schuster. Far from being a childrens' book, this is a whole set of field guides in one. Not only does it cover identification of birds, reptiles, mammals etc. and their habitat, it also branches out to concerns which Boy Scouts in past days never thought about: the environment, conservation, energy, community problems. Today's scout's motto, "be prepared," has not changed, and by following the instructions and diagrams here, he is prepared to help in a startling variety of emergency situations, among them: flood, broken bones, fire. There seems to be too much space allotted to cutting trees for various purposes and the tools needed for this, but other than that, this is a surprisingly up-to-date little book at an equally surprisingly low price. Norman Rockwell's scouting paintings reproduced in full color make this an attractive small volume for any camper.

Great Outdoors Guide to the U.S.A. & Canada, by Val Landi, Bantam Books. This enormous 854 page book is the most complete guide to all the U.S. (including Alaska but not Hawaii) and Canada available. In an area by area order each state or province is described as to terrain, history (both natural and man-made), weather and hunting, fishing, camping, backpacking and most other outdoor activities one can imagine. Charts of trophy fish taken, lists of booklets to send for and areas of special interest are clearly listed. For such a massive undertaking, a surprisingly large percentage of the information is accurate. The great problem with "current" guides is that they are soon out-of-date and so it is with this one in certain areas. The book has several beautifully drawn maps but unfortunately they are too small in scale to be of much use. Soft pencil drawings by Gordon Allen of animals, still lifes, and scenes are found throughout. These and the black and white photos add much to the reader's sense of place.

Two in the Far North, by Margaret E. Murie, Illustrated by Olaus J. Murie, Alaska Northwest Publishing Co. (second edition). This delightful book could be categorized as adventure, a love story, a travelogue or an environmental plea. It is all of these and more. Here young Margaret arrived in the Far North (Alaska) in 1911. In winter any blankets touching an outside wall in the Fairbanks home are stuck fast with frost by morning. "We all learned to be fast walkers, growing up in Fairbanks," Mrs. Murie states while describing the daily winter journey to school with her three friends. Later she falls in love with and marries Olaus Murie, distinguished biologist, and describes their travels in the vastness of wilderness Alaska, its grandeur and beauty. We learn of gold mining, dog sleds and of her own changing role from timorous bride to full partner with her husband. How does the frontier woman feed a husband (and later a family) while maintaining a trapline? She describes the precious personal relationships that develop between people when population is thin and meetings few. In this new edition additional chapters are added concerning the tremendously important D-2 lands and parks issue which concerns not only Alaskans but all of us. These magnificent areas can be preserved for future generations just as the young couple found them so long ago if we act wisely now. Anyone with a bit of adventure in his soul, with the smallest dollop of heart, will enjoy this little brown covered book.

Trees of North America and Europe, by Roger Phillips, Random House Inc. Over 500 species of trees common to the temperate regions of the world can be easily and quickly identified with the aid of this full color photographic guide. To use it the reader matches the leaf of the tree in question with its photograph in the front of the book. He then turns to the indicated page in the rear where the trees are listed alphabetically by Latin name and where it is illustrated by flower, fruit, bark and mature silhouette. An index of common names is also included. Interesting bits of information may be learned: the monkey puzzle tree for example, originated in Chile and Argentina and its nuts were served as a dessert in that area. In the 19th century a visiting Englishman slipped a few into his pocket and brought them back home to Britain where the tree was successfully cultivated.

The Natural World of the Texas Big Thicket, Photographs by Blair Pittman, Texas A & M Univ. Press. This is a book to be enjoyed at leisure. The green and delicate floor of the thicket, its birds, mammals, and plant life are all here. The forward by William A. Owens describes this unique area and the obstacles overcome to preserve it for the future in the face of industrial greed and personal cussedness. Whether one knows the Big Thicket already or not this book will help the camper better appreciate whatever he will see in his journeys anywhere.

Guide to Rocks & Minerals, Edited by Martin Prinz, George Harlow and Joseph Peters. The American Museum of Natural History, Simon & Schuster. With over 600 pages this guide is an entire geology course. It is divided into two sections: the first concerns minerals with a text and diagrams far too involved for the casual reader. But this is followed by 276 entries, each with a stunning color photograph of a single mineral and information on its rarity, uses and history. The second section on rocks follows the same plan and describes 101 of them under the three basic categories: igneous, sedimentary and metamorphic. The rank amateur rockhound will page through this book looking for a particular specimen, but he is soon seduced into reading more about rocks and minerals in general. Everything he might like to learn is included in this single volume.

Whitewater!, by Norman Strung, Sam Curtis and Earl Perry. Macmillan. Recently there have been numberless books published on this subject, but this is the one to select. Beginning with the hydraulics of water itself complete with diagrams and directional arrows and proceeding to boating techniques, *Whitewater!* takes the would-be boater to any river or stream and shows him—before he begins—what the water holds and how to work with the forces involved. Inflatable rubber rafts, canoes and kayaks are each discussed with information on their characteristics, limitations, selection and care. Black and white photographs and line drawings illustrate better than the written word just what is involved. And what is involved is probably more than you thought!

Guide to Natural Wonders of the West, by George Sykes and David Sumner. Stackpole. From the title one would expect this guide to include Grand Canyon, Yosemite and Yellowstone Park. It mentions none of these, for this is a volume of what the authors call "alternatives." Here are areas of great beauty and wonder which are in a vast network of unspoiled and under-publicized publically owned domains. They belong to us all. Red Rock Canyon for example, only 15 miles from the throbbing casinos of Las Vegas, offers a magnificent setting for the archaeologist who can find evidence of prehistoric cultures dating back to 8,000 B.C. A remnant of the Old Spanish Trail can be seen as well as wildlife including bobcats, badgers and coyotes. There are also feral burros which destroy vegetation and foul waterholes driving off the native desert bighorn sheep which the Indians knew. There is spectacular geology and a fine assortment of wild flowers in the early spring. Never heard of it? That's why it is in the book along with all the others. The authors plead that users of these areas preserve them for others to come, both by their deportment at the time and by prodding Congress to continue to protect them from intrusion and development in the future. This book should be consulted before any western vacation, especially by those who have seen the "name" places and yearn for a less crowded, more leisurely pace.

The Milepost, Alaska Northwest Pub. Co. An indispensible guide for anyone going to the Great Land, Alaska. Now in its 31st edition this guide to everything covers not only Alaska, but also Yukon Territory, British Columbia, Northwest Territories and Alberta. There are maps and mile-by-mile logs of every major highway in Alaska as well as major travel routes through western Canada. The traveler knows exactly what to expect: camping, fishing, gasoline, food, motels and major attractions. Ferry schedules and tariffs are listed as well as all railroad information. Areas, cities and tiny hamlets are listed with all pertinent information. There simply is nothing you could want to know about travel in Alaska that you couldn't find in this justly famous large-size paperback.

Wildlife Country. How to Enjoy It. National Wildlife Federation. Leaping from subject to seemingly unrelated subject, this book, with its profusion of beautiful photographs, includes chapters on adventurous trips with the whole family, high country horseback, wildlife photography, equipment and a host of other information including recipes for use in the outback and the use of map and compass. For every kind of camper from the winter cross-country ski tourer to the velvet footed bird watcher this volume offers valuable information.

Take Your Boat
—or Any Boat—
Camping

by TOM HARDIN

ONE BRIGHT and balmy day last spring a Florida carpenter, Will Svoboda, announced that he was taking a week's vacation with his wife Olive. He had recently traded a smaller boat for an 18-foot runabout and was in the mood to take it fishing. After all, fishing is never better in the Sunshine State than it is in springtime.

But when a week and eventually 10 days passed, and Bill did not return to work, his employer notified authorities that he was unaccountably missing. A search and rescue operation began immediately. Friends feared the couple was lost. But when they were finally "rescued" by a team of game wardens, the Svobodas couldn't have been healthier or having a happier time.

The new runabout was anchored in a quiet bay when the wardens found it. Will was lolling in the sun on a sleeping bag and foam mattress while Olive cooked breakfast on a small camp stove. Soft music from a Cuban station was coming from a portable transistor radio. It was an idyllic scene and certainly a neat way to be "missing."

"Suddenly we just discovered boat camping," is the way Bill explained his absence to his worried boss and to newsmen. "And I'm sick that we didn't try it a long time ago."

But Bill wasn't speaking for himself alone. In recent years more and more Americans are learning about this new kind of holiday on the water. Camping from a boat is high adventure which any boat owner can enjoy. More importantly, it is also a way to explore and see our country's greatest natural wonders from an entirely fresh viewpoint. Most of all, it is the one sure way to escape crowded highways and the congestion of land-bound camping which is sometimes a fact of summer life.

There is no single formula or pattern for a boat-camping holiday. You can sleep and live aboard the boat or go ashore at night to make your camp; this depends on the number in the party and the size of the boat. Perhaps you can even sleep aboard the boat while trailering it to a boat-camping destination. The latter is worth considering, if only for the lodging bill it saves.

Many boat campers may prefer to pitch a permanent camp at one especially attractive site and then to use it as headquarters for fishing, swimming, beachcombing, waterskiing or whatever. Others would rather go vagabonding every night. Either plan is possible because of the vast water areas which are scattered so conveniently across North America.

What equipment does anyone need to go boat camping? It depends, of course, but the case of my neighbor, Lou Sands, is a good illustration. Lou already owned a fishing boat, and had a wife, two small, active boys, and a beagle. He also had the same equipment—a light tent, sleeping bags, stove, cooler—he had purchased for car camping trips 2 years before. Early one Sunday morning he loaded the whole works, dog included, into his boat and started on a camping trip to Fort Peck Reservoir in Montana.

During the next 2 weeks the Sands were soaked by a summer storm, suffered now and then from mosquito bites and sunburn, dropped a camera overboard, and once were temporarily lost. Inexperience worked against them at first. But they never knew a holiday exactly like it. Each night they beached their boat and

Most boats can be modified slightly to carry tents and cooking gear. This way each night can be spent at a different place with no crowded highways to worry about.

camped in a different lonely bay, often while mule deer watched them from the bluffs above. The kids hunted for fossils and agates. They returned tanned and tired and already planning when and where to make the next boat camping trip.

All hands learned a lot from that first venture because boat camping is a real course in self-sufficiency. Lou is handy with tools and has considerable ingenuity—and so he figured out how to make better use of odd spaces for storage in his boat. He traded a 3-burner stove for a 2-burner model because it better fitted one of these odd spaces. He also installed a cooler beneath a boat seat, figuring it could double as a bait box when he went on fishing trips. Finally Lou swapped the dinnerware for a nesting set of dishes and utensils which required only half the space. The tinkering can go on long after the trip is finished.

With few exceptions, boat camping is not an expensive holiday. It may be necessary to acquire some extra camping equipment, but all of it can be used for a long, long time. You already have the boat, so why not use it? And any boat from canoe to luxury cabin cruiser can be converted to a camper.

For one or two persons on inland waters, a canoe is a

(Right) To keep cameras dry and film in one place, use heavy plastic bags like these Zip-Locks.

39

These bags not only keep the contents absolutely dry but even float if accidentally dropped overboard. They consist of an inner compartment surrounded by an air bag. The air cushion guards against bumps, too.

Simply planning a trip can be fascinating for everyone in the family. Once you have selected the area, make out a grocery list. Calculate next your fuel requirements and then add extra for emergencies. Gasoline is readily available on most boating waters, but be sure you know exactly where and carry along a few extra gallons anyway.

It is unfortunate for boat campers that we have not kept our waters cleaner than they are today, for drinking water can be a problem. Always carry your own supply if you plan to camp away from approved and improved campgrounds. Sometimes lake or river water is safe enough for cooking if vigorously boiled. But why take chances. Carry along the water you need or buy a portable purification outfit. Plastic bleach bottles with handles are excellent for carrying water aboard a boat.

About the only problem with food is having enough on hand for huge appetites. It's good advice to depend on non-perishables—canned, concentrated and freeze-dried foods. Then supplement by buying fresh foods whenever possible along the way. Shoreline farmers are happy to sell fresh eggs, green garden veg-

Boat campers can spend the night or a weekend, on shore in a roomy tent while fishing the shoreline or motorboating to neighboring areas during the day.

dream to use. If it is square-ended and you have a small outboard to fit, so much the better. With such a combination you can pitch your tent and build your campfire on remote shores which even the other boatmen cannot reach. By the same token, larger boats can safely cross larger water areas to reach places the canoe can't.

Generally speaking, small boat owners will have to do their camping on shore while large boat owners can unroll sleeping bags on deck when night begins to fall. In the morning the beds are rolled up again and the same deck becomes a breakfast area—and later a living room. However, it is possible to convert even small boats into sleepers for one or two campers. The trick is to make a hinged plywood sandwich board which fits out of the way on the boat floor during the daytime. At night it is opened and spread across two or more boat seats and then beds are unrolled on top of it. An overhead canopy is easy to rig with a sheet of canvas, ropes and perhaps using oars or paddles as tent poles.

As in any other kind of outdoor adventure, planning is important. First, you decide where to go. Next, if the area is large or unfamiliar, you'll need charts and maps. That's easy enough because most state watercraft or conservation departments have boating water maps which are available free or at little cost. Many petroleum companies also offer boating charts of important recreational waters. These are very handy because they show launching sites, marinas and fuel depots as well as campgrounds. More and more campgrounds are being built for exclusive use of boaters.

etables, smoked country sausage or bacon, butter, honey, cold cider, roasting ears of corn or frying chickens.

On one Wisconsin boat-camping trip I will never forget, Frank Hanson and I made a game of trying to live off the land. Other boat campers might give it a whirl too. Fortunately fishing was good and we always had plenty of walleye fillets on hand. But we also gathered wild greens, mushrooms, froglegs, and enjoyed a rich turtle soup. Frank had caught the main ingredient—a large snapper—by setting a baited bankline overnight. At other times on other waters, a boat camper might find nuts or oysters, clams or crayfish, wild berries or fruits.

A great deal of experience in either boating or camping is not necessary to try this exciting kind of holiday, but certainly it helps. It's very sound advice for beginners to try a short shakedown trip before proceeding on an extended cruise. Weekends are great for this; one weekend trip will give every member of the family a chance to adjust, and it will reveal any deficiencies in equipment.

An inflatable rubber boat collapses into a bundle the size of a suitcase and can be stowed in the car's trunk.

A foot pump inflates this Explorer Sea Eagle. With its shallow draft it can drift up to lunkers in weedy edges and float over just submerged fences and tree stumps found in impoundments.

41

Lightweight boats can be used to shield campers from a chill wind off the water.

Each year more and more group boat-camping trips or cruises are organized, usually by boating clubs, and these are good opportunities for beginners to quickly learn from experts. If you do not already belong to a club which sponsors camping cruises, watch the outdoor or boating columns of local newspapers for announcements. Local boat and marine dealers also can supply information on such trips.

Group trips are particularly pleasant experiences for more gregarious boat campers. They combine the extreme sociability that exists around every campground with the convivality of an evening around a typical yacht basin with cocktail flags flying and somebody strumming a guitar. Some groups trips are ambitious and cover vast distances of difficult water, while others are leisurely and nobody works hard at anything except getting a suntan. But it is all great fun.

Just as many boaters, however, see summertime as a chance for delicious escape. Having camping gear aboard makes it all the easier. If they choose, these escape-boaters can see magnificent corners of America which too few of their fellow citizens ever see. Take Yellowstone Park for one example: In an average summer, 2 million people visit the park, although only a handful ever leave the pavement. But with any craft from canoe to cruiser, it's possible to see the lonely,

lovely backcountry around Yellowstone Lake. Here it is also possible to see an extraordinary amount of wildlife in its undisturbed natural habitat, some of it close to Plover Point campground, located near the center of the lake. While other campgrounds are bulging, you can usually have Plover to yourself because it is only accessible by boat.

Or for even higher adventure, how about a boat-camping trip through the labyrinthine waters of Everglades National Park, down the Rio Grande through the deep canyons of Big Bend National Park, Texas, or up through the inland waterway past British Columbia to Alaska? All of these would require more elaborate planning, but all have been done before, and the doing becomes an incredible memory.

I have been lucky enough to wander widely around the world, in boats as well as by other transportation, but one adventure which must rank with the most memorable of all was a short boat-camping trip through what is now Canyonlands National Park in Utah. The cast included father and son, Beaver Bill and Lee Howland, my oldest son Paul, and me. The time was in June, just a few summers ago.

Fifty years before, Beaver Bill had made the same 196-mile trip down the Green River (from Green River village) to its junction with the Colorado River and up

Modern boat trailers can carry even large boats easily and safely over any moderately good road.

the Colorado to Moab. He had no motor on his wooden rowboat, and spent 15 days on the journey. We had sleek new outboards on two fiberglass boats and took only 5 days, although we could have done it in one. Still, 5 days was a short time to explore such country.

Besides our camping gear, we carried food, water, fishing tackle and a Geiger counter to prospect for uranium. Catfish were about as hard to catch as getting a bait in the water, and one awesome canyon scene followed another as we traveled deeper down the Green, almost to impassable Cataract Canyon, where it was necessary to turn sharply left and begin laboring up the murky Colorado.

We poked into lost mines and explored the ruins of the Mokis, a race of cliff dwellers which mysteriously vanished from this stark land centuries ago. We also examined Moki petroglyphs on red canyon walls. These revealed that bighorn sheep, deer and bears lived there in primitive times. Only the deer remain today.

We camped wherever night caught up with us. The first chore after pulling ashore was to build a big driftwood fire for cooking and to ward off the chill of a desert after dark. Then Beaver Bill would dig the Dutch ovens from under a pile of duffle and begin cooking a dinner ample enough for twice as many campers. Finally we unrolled sleeping bags on the ground and slept under the Utah stars. If it happened to rain, which it didn't, a tent was handy in the boat.

Long before sunlight ever penetrated into the canyon the next morning, Beaver Bill had another fire and another tasty meal cooking. Soon we were underway again, past such picturesque places as Anderson Bottom, Rattler Gulch, The Slide and Deadhorse Point. The trip seemed to end as soon as it began.

Boat-camping trips too often end that way. But then you have a boat, why not discover that for yourself?

A lightweight aluminum boat is easily transported either on a boat trailer or on top of the vehicle. With a little motor it can take anglers to secluded coves like these in the northwoods.

TENTS

What's Available, How to Choose

IF OMAR the Tent Maker were alive today, he would be a very busy man indeed. Never has there been greater interest in the outdoors, in fact some of our public lands are being loved to death. There is scarcely a new labor contract drawn which doesn't add another holiday or two to the calendar and more leisure hours plus a population whose age bulge is now entering the 15- to 40-year group just adds to the potential tent user pool.

A great number of manufacturers have come into the recreational equipment field in recent years and there is keen competition among them to produce a better, more innovative product at a lower price. They join the traditional manufacturers. It is private enterprise at its best and the customer, the tent buyer in particular, benefits.

What's Available

A walk through the tent section of a sporting goods store or a browse through the catalogs shows a staggering number of shelters from a tiny 3-pound, 10-ounce nylon backpacker tent to a magnificent canvas wall tent weighing 60 pounds, and that's without the floor piece or the poles! Nothing between has been omitted, either. Costs run from under $50 to nearly $500; shapes can be the conventional rectangle with V-roof, a dome, a tun-

nel or A-frame. They come in many different fabrics. But how to choose? What to look for. First think of the exact purpose of your tent.

There are campers who want a large canvas walled shelter which will be erected only once a season, the kind of tent found in a professional hunting camp. This can hold everything: a full size stove/oven, table and benches and even off-the-ground cots. Little has changed in this shelter since early in the century. There they stand, supported by poles cut at the site, able to support 500 pounds of new fallen snow. There's plenty of room to stand and move around and that's important during long rainy spells. On balmy days they are a shady refuge from high sun and a breeze wafts from end to open end. An entire family can spend a whole season in one of these large, sturdy tents. One fine manufacturer is Bob Beckel (Beckel Canvas Products, P.O. Box 20491, Portland, OR 97220). The camper may order any size from 9'x9' to 15'x21'. Optional windows, stove pipe holes, ropes, etc., are ordered as desired. A good sized tent with all the needed extras can cost about $500. That's a lot of money but consider that this is like a summer cottage for the whole family and compare this cost to motels night after night. It could be a very good investment.

For the mobile camper consider a fold-down camping

(Opposite page, left) As a backpacking tent or an auxiliary tent, the Chateau by Holubar can be bought ready-made or in kit form.

(Opposite page, right) Probably the best small, lightweight tent on the market today is Early Winter's Gore-Tex Light Dimention. It goes up in a wink with only two shock-corded fiberglass poles and three stakes. It weighs only 3¾ pounds.

(Right) A mid-size tent which we use often is the Great Western by Eureka. It comes in several sizes and has an unobstructed doorway.

the Right One, and Care for It

trailer. With fuel economy more and more important, these "tents" are being made smaller and lighter to be towed by a compact auto. Their design has been slimmed down too, to offer less wind resistance.

Viking (a subsidiary of Coachman) now has a mid-size 17-foot Saga XL fold-down trailer which has a galley with either an inside or outside stove mount. It can sleep four comfortably, or more if some are children. They also offer larger models.

Old reliable Coleman makes 10 models each weighing less than 1,000 pounds and with a low profile would cost the tower only about one extra gallon of gas per 100 miles of highway travel. Each has an icebox, dining table which can be used inside or out, 4-inch thick mattresses and a galley. These are remarkably well designed and for the camper who wants comfort this is a good choice.

For pickup campers Coleman makes the Country Squire, a fold-out which nearly doubles the size of the truck bed. It flips up and out easily, has a galley, table, storage space and comfortable beds. Coleman too, is looking to the dim fuel future and now makes the Country Squire Jr. to fit the new mini-pickups with either the regular or long beds. Of course these are smaller, but when the more efficient little pickup with everything you need can get 25 mpg, it's easy to forgive

the lack of a few extra feet of camper space.

Families with an ordinary sedan or stationwagon usually opt to stay in campgrounds with fireplaces, picnic tables and toilet facilities. An excellent choice for them is the large square or rectangular tent. Most come in several sizes.

One which we have had and enjoyed for several years is Eureka's Great Western 10. It is slightly less than 10 feet square and has plenty of room for a man well over 6 feet to stand comfortably. The large triangular windows open easily with zippers and there is no annoying pole centered in the middle of the doorway. It is easy to set up with an exterior umbrella pole design. We have used it camping in the desert in southern Utah and during a snowfall in the Absarokas in Wyoming and of course under just average conditions. Probably the only drawback is that nice large awning extending outward from the door. We just never could get the thing to stay up without a lot more trouble than it seemed worth. It is claimed this size will accommodate four to six persons, and so it will, but it would be a cramped situation tolerable for a group of backpackers but not for a family on vacation. It weighs 25½ pounds.

Another Eureka tent is the very large Teton, with a 9'x12' or 8'x10' floor space and headroom of 7 feet. This is made as conscienciously as the Great Western

Just the right size to be towed by a compact car, the Viking Saga XL, a 17-foot fold-out tent trailer makes a cozy vacation home that travels.

(Above and below) Coleman's Villa Del Mar can be attached to a van with an optional van conversion kit. A "single" becomes a "suite."

but is larger and has V-shaped roof with a central ridge pole and two end eve poles slightly lower. Unfortunately this has the pole bisecting the doorway. For a large family or a group the Teton makes a roomy shelter with surprisingly little weight.

Coleman specializes in family camping, and we have found their 9'x12' Villa Del Mar tent one of the finest larger tents on the market. The light colored roof reflects heat, there is lots of window area and the doors (there are two in this one) are unobstructed. An added feature is the Van Conversion Kit which can be purchased to go with the tent. This connects the tent (one of the doors) with the van by a completely enclosed, freestanding connection somewhat larger than a phone booth. Using this, a group of children can sleep in the tent while the parents luxuriate in the van. Our only complaint with the Villa Del Mar is the instructions for setting up the tent. They are unnecessarily complicated. Poles should have coded colored markings where they meet and indicators as to where they should be placed. I have marked our poles with tapes of various colors and when lending the tent to friends I caution them to set it up first at home, to watch my colors and the picture, but under no circumstances read Coleman's directions!

There are dozens of smaller mountain tents on the market and these are perfect for the backpacker or for family campers who bring them along to use in addition to a tent camper, van or another tent. A separate tent is a fine idea since it gives privacy and a place for the youngsters to sleep while the adults are still up nearby.

Making these tents at home from a kit is not difficult once the sewer can visualize the tent and isn't intimidated by the yards and yards of fabric. It saves money and is even fun. Holubar offers a few tents either ready made or in kit form. In the two-person Chateau Tent the ready-made item is over $200 while the kit (which comes with poles and stakes) sells for only about $150. Frostline offers four tent kits for the home sewer, the cheapest being the Kodiak for about $100. This will sleep two and includes a rain fly.

Our favorite mid-size tent is REI's Great Pyramid. It will sleep four and is absolutely spacious for two. It is a rounded pyramid shape with exterior fiberglass poles radiating from the apex. These run through loops on the tent to the ground. Just below the center line a hoop of the same poles holds the sides taut. The poles are all alike (no looking for the "slightly shorter, thicker one") and fit together easily. The tent is up in no time, even the first time. (Recreational Equipment, Inc., P.O. Box C-88125, Seattle, WA 98188) This tent was chosen to go to K2 with the 1978 American expedition. Although

Reliable Coleman makes several camping trailers for family camping. Here the smaller "Ligonier" sleeps six and in the background, the larger Brandywine, Ltd. to be towed by a larger vehicle, sleeps eight.

you may not need these capabilities of wind resistance, strength, lightweight, etc., it's nice to know it's there, anyhow.

Our favorite small tent, and we use it when backpacking for any distance, is the Light Dimention. This little whizz weighs only 3¾ pounds and sets up in a wink (1 minute on average) with only two hoops. It folds into a compact 7″x16″ bundle. Three stakes hold it fast under most weather conditions, but there are side guy lines included for extremes. It is made of Gore-Tex. We've used it for 4 years and aren't nearly done yet! A larger tent which is almost identical, but large enough to hold two plus backpacks and weighing 4½ pounds is the Winterlight. Anyone hiking or cross-country skiing and camping in winter should have the Omnipotent with an integral double wall. No fly to set up separately, this truly 4-season tent is tunnel shaped and made to deal with the worst weather conditions one could encounter. It is not cheap either. All these tents are from Early Winters Ltd., 110 Prefontaine Place South, Seattle, WA 98104.

Another fine new small tent is Eureka's Caddis with its super insulation from a large, well-shaped fly. It comes in two sizes.

Tent Fabrics

The kind of tent you choose for yourself or your family is generally determined by the fabric. Tents made for backpacking would never be constructed from a heavy cotton, for instance. On the other hand this is the most common fabric used in large family tents.

There is cotton duck, a good sturdy material, or Army duck which is such a tight weave that no sizing is necessary. Drill has a diagonal weave tighter than regular duck and is a good choice. The top cotton however is poplin, lightweight and strong. Cotton has the advantage of swelling when wet to be quite waterproof. It is also porous when dry which is good for ventilation, and it resists abrasion well.

Nylon is the choice for strength and light weight and is used in all smaller tents. A breathable nylon is used for the tent proper while a waterproofed nylon is used for the fly. The fly is important since water vapor expired through the tent roof condenses on this rather than inside the tent. The fly also provides a layer of

Eureka's Teton is a fine shelter for a small family. Note large doorways and windows for good ventilation.

47

For small pickups, the Country Squire and Country Squire, Jr. can accommodate four adults. When folded for travel, the low profile offers minimum wind resistance for better gas mileage. Made by the Coleman Company.

to treat a tent, wet and dry. In the wet process (the most usual) a solution is applied after weaving, and it leaves the surface slightly sticky and with a characteristic smell. This treatment will stiffen in cold weather, lessen the breathability and sag in the heat. It also adds greatly to the weight of the tent. Tents are weighed before this treatment, so be sure to consider what this flame-retardant process will add before buying any such tent. The dry treatment is more expensive but has none of the drawbacks of the wet treatment. Unfortunately, it is rarely used.

Whether or not to spend the extra money on a tent fabricated of Gore-Tex is also an individual matter. As by now almost everyone knows, Gore-Tex is a laminate which allows water vapor to pass through, but not water droplets since these are much larger particles. The principle is the same as pouring a pot of cooked peas into a strainer. The water passes through the holes but the peas, being larger, do not.

On the plus side Gore-Tex generally means that the

One of the truly fine tents we have used in REI's Great Pyramid. It has lots of usable space, standing room and is easy to set up with identical fiberglass poles.

dead air important for the insulation of either the winter or summer camper. Sometimes tents (such as the Omnipotent mentioned earlier) are constructed of a double layer so no separate piece is necessary. This adds to the cost, but substracts from the work! Nylon will leak along the seams if a sealer is not applied to the needle holes. It also should be protected from abrasion.

The question of flame retardancy is one with two sides. One side states that fabrics which meet the C.P.A.I. 84 standards only guarantee a very slow burn immediately after the treatment. They further state that no one knows how long this will last on a tent exposed to the elements year after year and that the treatment only adds to the cost (and almost always) to the weight of the product. Others feel we need all the protection we can get and that only a fool would camp in a non-treated tent. Several manufacturers (Eureka is one) offer both treated and untreated tents.

Treated or not, no tent is flame *proof* and care must be exercised by the occupants. There are two methods

(Above) Sears, Roebuck and Co. offers the Sir Edmund Hillary Tent. It measures 10 feet x 14 feet and is sold at retail stores and through catalog outlets. It is flame-resistant.

Only slightly larger than the Light Dimention is the Winterlight (also made by Early Winters, Seattle). It has three poles, four stakes and sleeps two plus two backpacks. It is made of Gore-Tex, too.

tent will not need a fly, and it is therefore lighter in weight and faster and easier to erect. Even when completely zipped vapor will not condense inside. On the minus side is its high cost and the fact that it must be reasonably clean to work. Imbedded dirt or grease makes it leak and these should be removed by gentle washing with soap (not detergent). Needle holes should also be filled with a sealer which comes with the tent. This is a slow process which it seems should be done at the factory, but it never is. Often the sealer is inexpertly applied (especially the first few feet) and leaves whitish patches where it is inadvertently smeared. A pity on such a beautiful and expensive tent. There are also occasions when the temperature drops very low during the night and the vapor, instead of passing through the tent, freezes on it instead resulting in a frosty crust inside and out. In spite of these problems, we usually choose the Gore-Tex since we feel that the advantages outweigh the drawbacks.

All tent floors are of a durable, waterproof material which usually extends up the side walls from 8 to 18 inches. This keeps dampness from the ground from working its way inside and also keeps any moisture which drips on it from the edge of the fly from reaching the inside of the tent. Of course this tub bottom also keeps any spilled puddles trapped inside and makes sweeping out the floor very difficult. Some campers just

49

ignore this, others lay a tarp inside which is lifted carefully out the door and shaken clean from time to time.

Care Of Your Tent

Before you ever take your tent camping set it up in the backyard. This way you will learn just how it goes together, and how to recognize its various components. If necessary mark certain poles or tent corners for easy identification when the real test comes. Now hose the tent down and let it dry. Do this twice if it is cotton. This will swell the weave to prevent leakage which would otherwise occur during the first rain.

By far the worst enemy of the cotton tent is mildew. Not only does mildew make a stain and have an odor, it also weakens the fabric which is its worst aspect. Mildew can only grow in a moist atmosphere, so *never* store a damp tent. Nearly every tent will have some moist areas when it's brought home after a camping trip and it must be dried out thoroughly. Hang it in the basement, dry it in the sun or even in one of the large commercial dryers. But never put it away damp. Test the double areas such as the reinforced corners.

Other things which you should do to insure a tent's long life is to vacuum or brush out all debris. Use the garden hose and a brush on bird droppings and a little mild soap on greasy spots. Just leave the tree sap alone. Anything strong enough to move it will destroy any water repellency or mildew proofing. Mud should be allowed to dry and then the dirt brushed away.

Nylon tents should be wiped with a damp sponge and allowed to dry before storage. Be especially careful about the zipper tapes. These usually contain some cotton and will dry much more slowly than the nylon.

On any tent with stubborn zippers, rub the teeth with a candle or crayon and then slide the handle back and forth briskly until it runs smooth. Any grit should be brushed away with a toothbrush. Needle holes which have been seen to leak can be sealed at this time too with the candle or better yet, with a special sealant.

Now that the tent is clean and thoroughly dry it should be folded loosely and stored in a dry place. Don't fold it on the same lines each time as the creases will become weakened. And be sure mice which just love to nest in tents are prevented from doing so.

Stakes and poles, wiped clean, should be wrapped separately in a piece of canvas or placed in a small nylon sack and wrapped with the tent.

The average camper uses his tent for 3 weeks each year. With proper care it can last 10 to 15 years or even longer. However a tent that is in use for whole seasons and exposed to lots of sun, wind and rain may only last up to 3 years. Erecting the whole-season tent where it is protected from the elements, making necessary repairs immediately and taking care to keep it moderately clean can greatly lengthen the life of any tent.

The right tent for the camper's needs plus the right care can equal years of satisfactory tent camping.

A practical family tent made for years of enjoyment is the American Heritage. It comes in three sizes. The largest is 10 feet x 13 feet. By Coleman.

Under the

Maple Leaf Flag

HERE ARE CANADA'S 11 TOP NATIONAL FORESTS FOR CAMPING
by JEROME KNAP

WE CANADIANS are an outdoors people. Our nation was founded on a wealth of furs, fish and forests. The blood of fur traders, trappers, voyagers and *coureurs-de-bois*—runners of the forests—flows through our veins. Our love for the outdoors is part of our heritage and nowhere does it show better than in our national parks system, which now includes areas in each of Canada's 10 provinces and the northern territories.

There are 28 national parks in Canada, stretching from Terra Nova on the rugged and rocky Atlantic coast to the seemingly endless white beaches of the Pacific Rim and from Auyuittuq in the north on Artic's Baffin Island to the unique Point Pelee, jutting into Lake Erie.

The parks vary in size from a mere 1.6 square miles in the case of the St. Lawrence Islands National Park, to the immense Wood Buffalo National Park whose 17,300-square-mile size makes it the biggest national park in the world. The park in fact is bigger than such European countries as Switzerland, Denmark or Holland.

According to the National Park's Act, every one of Canada's 28 national parks is a special place, set aside for the "benefit, education and enjoyment" of Canadians. Trying to pick the 11 best is a subjective exercise, but here are my choices, starting with Terra Nova in Newfoundland.

1. TERRA NOVA, situated on rugged, forested hills on Newfoundland's east coast. Known for its rocky coastline with spectacular inlets, the parkland is covered by typical boreal forest of spruce and bogs. The cold Labrador Current gives the park cool summers. Icebergs often float in the ocean from May to August.

The park has many peat bogs where delicate orchids grow in profusion as well as the carniverous pitcher plants. Moose are frequently seen in the park along with a host of smaller mammals. Bird life is rich, characterized by myriads of shore birds along the seashores and coveys of willow ptarmigan in the uplands. There is excellent brook trout and good Arctic char fishing in and around the 150-square-mile park. The park also has a nature interpretive program, campgrounds and bun-

51

galows. For more information write Superintendent, Terra Nova National Park, Glovertown, Newfoundland, Canada, AOG 2LO.

2. CAPE BRETON HIGHLANDS is one of Canada's most scenic parks. The area is set on tablelands, some of which rise 1,700 feet above the sea level. The rugged Atlantic coastline is contrasted with forested hills that flow to the coastline, frequently dropping over 1,000 feet to the sea. Cabot Trail, a 180-mile highway, leads through the park. It is regarded as one of the most scenic drives on the continent.

The seascapes in Cape Breston Highlands National Park are magnificent. The park is rich in wildlife and

Lucky campers may see a black bear at Terra Nova.

Terra Nova National Park on Canada's rugged Atlantic coastline has a rocky, forested character with many small waterfalls.

The dark Red River twists between mountain banks along the Cabot Trail in Cape Breton Highlands National Park. The wild splendor of the glens and pebble-bedded rivers reminds many of Scotland's western highlands.

has several interesting nature trails and some outstanding hiking trails. There is a nature interpretive program and camping grounds. For more information write Superintendent, Cape Breton Highlands National Park, Ingonish Beach, Nova Scotia, Canada, BOC 1LO

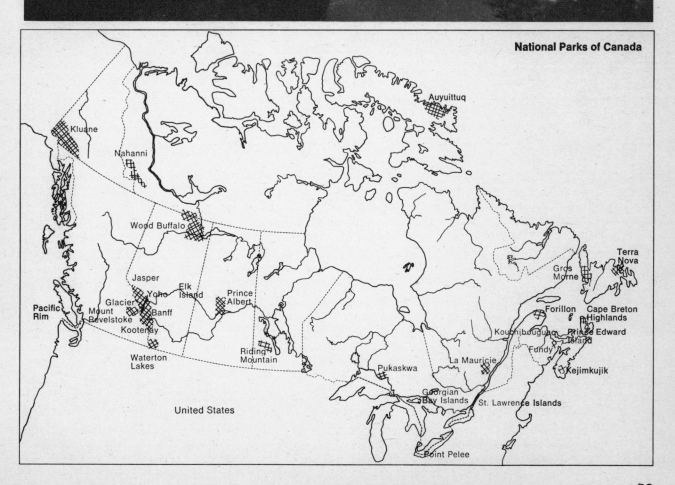

National Parks of Canada

Auyuittuq

Kluane

Nahanni

Wood Buffalo

Terra Nova

Gros Morne

Jasper

Elk Island

Prince Albert

Pacific Rim

Glacier

Yoho

Mount Revelstoke

Banff

Kootenay

Forillon

Cape Breton Highlands

Kouchibouguac

Prince Edward Island

Waterton Lakes

Riding Mountain

Fundy

La Mauricie

Pukaskwa

Kejimkujik

Georgian Bay Islands

St. Lawrence Islands

United States

Point Pelee

3. FORILLON, on Quebec's scenic Gaspe Peninsula has a striking blend of limestone cliffs that plunge steeply into the sea, and charming coves and bays that give the impression of tranquility.

The park offers a surprising variety of habitats and ecosystems each of which harbors its own wildlife. It is a bird watcher's paradise, with over 200 species recorded. In the summer vast numbers of cormorants, kittiwakes and guillemots nest on the seaside steep cliffs. Whales can be seen passing the tip of the park and harbor seals are common.

The 92-square-mile Forillon National Park has a nature interpretive program and campgrounds. There are other forms of accommodations in the charming Gaspe villages nearby. For more information write Superintendent, Forillon National Park, P.O. Box 1220, Gaspe, Quebec, Canada, GOC 1RO.

4. ST. LAWRENCE ISLANDS is Canada's smallest national park. The islands of this park are part of the "Thousand Islands" chain in the upper reaches of the St. Lawrence River. They offer captivating scenery and a setting that is ideal for all water sports. Fishing for smallmouth bass is excellent in the rock studded waters. In fact, the St. Lawrence River here is rated as one of the best bassing spots on the continent.

Another game fish that's found in the local waters is the muskallunge. This is where the 69-pound, 13-ounce world record musky was caught.

For the non-fisherman, there are historic sites, river cruises and scenic drives near the park. There is a good campground with a boat launching ramp. For more information write Superintendent, St. Lawrence Islands National Park, P.O. Box 469, R.R. No. 3, Mallorytown, Ontario, Canada KOE 1RO.

Forillon, on Quebec's scenic Gaspé Peninsula has spacious picnic and camping areas for the visiting camper.

5. GEORGIAN BAY ISLANDS

5. GEORGIAN BAY ISLANDS is one of the smallest of Canada's national parks. It is 5.4 square miles, made up of scenic islands at the southern end of Georgian Bay and off the tip of the Bruce Peninsula. The park includes the unique Flowerpot Island. The park islands are part of the Thirty Thousand Islands vacation area.

The costal scenery of the Georgian Bay Islands National Park is enchanting. It offers unique boating and sailing opportunities. There is camping on Beausoleil Island which can be reached only by boat. There are no campgrounds per se but organized camping sites are situated completely around the shoreline. The fishing is excellent for smallmouth bass and northern pike off the rocky reefs and in the many bays. The park islands are rich in wildlife with whitetail deer, red fox and raccoon being surprisingly abundant. The wildlife repertoire on the islands includes the small, timid, and not very hazardous massasauga rattlesnake which is an endangered species in Canada. Beausoleil Island was a home of the Chippewa Indians. The sites of their encampments can still be seen. The French explorer, Champlain, is believed to have spent the winter of 1615 on the island while exploring the Great Lakes. For more information write Superintendent, Georgian Bay National Park, Honey Harbour, Ontario, Canada, POE 1EO.

(Left) Unusual rock formations resembling mammoth stone flower pots are found on Flower Pot Island, a national park 4 miles from Tobermory in Georgian Bay. (Photo courtesy of Georgian Bay Islands National Park)

(Below) One of the famous "flower pots" in Georgian Bay Islands N.P.

(Below) A serene sunset from one of the campsites on the shore of Beausoleil Island in Georgian Bay.

6. NAHANNI gets its name from the South Nahanni River which winds through the Northwest Territories for some 200 miles. This is a magnificent land of mountain wilderness and spectacular canyons. One of the park's scenic highlights is Virginia Falls which plummets for 300 feet to the canyon below. The legendary Headless Valley, into which only courageous men once ventured lies within the park.

Nahanni National Park is a true wilderness. The best way to see it is by taking a tour in a steel-clad river boat from the Indian village of Nahanni Butte on the Laird River bringing everything you will need. There are no organized campgrounds in the park. In fact, the park cannot be reached by road. Nahanni is rich in wildlife. Over 30 different species of mammals have been recorded here, including herds of white Dall sheep, along with moose, mountain caribou, grizzly and wolves. For more information write Superintendent, Nahanni National Park, Postal Bag 300, Fort Simpson, Northwest Territories, Canada, LOE ONO.

7. KLUANE in Yukon boasts Canada's highest mountains, the St. Elias Range which includes the 19,850-foot Mount Logan. More than half of this magnificent park's area of 8,500 square miles is covered by ice fields and glaciers. But there are also lush valleys of vast forests plus mountain meadows and tundra. All these support a variety of wildlife including mountain goats, Dall sheep, caribou, black bear, grizzly. Moose are very common in the park, and they are particularly abundant on the flats of the Donjek River. There are also wolves, coyotes and wolverines plus a host of smaller mammals.

The Kluane National Park is accessible by highway. It offers nature interpretive programs, organized campgrounds, hiking and horseback trails. Brewster brothers, well-known Yukon outfitters, have organized trail rides which take campers on horseback camping trips deep into the Kluane wilderness. The fishing is superb in many of the streams for grayling and trout. For more information write Superintendent, Kluane National Park, Haines Junction, Yukon Territory, Canada, Y0B 1L0.

8. BANFF was established in 1885, making it Canada's oldest national park. It is well-known for its resorts of Banff and Lake Louise, set among snow capped mountain peaks and deep valleys. The park has vast glaciers such as the Columbia Icefield. A host of

"The Gate," a famous scenic area in Canada's wilderness park of Nahanni in the Northwest Territories.

Canada's highest mountains, the St. Elias Range,
are included in its park in the Yukon, Kluane.

(Left) Cool summers make camping in Canada a favorite activity of citizens from each side of the border. Wood stoves like this make good cooking areas and radiate welcome heat in the evening.

(Below) RV campers at Kluane Lake, along the Alaska Highway in the Yukon Territory. The lake, on the border of Kluane National Park, is a favorite of fishermen.

The Giant Steps in Banff's Paradise Valley.

mountain streams cascade down the valleys forming cold mountain lakes with excellent trout fishing.

The park teems with wildlife and many of the western big games species including bighorn sheep can be seen from roads and highways. There are hiking trails, trail riding on horseback, and interpretive programs, plus many campgrounds, some of which are fully serviced, in this 2,560-square-mile park. The park's eastern gateway is only 75 miles west of Calgary. It is easily reached by an excellent highway. For more information write Superintendent, Banff National Park, Banff, Alberta, Canada, TOL OCO.

9. JASPER adjoins Banff National Park which lies just to the south. It vies with Banff for magnificent scenery, wildlife and cold mountain lakes. There is no scenery more stunning than Jasper's Ramparts Range, contrasted by the green Amethyst Lakes deep in the Tonquin Valley.

A typical U-shaped glaciated valley in Banff National Park.

Trail hikers are dwarfed by the majesty of the Canadian Rockies in Banff National Park, Alberta.

Canoeing on 5-mile-long Medicine Lake in Jasper National Park is just one of the many possible activities for the camper in this very popular Canadian park.

Campers of any age enjoy a visit to cool and beautiful Waterton Lakes Park.

Van camping with a tent erected on a special platform in Jasper National Park in Alberta.

The park is a backpackers' paradise and there are good reliable horseback outfitters who can take campers deep into the Jasper wilderness. Jasper is one of the best places to see mountain big game including bighorn sheep, and mountain goats along with mule deer, elk, moose and grizzly. There is an interpretive program and several campgrounds, some of which are fully serviced, in the 4,200-square-mile park. The park is easily reached from Edmonton on an excellent highway. For more information write Superintendent, Jasper National Park, Jasper, Alberta, Canada, TOE 1EO.

10. WATERTON LAKES is the Canadian section of Waterton-Glacier International Peace Park. As the name suggests, Waterton Lakes borders Glacier National Park in Montana. The park offers a spectacular contrast between mountains and grasslands. It is a colorful mountain park with scenic lakes and charming vistas. The small steamer, "The International," runs scenic cruises on Upper Waterton Lake. There is excellent trout fishing in the mountain streams in and around the park. Some of the oldest rocks in the Rocky Mountains dating back 100 million years are found here.

The park is rich in wildlife. Mule deer are very abundant, so are elk, mountain goats, bighorn sheep and grizzlies, plus smaller mammals and a host of birds. The park has excellent hiking trails, a nature interpretive program and campgrounds. For more information write Superintendent, Waterton Lakes National Park, Waterton Park, Alberta, Canada, TOK 2MO.

11. PACIFIC RIM streches along 65 miles of Vancouver Island's west coast. This unique Pacific coast

The western shore of Vancouver Island is a national park for 65 miles of its length. Forested islands dot the sea to the west and are part of the Pacific Rim Park.

park offers 7 miles of white sandy beach called Long Beach. A 45-mile route called the West Coast Trail winds between Bamfield and Port Renfrew. Another uniquely scenic feature of this park is a group of islands at the mouth of Berkley Sound which have nearly 100 plume sprays.

At low tide the marine life in shallow tidal pools is spectacular. The park is rich in bird life, with myriads of shorebirds plus thousands of ducks and geese which migrate long the park's seashore every spring and fall because of the park's strategic location on the Pacific Flyway. Sea lions gather on offshore rocks, gray whales rise off Long Beach and harbor seals are found in many of the quiet coves. A thick Pacific rain forest covers the 4,000-foot mountains which rise behind Long Beach. There are blacktail deer and cougars in the forested areas of the park. The 250-square-mile reserve also has a nature interpretive program and a camp-ground. For more information write Superintendent, Pacific Rim National Park, P.O. Box 280, Ucluelet, British Columbia, Canada, V0R 3AO.

Anyone planning their first camping trip into Canada should write to Canadian Government Office of Tourism, 235 Queen Street, Ottawa, Canada, K1A 0H6 for general travel and tourist information. Canadian Government Offices of Tourism also have highway maps. Incidentally, Canada has not experienced any gasoline or diesel fuel shortage. It produces enough petroleum of its own for its domestic needs. Gasoline in fact, is a little cheaper than in many areas of United States. Ours is an imperial gallon which is 5 quarts, not 4 as in the U.S.

For information on all of Canada's 28 National Parks, contact Parks Canada, 400 Laurier Avenue, West, Ottawa, Canada, K1A OH4.

The Lady

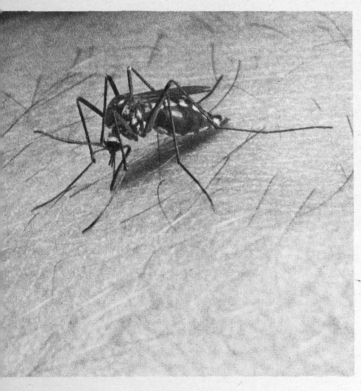

A mosquito caught in the act. First an anesthetic is injected so the victim often remains blissfully ignorant of the attack until too late. (Photo courtesy of Ed Hutchins)

by BARNEY PETERS

WHEN RESCUERS finally found the camper, who had been lost for a week in a remote Canadian wilderness, he was a sorry figure with a strange story to tell. "I was never hungry," he said, "because fish were plentiful. The bears didn't bother me and I never lacked for shelter. In a way it was high adventure—except for those maddening, murderous mosquitoes. I really thought they'd eat me alive!"

In Michigan, a friend of mine found a freshwater spring in a swamp that was full of fat native trout. But clouds of mosquitoes drove him away from the bonanza. In Ontario swarms of the tiny vampires tormented a hunter until he missed an easy shot at a trophy moose. I was that hunter. And in Tanzania I spooked a magnificent kudu by idly slapping a mosquito on the back of my neck. Something similar has happened—or will eventually happen—to anyone who ever pitched a tent in the great outdoors.

In the whole wonderful world of campers there's no greater nuisance than the mosquito. Neither heat nor cold, snow nor rain, has caused more headaches and discomfort. And you can't escape these pests because they're everywhere. Although they're small and frail, more legends and tall stories, some true and some false, have grown up about them than about all the killer bears and lions on two continents. And no wonder, because mosquitoes can be as deadly as rattlers or rhinos, or even gunfire.

Many of the stories started in World War II when most training camps were in the South, often in the dampest parts. When a man went AWOL, someone would laugh and remark that the mosquitoes carried him away. Or a soldier would wake up at night and swear he heard a giant mosquito talking. "Let's take this one in the upper bunk," the insect would say to his friends, "He's a sergeant, and no one will miss him." Such anecdotes were repeated and enlarged on without end.

Nobody Loves

Virtually no camper anywhere has escaped the attacks of these midget divebombers, which just happen to be among the most numerous and perhaps the most interesting residents on the face of the earth. There are, in fact, more than 3,000 catalogued species, with more still to be discovered—scientifically, that is, because sportsmen have already discovered them the hard way.

Among many living creatures the female is said to be more deadly than the male, and it was never truer than with mosquitoes. The male isn't even equipped to bite. But the lady may be deadly. Although her principal food is plant nectar, she needs the vitamins in an occasional swig of human or animal blood to sustain the breed. Luckily she needs the blood only once in every 25 generations or so. Otherwise mosquitoes might inherit the world.

Little is known about mosquitoes and what makes them tick. The harmless male has a short, happy life of 8 or 9 days, during which time he meets and woos a mate in midair. After that he retires to sipping fresh vegetable juice.

An average female lives 30 days and lays 100 eggs. In warm weather it takes 10 days for an egg to develop into an adult—and that means 15 new generations of mosquitoes are possible from spring to fall in temperate latitudes—from 20 to 30 generations in tropical regions. But think of this: In only six generations a single female can have 31 billion descendants! Fortunately there are frogs and toads, fish, birds and bats to eat most of them.

Mosquito eggs are usually laid on the surface of stagnant water, and in the larval or pupal stages they resemble tiny snorkel submarines. The snorkel is used to breathe air above the surface. Eventually the pupa splits wide open and a full-grown mosquito buzzes out of the shell, which is a sort of launching pad. The males emerge first and the females last, but that's of little interest to a camper caught without his repellent.

What is interesting, however, is that, like some other insects, all mosquitoes come fully equipped with chemoreceptors. These are nature's nearest approach to radar. They combine a sense of smell and "feel" that "beams" the mosquito toward the nearest fisherman via the odors and heat waves from his body. Ordinarily the chemoreceptors are located in the mosquito's whiskers, or antennae, but some also have substations in the hairs of their legs.

Most mosquitoes don't travel very widely; for a creature so small and frail 1,000 feet is almost an incredible journey. Not until the past few years was this range determined, and then in a unique manner. Mosquitoes were captured, brushed lightly with a radioactive substance, and released again. Then entomologists followed their meanderings with supersensitive Geiger counters. These clever scientists made a disconcerting discovery. A certain strain that breeds in saltwater marshes can make mass raids as far as 75 miles away!

The actual bite of a mosquito would be a blood-chilling spectacle to watch if one could see it vastly enlarged. The feet of a female are soled with friction pads and shod with hooks, the better to cling to tender skin. In her snout she carries a terrible kit of switch-blades, spuds, spikes, and a high-speed drill that zips easily into the toughest flesh. It works on moose, mice, and snakes as well as on a weekend angler.

Sometimes the drilling will hit a sensitive spot immediately; just as often it will go unnoticed. But the instant the skin is punctured the vampire administers a local anesthetic that deadens the victim's feelings as effectively as a shot of novocaine. The anesthetic, which also thins the blood, is delivered through a hollow needle in her tongue. This thinning makes it possible for the mosquito to suck blood, by means of a pump in her head. If undisturbed she will draw off three or four times her own weight.

Several summers ago I was fishing in the Louisiana bayou country with Rich and Gene Blanchard. Clouds

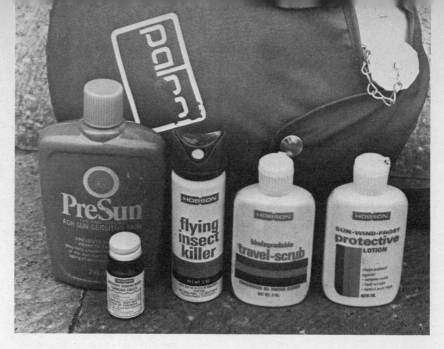

A camper's kit should contain these preparations. The flying insect killer can keep the inside of the tent insect-free but should not be sprayed directly on nylon fabric.

of mosquitoes whistled and whined about our ears, and only the fact that bass were striking made them tolerable. But Gene wasn't bothered.

"Why," Richard asked his brother, "do the mosquitoes attack me and leave you alone?"

"I owe it all," Gene laughed, "to good, clean liquor. And of course a clear conscience."

True, some people are vastly more susceptible to mosquito bites than others, but it's doubtful if either the brand of liquor or a man's conscience has anything to do with it. On the other hand, some rather dramatic experiments at Western Ontario University have revealed that the rate of breathing has much to do with attracting the pests. Rapid breathing attracts far more than calm or normal breathing.

And here's another point to think about. Those same tests in Ontario revealed that 10 times the number of mosquitoes landed on very dark clothing as against white clothing when worn side by side. In general the lighter the garment in color, the fewer the mosquitoes.

Although most mosquitoes cause only severe itching and discomfort, certain species around the world are known to carry dread diseases. As long ago as 1878 it was found in China that mosquitoes transmitted filariasis, and this often resulted in elephantiasis. Twenty years later anopheles mosquitoes were detected carrying malaria, and in 1900 *Aedes aegypti* mosquitoes were proved to be carriers of yellow fever. They've also been suspected of transmitting sleeping sickness.

But the species that torments the sportsmen in North America is a fellow called *Culex pipiens*. Largely nocturnal, this is the insect most likely to slip into camp or cabin after the lights are out. It has an uncanny ability to find the tiniest holes in walls, screens, or nettings. And it's even more uncanny how it can accomplish this after everything has been doused with repellent.

Some of today's sportsmen grew up in the days when most streams were cool and pure, and life outdoors was

a bit more rugged than it is now. Not remembered with sweet nostalgia were such early mosquito repellents as oil of citronella and oil of pine, both of which were far more formidable than the mosquitoes. Nonetheless I carried a supply of the sticky stuff on every outing—and hoped I wouldn't have to use it.

After the citronella era came World War II and new formulas developed by the Armed Forces. Compared to the repellents of boyhood days, these worked like magic, but the odor was as objectionable to the victims as to the mosquitoes. Fortunately for all of us the laboratory boys kept busy, and still more progress was made. Nowadays we can buy effective products, in spray cans as well as bottles, that are almost a pleasure to use.

Besieged in camp by bad weather, while vagrant mosquitoes infiltrated the tent, almost every sportsman has asked himself, "Are these damn things good for *anything*?"

The answer is yes. They're an important, easily captured part of the diet of many birds, reptiles, fish and even other insects. Some insect-eating birds (including several game species in springtime) depend on them almost entirely, and other critters depend on these insect-eating birds. To suddenly eliminate all of the mosquitoes on earth would probably eliminate other wildlife as well.

Mosquitoes have still another, almost immeasurable value that a serious outdoorsman can appreciate. They have discouraged, and even stopped, the exploration, development and settlement in remote places that otherwise wouldn't be remote today. This is important to the man who wants to vanish for a spell from all that's familiar and to cast a fly far from any blacktop highways. Mosquitoes have saved a few such areas for the future. And all they ask in return is to make an occasional withdrawal from a walking blood bank, which will probably be you.

Take the ROUGH Out of Roughing It

by JAMES TALLON

Rafting down wild rivers can be super fun if you're well-fed and get plenty of liquids and rest. Trapped by canyon walls you don't run down to a restaurant or hotel. These river-runners are in Grand Canyon.

IN THE remaining twilight I washed chicken blood off a fist-sized piece of ice. It had fallen from an orange crate of cold grub lugged from the rafts to our campsite. Right now it was more valuable than gold. This was the seventh day on a Colorado River run through the Grand Canyon. Summer storms had dumped tons of silt into the river—our drinking water source. I could taste and re-taste the mud. Most of us were sorely dehydrated by the super-dry Arizona air. In the evenings our boatmen-guides would sip cold beer. Sorry, there wasn't enough for the passengers. The drinkers joked and laughed. The passengers didn't. I fantasized cold, clean liquid swishing about in my mouth. Trickling down my throat. So satisfying. So necessary for the spirit as well as the body.

Now the ice was reasonably clean. I held it behind me and approached an elderly but wise lady who had become my friend. "If you'll give me a tiny bit of your rum, I'll give you half my ice." A small campfire lit her smile. "You can have some of the rum anytime," she said, and poured some into my cup. I brought the ice into view and broke it with the handle of my belt knife. She was astounded; she thought I had been kidding about the ice. She needed it worse than I wanted the rum. "Marvelous, marvelous," she said, and we hugged and laughed with a touch of hysteria. We toasted each other, and I vowed that I would never again be

65

In North Dakota, members of a recreational vehicle caravan pitch in to have a super lunch.

trapped with such a slipshod, inconsiderate outfitter, that I would always be in charge of my personal comfort. From now on I would even upgrade my backyard cookouts.

That was 14 years ago. The details are still vivid. All negative. But they have kept, and keep, me thinking positively. Not one of the many, many outdoor trips I've made, as vowed, has approached the low level of that Colorado River trip. In fact, I have made the run twice more and both trips had to be classified as super. I have learned to take the rough out of roughing it.

Just because you're outdoors it makes no sense to punish your body inside and out, and cloud your thinking. A friend of mine says the only woman he could ever love is one who will sleep in the mud with him and eat sun-dried goat meat. (One said she would, but as far as I know they haven't teamed up.) He is an extremist. On the other end of the spectrum I know a true story about a famous TV outdoor personality who was on a 3-day fishing trip at Yellowstone Lake's South Arm. Every evening he insisted on being boated back to town for dinner and beddy-bye. No sleeping in a tent or camp-chow for him.

But there is a very happy middleground where I believe most of us fit. We *like* camping. A lot. It is recreation and re-creation. Sort of a restoreth-our-soul event. Al Gillie, an avid fisherman, was tuned to the outdoors but had different ideas about camping until he got an example of the new outdoor me. We fished for rainbow trout at that outstanding 14 miles of Colorado River known as Glen Canyon. (There are always a few flashes of irony here because Lee's Ferry, the entrance to Glen Canyon, is also the jumping-off place for Grand Canyon river runners. Fishermen go upstream and rafters go down.) The first day we had breakfast at home and lunch at a beef house in Flagstaff. As host I would prepare dinner in camp. I feel Al was expecting cold beans on a paper plate and cowboy coffee.

At the time I owned a ½-ton Ford pickup truck with a cab-high camper shell. Besides a folding bed for two with 4-inch foam mattresses, I had built in plenty of cubbyholes for storing outdoor necessities. Al watched with a certain fascination as I dug out items that were going to let us live most comfortably for our 3-day stay.

I washed off our campground table, removing the sticky crud left by outdoor inconsiderates, and covered it with a clean table cloth. I fired up a four-steak hibachi and completely covered it with two steaks, liberally seasoned with garlic salt and pepper from a mill. To speed the rest of the tale, we also had corn on the cob, foil-baked potatoes, a salad of Romaine lettuce, tomatoes and diced shallots, hard dinner rolls and a bottle of good red wine served in real wine glasses. Afterwards Al patted his stomach and shook his head unbelievingly. He said, "I thought we would be roughing it."

In truth, the dinner at Lee's Ferry was relatively simple and easy to make. Together, my wife, Vicki and I have put on some awfully elaborate camp meals for friends. Some of the best were on the remote beaches of the Sea of Cortez in Sonora, Mexico. The nearest stores and restaurants were 60 or more miles away. We took everything from this side of the border. Some of the things we prepared were for effect: We liked to see our guests' surprised expressions. Now we've backed off from Coq au Vin and strawberry crepes. We're more realistic. But no one ever complains.

Complete enjoyment of an outdoor venture is directly linked to plenty of good food and drink and proper rest. Put people into a demanding physical situ-

Fishing the Roaring Fork Ranch, near Carbondale, Colorado, these fly-fishermen take the rough out of roughing it with a motorhome well loaded with good food and drink.

At a shady ramada in Organ Pipe Cactus National Monument, the Tallon family prepares to have a satisfying lunch.

ation and see that they get these three main requisites and they'll come through, for the most part, in good humor. Reflecting back to my first Grand Canyon run I have to say that, though there wasn't enough of it, the food was okay. I had brought along a waffle air mattress but it was the intense dehydration that axed me. Now when I'm planning a trip, whether I'm running it or an outfitter is, I look at the liquid situation first. I want hot drinks and cold and some at room temperature.

In our van conversion we can carry 30 gallons of water and that, theoretically, solves our wet needs. But don't forget the importance of "satisfaction." After being indoctrinated to the beverages of modern times, you invariably crave a variety. We take along fruit juices, some pop—although we dislike most artificially-carbonated drinks—beer and wine for dinner and a little sipping afterwards. We're not much on hard liquor but do tilt an occasional Margarita and a few fruity rum drinks.

Three years ago, along with 26 other nature-lovers, I found myself with Baja Expeditions on Isla Partida, a deserted island in the Sea of Cortez, just off La Paz, Baja. One of our four 22-foot *pangas* (a very stable Mexican open boat) held a truck-load of food, ice, beer and water. The water was in 10-gallon plastic containers with spigots at the bottom. It had a disconcerting smell, and though it was okay in strong Mexican coffee, it tasted awful otherwise.

Knowing this, our group leaned heavily on the beer to satisfy their thirst, a brand called "Corona." Twenty-five years of sampling Mexican brew has educated me on that subject. Corona is okay for a bottle or two, then YUCKS. Soon I was eyeballing the water containers. A pretty thing known as Lori Chew beat me to them. She stood there pouring beer on the ground and wrinkling her nose in anticipation of what was to come. Our Mexican cook had dumped perhaps 100 *limons* (looking like a cross between lemons and limes) on a nearby table. I cut one in half and squeezed it into Lori's cup. She added water, stirred and tasted. Her eyebrows raised in approval. "That helps a lot," she said. Actually, it was a shot in the dark. But it helped take the rough out of roughing it.

The complete answer to clean, pure, sweet-tasting water lay on my desk at home. It was a flyer from American Water Purification, 1990 Olivera Road, Concord CA 94520. One of their "Water Washers" offered for sale was no bigger than a couple of stacked coffee cups. The cost is around $20, and it will filter 1,000 gallons of water before you have to replace the filter. Included are some "booster chemicals" that will make questionable water safe by killing bacteria. We never go anywhere without this great invention. It takes the "tank taste" out of our van water and the chlorine flavor out of our home tap water. It also removes organic chemicals, viruses and other pollutants.

With the liquid problem solved, I figure 8 hours of solid snoozing is more important than deluxe meals. Fortunately I recognized that fact a long time ago and have missed very few good nights' sleep. The waffle air mattress has been shelved because of weight. I tried one of those high-density foam pads the backpackers like. A joke. They take up too much space and by morning a pea-sized pebble under it feels like the Great White Throne in Zion National Park. Now when I'm on deserted islands, at backcountry lakes, or rafting down rivers, a ¾-length, pool mattress does the job. The purchase of a raft includes patching, but in 4 years of hard use, it has never had a flat. This one deflates into a small package 8x6x1½ inches.

Strangely, I always sleep better in a sleeping bag. Even at home. (As an experiment I tried it, but stay traditional for fear of being ridiculed.) We could use standard bedding in our van conversion, but prefer bags. At last count, the sporting goods closet showed six rated for three different temperature ranges. A good rule of thumb is always take a heavier bag than you think you'll need. If it becomes too warm you can regulate it with the zipper opening. Sometime back in a Mexican coastal camping situation, most of our group thought below-the-border temperatures would be much higher. They brought light bags. By morning after the first night the air echoed with sounds of castanets. You guessed it . . . chattering teeth. Some people don't learn very fast and a few of that caliber were with us. They had to be told the next night to sleep in their clothes, inside the sleeping bag, to ward off the chill. Since a great deal of body heat can be lost through the top of the head, I always take along a nightcap—a navy-style watch cap. One guy, because of that tip, said I saved his life.

Another item often vital to sleeping comfort is a

Wise backpackers always consider weight, but remember the body and spirit need to be satisfied daily. Take along thought-out necessities to do it.

waterproof cover, or at least one that is water repellant. Nothing seems to work better than a standard army surplus poncho. Cost is pennies. Half the poncho goes under your mattress (or pad if you insist), which serves as a ground cloth and also keeps the poncho from blowing away if the wind comes up. The other half, of course, goes over you. Even though you may not get caught in the rain, fog and dew can make you think you were. Use the poncho every night, just in case. Prop it up away from your bag for air circulation, to keep condensation at a minimum. A couple of sticks about 18 inches long will do it and are usually available even on desert islands. Carry several short pieces of nylon line to tie down the poncho on the long, open side.

I've already let you know basically how I feel about camp foods. But I need to elaborate a bit more so you'll get the full gist of interpreting "taking the rough out of roughing it." Food is no less an essential to a good-

It's a long haul, pal. And you'd better be ready for it. You don't tackle the Grand Canyon unless you're properly outfitted. Rescues are expensive.

time-was-had-by-all than sufficient drink and sleep. It is a matter of personal priority. Most outfitters now recognize the importance of competing with others and thus tout good meals as part of their package. Some go beyond that and emphasize their food is outstanding. I have to name H & M Landing, a sportfishing and natural history cruise company based in San Diego, as a prime example. Aboard their craft you'll be eating steak and lobster, beef Stroganoff and other sophisticated dishes. Some kind of goodies are always out for you to snack on: fresh fruit, potato chips, peanuts, individually wrapped sweets and lots of coffee, tea and hot chocolate. Other outfitters I've no less respect for though their bill-of-fares are far less impressive. But who can drag a Thanksgiving turkey oven or a deep-freeze into the outback? Sanderson Brothers, a river-rafting concern (not to be confused with the baddies mentioned earlier), irk me with some of their less-

than-professional business practices but make up for them with excellent chow. Their boatmen do fantastic cooking things with dutch ovens and they even make fresh ice cream every third day in Grand Canyon.

Anyway, this is the kind of outdoor adventure I look for today. It gets me off the cooking hook, out of chasing down food and supplies, out of making up menus and out of sudsing pots and pans. But not entirely. And I don't ever want to be. I think I cook a darn good steak and make the best guacamole in the world.

Vicki knows how picky I am. (I explain that I picked her, despite the hazards involved.) She has taken over most of the shopping, but I get to study the menu a day or two prior. That way I can make changes or add items she may have overlooked.

Steaks almost always go on the list first. They keep better than hamburger, taste a whole lot better, and if you consider the fat content that burns away, much cheaper. We take along canned fruits and vegetables, but most often eat fresh frozen. Vicki likes to make bisquits and our daughter, Rachel, and I love to eat them. They can show up at both breakfast and dinner. Fresh salads rate high with us, and we can get very fancy with them.

Breakfasts are relatively standard fare of bacon (although we're boycotting it right now because of the high price for what you get) or sausage and eggs, flap-jacks, French toast, waffles, once-in-awhile cereals, coffee, tea, milk and juices.

We tend to dilly-dally over breakfast and dinner. But lunches are prepared quickly and usually consist of foods that need not be cooked. We belong to an international cheese club (although my favorite is a smokey white that comes from Logan, Utah) and we're on a first name basis with the folks at the Metrocenter Brookside Winery. I'll tell you, our lunches can be quite tasty.

With the exception of one or two long trips per year, such as exploring desert islands, our backpack trips fall under the head "day hiking." Similar lunches to those mentioned earlier go into our packs and may take up most of the space. On week or longer hauls, I probably do more thinking about grub—having worked the bugs out of drinking and sleeping—than any other phase of camping. Being isolated by sea or canyon or simply distance means you can't quit when you feel like it. Staying in a pleasant frame of mind helps me to make it. I always take along special treats to bolster my spirit. Modern supermarkets and backpacker stores are shelved with hundreds of lightweight foods and goodies that can turn the mental tide for you. Think up what will do the job for you and take it, even if it adds noticeably to your load.

Taking the rough out of roughing it is pure common sense. There's no mud in my drinking water now, and I've not had to scrounge for ice again. You just can't count on someone else to take care of you. You have to look out for yourself.

AMERICA'S GREATEST CAMPERS AND OUTDOORSMEN

This buckskinned rider looks much as his predecessors did with a coyote fur hat, buckskin clothing and powderhorn suspended from his shoulder. Even the saddlebags were hand made from a durable hide, perhaps elk.

by ERWIN A. BAUER

THROUGHOUT the endless brutally cold day, a dry snow fell and the wind-driven pellets stung Joe Meek's taut, bearded face beneath a wolf skin cap. Sometimes he rode his weary mule; otherwise he walked briskly to keep warm. But from dawn until late afternoon, Meek never crossed a single fresh track of any game. ''Not a damn thing moving,'' he muttered to himself. Anyway he knew that the swirling snow would quickly cover any sign. Toward dusk Meek realized he must hurry back to camp empty handed—to a camp of mountain men, fellow beaver trappers, who huddled around wood fires in desperate straits for lack of meat.

The time was early winter, 1829 and near Cinnabar Mountain along the upper Yellowstone River on the way to Jackson's Hole. Joe Meek was 19 and little more than a year before, tired of plowing hardscrabble, had walked away forever from the family farm in western Virginia to seek a more exciting life in the then mysterious West. In the frontier town of St. Louis, he met William Sublette, a new legendary figure who was recruiting men to trek to the Rocky Mountains to trap beavers. Beaver pelts then were almost worth their weight in gold on European markets and expeditions were being organized wholesale to head westward where, Lewis and Clark had reported, the strange aquatic animals existed in unlimited numbers. This was the dream of riches and adventure which drew Joe Meek, who had cut his teeth on hunting squirrels and whitetail deer with a Kentucky long rifle, to a land far more awesome, far more formidable than the Appalachian hardwood hills of home.

Although he was hunting in unfamiliar country, Meek was woodsman enough to know he was very near his trapper camp when in the gloom he spotted the first fresh tracks of the day etched in the soft snow. For a moment, elation! But not even the trail of a giant grizzly could have made his blood run colder because these were the moccasin prints of many Blackfoot Indians. From top to bottom of the Rockies no Indians were more hostile, more terrible, than these to whom the warpath was a way of life. Beaver trappers with their efficient steel-jawed traps were especially unwelcome in Blackfoot country. Not far from where he first crossed the unmistakable tracks, Joe Meek reached a familiar ridge from which he could look down on camp. The place was surrounded and under siege in the gathering darkness.

Meek had no option but to back away. He was no match for the Blackfeet and could never get past them to join his fellows who might be doomed anyway. So he simply headed southward toward Jackson's Hole alone, through unexplored country and a sub-zero night, with a rifle, the buckskins he wore, a half-dead mule and nothing else. There was only a faint chance he might meet his party, or another, later if he could somehow avoid meeting more Indians. But it was a chance.

It isn't clear exactly how long Meek traveled, never stopping even to sleep for fear he might freeze to death. He plodded southward, upstream and parallel to the course of the Yellowstone River, but deep in deadfall timber well away from the bottomlands to avoid Indians and Indian trails where the going would have been faster. He couldn't even risk building a fire or firing his rifle for several days. Meek's mule soon expired and the man probably paused long enough to strip off some of the lean meat and eat it raw before pushing on. Later, almost dead from hunger, he risked a shot at a bighorn ewe, gorged and carried along as best he could.

Altogether Meek covered about 100 miles to reach what is now the heart—the main hot springs area—of Yellowstone Park. One morning as he staggered and stumbled along the thermal wonders, a rifle shot rang out and Meek hit the ground. But the rifleman turned out to be a trapper-scout of the Sublette party which had managed to survive the Blackfoot raid. It was also only the first of several brushes with death—with miracles, really—in the life of beaver trapper Joe Meek.

But the escape of Joe Meek was no isolated incident, it was merely typical of a time and a place and a unique breed of humans. That time was the first half of the 19th century when the place, America west of the Mississippi, was still mostly a wilderness, teeming with as much wildlife as anywhere on earth. The men were the beaver trappers, some free-trappers (we might call them free-lancers today) who wandered alone and some were members of organized trapping parties, even of large companies. Some of the names are familiar and perhaps will always be: Sublette, Jedadiah Smith, Davey Jackson, Hugh Glass, Jim Bridger, Kit Carson, Manual Lisa.

These trappers came from many backgrounds and circumstances. Most were young, in their late teens when they left home, which most likely was rural Pennsylvania, Kentucky, Virginia or Tennessee. Some were misfits, perhaps running from the law, a bill collector or a shotgun wedding. But most were restless men who simply felt more comfortable roaming in the outdoors than living in a civilized place—and the eastern United States in the early 1800s was getting far too civilized.

Others such as the U.S. Cavalry, cattlemen and traders are sometimes given credit (especially in motion pictures) for first exploring—for "opening up"—the Rockies, but those buckskinners we call mountain men were everywhere the true pioneers. Perhaps no single small group in American history suffered such hardship or lived such precarious lives. As woodsmen, campers, hunters and survivors, they matched (because they *had* to) the western Indians in skill and at the Indians' own games. The mountain men rank among the greatest outdoorsmen of all times and their story should fascinate anyone who loves the wilderness—who ever goes hunting, fishing or camping today.

Beaver trapping is really as old as America. The mammal, *Castor canadensis,* which builds stick and mud dams, and log lodges along rivers, was native to a large part of the New World from the Atlantic to the Pacific and from the Gulf of Mexico northward well into the sub-Arctic. The first settlers who waded ashore at Plymouth Rock trapped and otherwise quickly eliminated beavers which were only a nuisance to planting crops. Eastern Indians had largely ignored beavers because there were bigger animals in the woods with more meat on their bones and easier to kill. And they had no traps.

But beaver fur being of the luxurious quality it is, there was indeed a modest beaver pelt "industry" in the Northeast through the Revolutionary period and beyond. But trapping was more a by-product of other land use, mostly of clearing and draining, than a primary occupation. By the time Lewis and Clark began their cross-country journey in 1805, beavers were already few and far between in the United States east of the Mississippi, except in the upper Midwest. Trapping flourished for a time longer in Michigan, Wisconsin, Minnesota, and of course over a large chunk of Canada where colorful French trappers, the Voyageurs, had been the pioneers. The biggest beaver bonanza still remained untapped however—completely unexploited —in the countless valleys of the Rocky Mountains and on both sides of the Continental Divide.

When you drive through, or hike at trail level, or

Warmed by a buffalo robe and Hudson's Bay blanket two mountain men of today re-create the late winter camp of the beaver trapper. Coyote hides and beaver traps can be seen. The trappers are clothed in buckskins which were often made by squaws.

camp along the waterways of the West today, you may see some scattered sign of beaver, here or there a small dam or a house of alder and cottonwood cuttings on a landscape which seems to be mostly gray-green sagebrush rising up to meet evergreen foothills. Few beavers live there, you assume. But climb with me on up a Teton National Park trail and look back down onto these same sagebrush flats. Now suddenly from this vantage point you soon see that the country is laced with a necklace of dams and beaver workings. That's the way it was when Joe Meek and his friends first entered Jackson's (now Jackson) Hole and in fact the entire northern Rocky Mountain region. Beavers not only dominated a lot of the landscape, they created it.

Still, with all of the super-abundance, beaver trapping, even without the Blackfeet, was a hard, perilous way to make a living. Each trapper soon became a survival expert . . . or else. Pelts, called plews (from the French *plus*), were prime, of maximum value and trappable at only two times of the year: during late

autumn just before freezeup and toward the tag end of winter when ice on beaver ponds began to break up. Every man was worse off than any Mississippi slave during the actual trapping. Winters were spent "holed up," living alone, or with such friendly Indians as the Crows, or with an Indian bride, just trying to avoid freezing. Summers made the rest worthwhile; the weather was warm and the trappers gathered at a rendezvous point, about which we'll say more later.

Company trappers usually worked in twos, each with a pack animal, six or eight traps and "full kit" for safety, efficiency and often because in this way an experienced older man could train a beginner. The buddy system was sound psychologically, too, because not too many men could bear to be totally alone for months on end. However, a few did thrive on the isolation. Still others traveled with an Indian squaw who may have been a wife or a companion. Often a squaw was far better survival insurance (particularly in her own home territory) than a white companion. For one

At a modern Rendezvous beaver trappers recreate the bidding which went on at the original meetings for an Indian bride. This was at the Green River Rendezvous in Pinedale, Wyoming.

thing she was the equivalent to today's field guide to edible plants; almost anywhere she could find roots or seeds or berries to keep a body alive. She could also sew, pitch camp, collect firewood, cook, tan leather (with beaver brains and wood ashes), skin and stretch plews. A trapper would also wear out several pairs of moccasins a year and a squaw could keep him supplied with the best, which fit the foot like a glove, made from the smoked skin which once covered her tipi.

Let's examine, but just briefly, how beavers were trapped. Once the territory of a beaver family—an impoundment—is located, the trapper heads upstream, following the animal's own slick trail to a place in the stream where shallow water drops off abruptly into deep water. There a stout, sharpened stake is driven into the streambed to serve as a solid anchor for a trap with a 5-foot chain and swivel. The trap itself is placed in very shallow water so that the trip pan is level with the gravel and the jaws are hidden. Next a strong smelling "medicine," which is the castoreum derived from a

beaver's scent glands, is daubed on the stake. When a resident beaver comes along, he is fatally attracted to the false smell of a stranger—an interloper—and he is trapped and drowned.

The overall aim was to trap out as many beavers as quickly as possible from an area and then to move on, while the trapping season lasted. It meant that a man constantly had to be wading in and out of crotch-deep, almost freezing water with only buckskin moccasins on his feet. Even at night and around a campfire he couldn't take off the moccasins to dry quickly because the skin would shrink and never fit well again. Especially an older trapper's legs might torture him all winter following a fall season of trapping. Except during midsummer his feet might never be totally dry.

Because every plew meant money enough to pay off his grubstake, his debts and provide enough cash to trap another year, it was a great loss to lose just one trapped beaver, either through carelessness or to a wandering wolverine. But to lose a trap was even worse because no replacements existed west of St. Louis. An unlucky man might have to dive deep to the bottom of a beaver pond to retrieve a lost trap. Or if Indians managed to steal his entire supply, which wasn't all that rare, he would have to resort to beaver catching Indian-style. That meant tearing out the beaver dam to drain the pond, then waiting to spear or club to death the beavers as they tried to escape a lodge left high and dry. This was even slower, more tedious than trapping. Anyone who has ever tried to remove a beaver dam will understand how difficult it is.

There was one time every year on which the beaver trapper's life was focused—Rendezvous Time. Every summer the exact site was decided for the next year's meeting. It would be in a suitable place such as Fort Bridger or Green River (at present day Pinedale, Wyoming), or at Pierre's Hole (Driggs, Idaho, today). All the trappers would converge here for several weeks to meet with traders who came from the East. Friendly Indians (and sometimes not so friendly) would also assemble on the spot to trade and an annual rendezvous might become a settlement of more than 5,000 tipis and wagons.

It is difficult to describe a typical rendezvous which may have been more colorful and brawling than anything modern man can imagine. It was Mardi Gras, Christmas and Super Bowl Sunday put together. Thousands of beaver plews collected from New Mexico to Alberta were sold and bartered by the mountain men. Indians in fantastic plumage traded their own skins for blankets, guns, powder and bad whiskey. There was drinking, dancing, carousing, wenching, games (target shooting, knife and skillet throwing) fighting; and once Kit Carson (among many others not as well known) killed another trapper in a savage fight. No one remembered the reason it began. But still an extraordinary amount of business was transacted for everything from flintstones to start fires, to pack horses, tobacco and pipes, and Dutch ovens. Some trappers bargained for squaws who would become their wives.

Even medical operations were performed. Try to visualize the rendezvous where painted Indians speaking a dozen different tongues sat watching fascinated, astounded, in a circle around a blazing fire, while Dr. Marcus Whitman removed an arrowhead which Jim Bridger had carried in his back for three winters. The only anesthetic was a belt of corn whiskey and a bullet to bite. Whitman was a pioneer doctor-missionary; he marvelled that the wound had never become infected.

"Lean meat doesn't spoil in the mountains," Bridger commented.

But the rendezvous and its revelry ended, the tipis were struck and it was back to the drudgery and dangers of beaver trapping. And one of those ever-present dangers was the grizzly bear which was called Old Ephriam or the "white bear" by the mountain men and which in their heyday lurked just about everywhere. Merriwether Lewis said he would "far rather fight two Indians than one bruin." Not many disagreed with him. Consider one extraordinary incident which illustrates both the role of the grizzly and the perilous life of the mountain man.

Nobody ever knew exactly where Hugh Glass was born, but it was probably Pennsylvania, and he was older than most trappers by the time he arrived in the West. But he had lived as an Indian for a time with the Pawneees, had been on war parties with them, and was an extremely skilled woodsman. A companion said that Glass could silently follow his own footprints (or an Indian's) in total darkness with his sensitive moccasined feet alone. He could smell wild animals and humans as well as a hound dog. Like Bridger he once sat impassive while another trapper cut an arrowhead, this one badly infected, from his spine with a straight razor. One day along the upper Missouri while out hunting meat for the rest of his party of trappers, he encountered a grizzly, shot and mortally wounded it. But before that bear died, it almost tore Glass apart.

The grizzly clawed away his scalp and bit completely through his throat. It ripped the flesh from his back, from a shoulder, arm and thigh. When the animal fell dead, Glass was also practically finished. His companions found him in deep shock, hanging onto life by a thin thread. Since the party was small and in forbidden Indian country, they couldn't tarry long and the hunter's condition was far too desperate for him to be carried. So for $80 apiece, then a great amount of money, two trappers volunteered to remain with Glass until he died and then bury him, while the rest went on. That might be only a few hours, at most a day or so. But somehow and although unconscious Glass's heart kept beating and in a situation of increasing terror, his two companions left him alone to die beside a spring. They took his gun, knife and other possessions, leaving only a flint and the black blood-caked clothes on his back.

Somehow Glass revived and racked with pain, managed to wash his wounds, except his back which he couldn't reach. Probably he passed out again. But when he woke, there was a rattlesnake nearby which was torpid from swallowing a rat and unable to move very well. That one fact proved to be the balance toward survival because Glass killed the snake and ate it. But because he could not chew, he had to pound the flesh on a rock to be able to swallow it, small bits at a time. In a day or so, the man could crawl on one hand and one knee, then hobble slowly for the first time upright. Wolves tracked him, or maybe he just dreamed it. In time, alone, unarmed in hostile Indian country, now feverish with worms and other parasites which infested the wound in his back, Hugh Glass lived on crushed buffalo berries and kept moving, maybe even gaining some strength.

Originally the Indians used hides to construct their tipis, but found the white man's canvas far superior since it was lightweight and admitted light. They were typically supported by 16 peeled lodgepole pine trunks. Some were decorated and others not. At the annual Rendezvous acres of tipis would spring up, always with the doorways facing the rising sun.

Once he watched a pack of wolves run down and kill a buffalo calf, but the trapper could not drive them away to get the meat. But Glass managed to make enough sparks with his flint, ignited a prairie fire and the resulting blaze did drive off the wolves. So he had precious, fresh and only slightly charred meat. Later he also managed to kill an Indian dog for food. Altogether Glass traveled—no, staggered—more than 100 miles before he met a Sioux war party cordial enough to take care of him and resupply him.

Although the man had often day-dreamed of revenge and perhaps had been nourished by the dreams, Glass did not take it when he caught up to his "friends" once more, 1,200 miles later. Instead he only retrieved his gun and went back to a lonely life of trapping beavers and camping in those picturesque valleys of the Rocky Mountains. Grizzlies gave him anxious moments, but were nothing compared to the brutal, snowy nights he spent in winter camps. Glass was murdered by Indians near Gardiner, Montana in 1833 or thereabouts.

At about the same time, beaver trapping also was coming to an end. Fashion in Europe was calling for silk hats instead of beaver hats and so a way of life was ending. But in all our history we have never known a band of finer outdoorsmen than the mountain men—the true buckskinners. Nor will we ever again know a world as pure and beautiful and wild as the Rocky Mountains of the beaver trappers.

Camp Historyland Trail—

This is the original brickwork of Jamestown, Virginia, first English settlement in America.

by CHUCK CADIEUX

SITTING IN the cool shade of tall trees on the bank of the James River we looked across the wide expanse of water and listened for the sounds of civilization. For one wonderful moment, we were alone with our thoughts, and for that wonderful moment we imagined ourselves in the shoes of the first English settlers in this nation. We could see only the broad river—no sign of mankind. We could hear only the wind sighing through trees—some of which were growing there when Captain John Smith first visited. More of those trees were growing when the first legislative assembly in America began its deliberations here in Jamestown, Virginia. We could walk the paths which served the settlers of the ill-fated Jamestown Colony during those terrible winters when they were the only Europeans in what is now the United States.

This place where America started is a good place to start your trip down Historyland Trail, a camping vacation which will take you where George Washington was born, to the place where Cornwallis surrendered at Yorktown, ending the American Revolution. This trail will take you through the length of Tidewater Virginia,

which produced many of the leaders of our infant nation and some of the leaders of both sides of the Civil War. Historyland Trail takes you to the birthplace of Robert E. Lee, and past Gunston Hall and into modern Washington, D.C., one of the most beautiful of the world's capitol cities.

Several months before you back your rig out of the driveway, you should start trip planning, to get the most out of your trip. Write to the state parks people in both Maryland and Virginia and get full information on all of their state parks which allow camping. Get a good campground directory—learn all there is to know about campgrounds along this historic route. If you make this trip in school vacation months, you'll find that we aren't the first to learn that this is a fascinating trip. All along the route you will be dependent upon advance reservations, or at least on "early in the day registration" to make sure that you have a place to camp at the end of the day's sightseeing. If you wait till mid-afternoon, you'll almost never find an empty space.

What is there to see and do? Starting at the south end of the trail you should visit Norfolk, Virginia, for a tour

Where America Began!

Tourists visiting Mount Vernon, home of George Washington.

There are lovely campgrounds in both Virginia and Maryland, but visitor use is heavy, and early registration is a must.

of some of its fine old antebellum homes, a visit to the Navy Yard, a trip across one of the engineering marvels of today's world—the Bay Bridge and Tunnel—maybe even some sea trout fishing near the bridge, or some offshore big game fishing out of Virginia Beach.

Then head upriver to Yorktown, one of the most interesting of America's National Battlefield Parks. Visit the Reception Center first to get oriented. Then rent a tape-recorded tour guide which will tell you where to drive and where to park as you tour the battlefield where Cornwallis surrendered to the Americans, ending the Revolution. The National Park Service operates a "Living History" demonstration here, which gives insight into the relationship between Tory and Rebel in those days, and a priceless history lesson.

Driving the Colonial Parkway from Yorktown to Williamsburg, you'll cross the narrow neck of land between the York and James Rivers, avenues of commerce in colonial days and still carrying a lot of boat traffic. Upon arriving in Williamsburg, you must first of all decide where to camp tonight. The crowds at Williamsburg will be the biggest you'll encounter on the trip, so don't be caught short. Register first, then go sightseeing.

This is reputed to be the best job of colonial restoration in our nation, and you should start your tour here by stopping at the Visitor Center for the excellent 1/2-hour movie which tells the story of Colonial Williamsburg and its place in history. Williamsburg was the capital of Virginia in colonial times, when its legislative halls rang with the impassioned oratory of Patrick Henry and the more solid counsel of Thomas Jefferson and George Washington. The House of Burgesses is the second oldest democratic legislative assembly in the world, older than our nation's Congress—second only to England's House of Commons.

Quaint shops and workshops, ornamental flower gardens, crafts and arts of the colonial period, even rides on the oxcarts on the Commons in front of the restored state legislature buildings—Williamsburg has something for everyone, and is well worth a long day of sightseeing. Colorful and interesting, the whole city is beautiful!

Just a few miles out of Williamsburg Highway 31 will bring you to Jamestown, the first permanent English settlement in what is now the United States. The National Park Service has done a lot of excellent restoration work here. Park Service Living History employees actually make glass as it was made in the early days— probably the first true manufacturing in America. You'll see the homes of the first settlers and see how they filled their daily needs. Take time to look at Jamestown, you'll feel a great respect for these people and admiration for the fortitude which they must have had just to stay alive. Near Jamestown, you'll find replicas of the original ships which brought the settlers to America, and even go aboard them. Try to imagine yourself making a transatlantic crossing cooped up in those quarters.

Before you leave this area, you really should visit one of the old colonial plantation homes, where Virginia planters lived like kings would like to live—absolute ruler of all they surveyed, growing rich from the fruits of this fertile land. Carters Grove is one of the best of these plantations; there's a charge for admission but it is well worth it, just to see how America's first aristocracy lived.

Next, head for Richmond where you should visit the National Battlefield Park while you decide whether or not to make the side trip to Monticello. The most beautiful home in colonial America, magnificent Monticello was built by Thomas Jefferson on a hill with a commanding view of the green valleys which surround it. A visit to Monticello will teach you more about this "complete colonial man," Thomas Jefferson, than you could learn in a full school year. Jefferson was not the

The national Capitol in Washington, part of Historyland Trail.

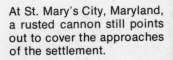

At St. Mary's City, Maryland, a rusted cannon still points out to cover the approaches of the settlement.

only great man produced here; it's but a short hop over to Ash Lawn, home of President James Monroe. Lewis and Clark, intrepid explorers who first crossed all of America to the Pacific, also came from this area.

Monticello is a long drive west of Richmond on super Highway 64. If your time is short, you'll probably leave Richmond on Highway 360 which leads northeast across Tidewater Virginia to the town of Tappahannock on the banks of the Rappahannock. You'll go through a series of small towns, steeped in colonial history, enroute to a good seafood dinner in Tappahannock, especially if you come in oyster season.

When you cross the Rappahannock, you are entering "old" Tidewater Virginia, truly the home of many of America's greatest people. This is the birthplace of presidents, the soil which produced most of the leaders of our nation's first 100 years. Stratford Hall, the birthplace of Robert E. Lee, and the birthplace of George Washington are well worth your visit. At the George Washington Birthplace National Monument, the National Park Service carries on one of its very best "Living History" demonstrations. You can watch the cook preparing meals from ingredients grown on the farm in the days of George himself, using only the spices and "savories" which were available to the cook of that day. Cooking is done on an open hearth fireplace, of course. The farm fields are being tilled by colonial methods, using oxen and horses to pull homemade implements. We watched the carpenter using hand tools to make the big wooden wheels of an ox cart.

Leaving the birthplace, it is a good idea to switch to Highway 301 and cross the high bridge over the

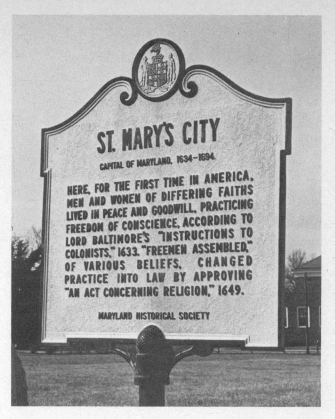

St. Mary's City, Maryland, was the start of religious freedom in the United States.

Potomac into Maryland. Turn sharply to the right and follow small town roads through Wicomico and Clements and Leonardtown into St. Mary's City, the first capitol of the state of Maryland. It's a beautiful little

You can still go for a horse-drawn carriage ride through the streets of Colonial Williamsburg, where Patrick Henry, Thomas Jefferson and George Washington once walked.

The manor house at Carters Grove, colonial plantation near Williamsburg, Virginia.

spot in a peaceful setting reminiscent of a life-style much less hectic than today's. Campgrounds in this area are hard to find, so set your travel plans accordingly.

Returning from St. Mary's City northbound on Highway 5, you'll go past the Naval Air Station at the Patuxent River Crossing, go through Charlotte Hall and on into the metropolitan area of Washington, D.C. Check your listings of Maryland State Parks and find a campsite there or go to a reserved space in a private campground. It's probably best to use the campground as a base of operations for several days of sightseeing in the capitol. Driving in Washington's traffic is difficult at any time and in a large recreational vehicle it is frustrating. We must admit, however, that we see large RV's parked near the Washington Monument every day of the year. Outside of the metropolitan beltway (Highways 295 and 495 around the city) there are many places where you can park in perimeter parking spaces and ride express buses right into the heart of the city. They'll take you in from 6:30 to 8:30 in the morning and bring you back, usually leaving downtown Washington at 4:30, 5:00 and 5:30 PM.

The list of things to do and things to see in Washington would fill a full length book. We'll list just a few ideas, knowing that no two people would agree exactly. First and second days: Bus in to the Washington Monument area and go sightseeing on foot. Ride the elevator to the top of the monument and pick out the places you want to visit from that fine observation point—the Lincoln Memorial, the Mall, the National Capitol, the White House. However, be sure you don't miss the National Space Museum. Its wonderful movie—*To Fly*—alone makes the trip worthwhile.

The steamer from Washington D.C. tied up at the dock of George Washington's estate, Mount Vernon.

Speaking of museums, the Natural History Museum, the Museum of Science and Technology, the Corcoran Art Gallery and dozens of others are within easy walking distance of the Mall. When your feet give out, look for the shuttle bus, operated by the NPS, for a quick ride to the next stop on the length of the Mall. At lunch time, try to find a cafeteria in one of the government buildings which will admit tourists. It's not gourmet fare by any means, but it is also not overpriced. From the Lincoln Memorial it's a short—but dangerous—dash across traffic to the Kennedy Center which was not built to be reached on foot. Our suggestion would be to find out what attractions are showing at the Center and get reserved tickets for one or more performances. Check the schedules for the free band concerts put on in the Mall area by the Navy and Marine Corps Bands—wonderful evening entertainment.

Ivy covered walls of Jamestown, Britain's first foothold in the Continental U.S.

Remember that Metro, the Washington subway system, serves all of this area. Find a campground or a parking area which is served by the Metro and the whole area is at your fingertips, via one of the best subway systems in the world.

Third day: Your feet will need a rest. Why not take the boat trip down the Potomac to Mount Vernon, George Washington's home? It leaves from its docks at the foot of Maine Avenue, just a short distance from the Jefferson Memorial and the Tidal Basin. Take the earliest run in the morning to avoid bigger crowds at Mount Vernon itself. The boat ride is fun, and it's a cool change from the city heat, and a good way to relax after a couple days of downtown Washington.

Fourth day: Drive your own rig to Annapolis, less than an hour east of Washington. This is the home of the U.S. Naval Academy, the one time capitol of Maryland, for a short time the capitol city of America. It's an excellent place to eat good seafood, but at high prices. This is a fascinating waterfront city where thousands of small craft ply the broad waters of the Severn River and nearby Chesapeake Bay. Sandy Point State Park, near the western edge of the Annapolis Bridge across Chesapeake Bay, doesn't allow overnight camping, so don't get your hopes up.

Fifth day: Take a look at the historic C & O Canal; walk a mile or so on its historic towpaths and you'll be 200 years back in history while still within 10 miles of downtown Washington. You might want to visit Arlington Cemetery, or Fort Sam Houston, or the Great Falls of the Potomac, or maybe visit Turkey Run National Park, right on the beltway around Washington.

Don't forget that there are campgrounds and state parks on the Virginia side of the river, also. You might have to camp 40 miles away from Washington, but it will be worth it in quiet camping and easy access to fascinating Washington.

Historyland Trail starts right where America started at Jamestown—where the United States started with the victory at Yorktown. It goes through the land which produced more of our nation's leaders than any other area, the land which gave birth to Washington and Lee, to Madison and Monroe, to Lewis and Clark, through the land where our democratic traditions got their start. Historyland Trail ends at our national capitol. the capitol of the free world, and one of the most interesting and beautiful of all capital cities in the world.

Many families report an added dividend. School age youngsters take more interest in history and in civics classes when they get back to school. It's much more meaningful when you've been there.

Camping makes it possible for the family of moderate means to make this tour. The camping can be fun, if it's planned right ahead of time. Start your tour planning 4 months in advance, then go camp the Historyland Trail—where America began!

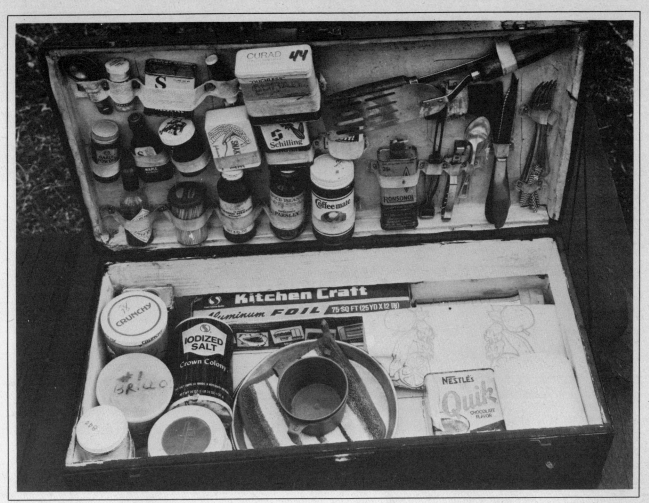

Campanions for the Camp Cook

by NORMAN STRUNG

THE CAMP KITCHEN is undoubtedly the most bothersome living unit to deal with when you're outdoors. The basic hardware required—eating and cooking utensils—takes up a lot of space and defies sane, sanitary storage when not in use.

More vexing are the "little things" like salt shakers, match cases, spices and can openers. They always seem to end up either missing or in the bottom of the box. Even big things like cans of pancake flour and coffee have a habit of being left behind or turning up empty once you get to camp.

These problems, and others that arose in the course of cooking a camp meal, provoked my wife, Sil, and me to customize a portable camp kitchen, complete with cupboard, closets and collapsible shelving. The entire kitchen cost us less than $60, and travels as a much more compact package than does the conventional cardboard box.

Sil gets the credit for the cupboard. Finding what she needed when she needed it was her biggest hassle, so she converted an old suitcase into a compartmented receptacle for spices, staples and clean-up gear. Putting

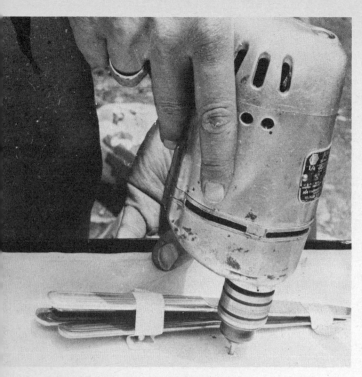

Begin by laying out all those small items that will best fit into the lid. Drill ⅛-inch holes on either side of the items.

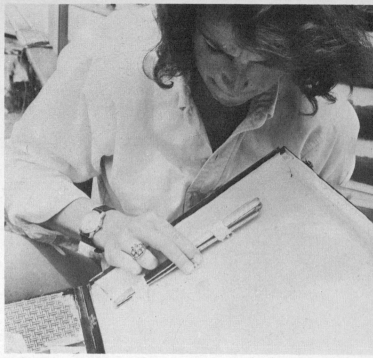

Run a ⅛-inch rivet through the top of the metal case, through the elastic banding, and face it with a washer. The washer keeps the elastic from pulling loose.

Blind riveters are the best tool for this job.

one together for yourself is really quite easy. It takes about 2 hours once you've assembled the necessary equipment. You start with a sturdy metal suitcase. The case that houses a defunct camp stove is another possibility. Begin by lining the inside with some sort of washable cloth material. A plastic table cloth is one possibility; a rubber baby's mattress liner is another. Glue it to the suitcase with contact cement. This not only facilitates the cleanup of inevitable maple syrup spills, it deters rust, and makes for an attractive background for the foods and utensils it will hold.

Next, you'll need a power drill with an ⅛-inch steel bit, ⅛-inch washers, a "blind" or "Pop" riveter with a batch of ⅛-inch rivets, and a ¾-inch wide elastic banding.

Once you've gathered these tools, assemble all those things you normally use for your camp cooking, and sort out the large items from the small ones. Begin with the small containers and utensils: things like knives and forks, can openers, spatulas, spices, toothpicks, and salt and pepper shakers. Lay them out on the inside of the open suitcase lid in whatever arrangement is most economical of the space available. Trace the outline of each item with a pen or an indelible marking pencil.

Once you've filled the space inside the lid, drill holes on either side of each outline. In most cases, you will be able to run a strip of elastic the length of the lid, so one hole will serve to fasten one side of two pockets. After all the holes are drilled, it's time to affix the elastic.

Start on the end, and poke a hole through the banding with an ice pick or an awl. Run the rivet from the outside of the lid, through the banding, through a washer, and pop the rivet in place.

To ensure a proper fit, take the item that particular pocket is to hold and put it in place. Stretch the banding over it so it is held snugly against the lid, and secure the loop with the second rivet. Lay the next item in place and repeat the process, until you've created a pocket for every outlined object.

In case you end up with more space than equipment this extra space is ideal for a first-aid kit, recipe notes, a deck of cards, a snakebite kit, and a pad and pencil. If it is practical and possible, you might also consider putting boxed goods into plastic containers. You can see their contents, they are more durable than paper, and they're fairly moisture proof.

When you've filled the lid, identify each nondescriptive outline with the name of the product inside the space. For example, the outline of a spatula is easy to identify, but several cans of spices in a row won't be. These labels make it easier to put everything back in its proper place when you're done.

The lower half of the case should be used for nonspoilable staples and kitchen aids like flour, sugar, coffee and paper towels. Packing them will be most economical if you use square plastic containers. Tupperware is one brand that comes to mind. The least desirable containers will be glass. They're heavy and prone to break even inside the stout case.

If the size and nature of the container lends itself to it, also secure them with elastic banding and label the space. When appropriate, Sil also wrote brief preparation directions, like a recipe for instant oatmeal with the amount of brown sugar and raisins we normally add. It's a big help to me when I solo as camp cook.

Depending upon the size of the suitcase you're adapting, this lower section might well also contain cups and plates, dish washing soap and scouring pads. Whatever consumable goods you stow there, remember to write it down. That way, when you use up a spice or a staple, all it takes is opening the cupboard before you leave on your next camping trip to know what needs replacing. It's all listed in easy-to-see empty spaces.

Storage and a handy check list of needed gear isn't

Fill the lid, outlining each item so you know exactly where it goes.

Larger items go in the body of the suitcase. Here too, it helps to identify what goes where. Note shock cord holding lid in upright open position.

Where practical, secure larger items with elastic banding just as you did on the lid.

The cupboard, fully stocked with spices, staples and utensils.

the cupboard's only function, however. You can work right from the opened case, like a spice rack at home. For it to serve this purpose lying flat on a picnic table, it's best to tie a short shock cord between the lid and the body. Just drill two holes, and rivet a chain or strip of leather in place. Even more simply, tie some nylon cording there. This keeps the lid up and open, with its contents in plain view and easy reach.

Another option is to hang the cupboard from the branch of a tree. It saves table and sitting space, and allows the cook to work at eye level, rather than from the ground. The best way to engineer this feature is to bolt two eye hooks on either side of the lid. With them, the cupboard can either be nailed in place, or suspended with a cord tied to one or two tree limbs.

Although Sil's cupboard solved some of the disorder common to camp kitchens, we still needed even more storage space. I grew weary of colliding at 3 AM nature calls with pots and pans that were left on the ground, and sharing table space with a sack of potatoes at meal time. What was needed was some shelving for the larger kitchen gear that was in daily use, so I devised collapsible camp shelves.

To build these, you'll need three, 3-foot long 1x12s, some lathe, 8 square feet of canvas and some shingle nails.

Cut the canvas into 1-foot x 4-foot strips. I'd also

With the lid in the open position, camp cooking items are in easy reach of the cook, and you know where they go when you're done.

recommend you hem the canvas on a sewing machine to prevent fraying. In addition, either sew buttonholes, or set eyelets into each corner of the strips.

Mark the canvas at 1-foot increments, and cut the lathe into foot lengths. Using shingle nails, tack the lathe to the butt-ends of the boards at the mark, sandwiching the canvas in between the lathe and butt. The net result will be collapsible shelves that resemble a venetian blind. They fold up into a 1-foot x 3-foot x 4-inch package. When you need shelving, just hang them between two tree limbs.

The cupboard can be hung in a tree, just like a spice rack at home.

Although it would be even simpler to fashion portable shelving from boards and rope, I strongly suspect rope fastenings would prove to be shaky. The canvas affords surprising rigidity, especially when you tie the shelving at four points.

You can eke even more storage space out of this concept by adding screw hooks to the underside of the bottom shelf. They're perfect for things like coffee cups, potholders and even clothing.

Two, stout wooden boxes were my final contribution. They serve to house the largest cooking utensils when you're on the road—pots, pans and basins to do the dishes.

Where there is nothing remarkable about a simple box, their size and sturdy construction represent surprising utility. They measure 14 inches x 14 inches x 20 inches. On the ground, with something like a boat cushion on top, they make for a serviceable seat. Stood on end, they raise a camp stove to a comfortable cooking height when picnic tables aren't available. They also fall nearly flush with the rear seat of my station wagon when stowed flat on the floor. By spanning the narrow space above the driveshaft tunnel with a piece of plyboard, it extends the size of the seat enough to make for a wide bed should someone want to snooze during a long day's drive. This arrangement is also an ideal way to sleep children—safe, secure, and quiet—should adult campers wish to burn the midnight oil.

If there is a key to camping with a minimum of hassles, it lies in adaptability and compactness; equipment capable of performing several tasks at once, that takes up a minimum of space. These additions to our camp kitchen surely fill that bill. "Camp-anions"—great things to have around at dinner time.

One of the good camping spots on the Suwanee River, this sand bar is just above Florida Highway 6 bridge.

CAMPING THE OKEFENOKEE AND SUWANNEE

by MAX HUNN

THE BEAUTIFUL Suwannee River rises in South Georgia's Okefenokee Swamp, and meandering out of the "land of the trembling earth" becomes a picturesque river as it journeys across Florida to the Gulf of Mexico.

Today the river which twists and turns for 265 miles enroute to the sea, is one of the nation's most famous streams. It's not famous because of its length or its width, but because of a song. Stephen Foster, the 19th century composer, brought undying fame to the stream with his song "Old Folks at Home," more often known as "Swanee River." Without ever seeing the beautiful waterway, merely because the name fit his song, Foster brought musical immortality to the river that begins in the Okefenokee and ends in the Gulf.

Today, more than a century and a quarter after Foster composed his famous song, the swamp and river can be the locale of an unusual camping-boating adventure, particularly if you travel the entire distance from the Waycross side of the Okefenokee to the little hamlet of

Suwannee on the Gulf. This is a camping trip requiring small boats. You can't operate in the swamp with big motors nor with big boats, both because of regulations of the Okefenokee National Wildlife Refuge, and because of the swampy terrain.

Once you see the shallow boat trails twisting across the beautiful, flower dotted prairies, or squirming through the cypress strands, it's obvious the boat must be narrow, too. Even then, you often have to get out and wade to lift your craft across sunken logs, cypress knees and other obstacles. This is, indeed, primitive boating.

The small boats are fine for maneuvering in the swamp, but the little motors are inadequate for the river's grander proportions. One possible remedy is to arrange to have a friend meet you with a larger motor where U.S. 441 crosses the river at Fargo, Georgia. An exchange here makes the rest of the expedition quicker and perhaps safer, too. You might ask the same friend to pick you up at the end of the journey at the hamlet of

The Minnies Lake area of the Okefenokee is known for its towering cypress trees. (Photos by Kit and Max Hunn)

Suwannee. Most campers find that a one-way expedition suits them well.

Don't think you're the first to camp in the Swamp or on the river. The Indians, followed by the Spanish, collected that honor centuries ago. Today, you're not really pioneering, although you are camping in a country where neighbors are mighty few.

The trip can be made by boat with outboard motor, or by canoe. Adventuresome canoeists, gung-ho with muscle, have made the long, long paddle but it's far more comfortable with outboards. It's a 7-day trip—6 overnights—using boats with motors and much longer by canoe, even with the favoring current. But whatever your means of transportation, it's an unforgettable camping experience.

This is a camping trip that requires extensive advance preparation, as we well know after having traveled the Suwannee from the Okefenokee to the Gulf. You must plan with reference to the height of the river. You cannot make the safari during flood conditions (most usual in the early spring), when the Suwannee frequently becomes a raging torrent. Neither can you make the cruise during extreme low water. At this time you can't get across the Okefenokee, and the river itself is studded with exposed rocks and rapids, particularly in the area around and above White Springs, Florida. These can be hazardous and at some points require portages. Even with prime conditions, there's one, unavoidable portage across the Sill as you leave the Okefenokee.

Another factor to consider is the heat. The most comfortable time of year to cross the Okefenokee is during April and May, and then again in October and November. However, the governing factor is the water level. But if the river is normal, the Swamp full or nearly full of water, these months are best so far as heat and insects are concerned.

You could, of course, make the camping trip during colder weather with satisfactory water levels but South Georgia and North Florida do get cold during the December-February period, too cold for most campers in tents.

Our experience on the 265-mile expedition highlight some of the facets of this camping expedition. The Okefenokee Swamp Park just south of Waycross, Georgia is the jumping off point for those planning to cross the Okefenokee and go down to the Suwanee. It's adviseable to have a knowledgeable "swamper" with you, for the Okefenokee has no traffic signs. We took no chances.

Our party leaving from the Swamp Park consisted of three veteran swampers: Johnny Hickox, chief Swamp Park guide; Jimmy Walker, Swamp Park Manager; and Johnny Seldeon, another guide; myself, and my wife, Kit. Our advance planning was detailed. Although we anticipated some tight places in the swamp, we decided to use 16-foot, semi-V, broad beam johnboats, rather

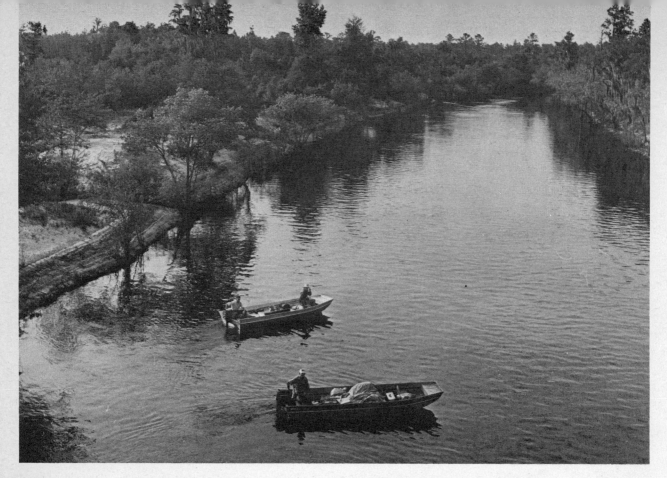

The Suwannee River is a broad, smooth avenue through northern Florida.

than narrower 14-foot models. You do need all the space possible for camping gear on such a long trip.

Because of the Wildlife regulations and the swampy terrain, you are limited to 9.8 horsepower outboard motors, which set no speed records with the heavy johnboats, but do the job. Fortunately, these motors aren't gas hogs, and our fuel calculations were perfect. Carrying two 6-gallon tanks for each motor—the tanks conveniently fit under the aft seats in the boats—we made the trip with three refueling stops: Fargo, Georgia, White Springs and Branford, Florida. We could have obtained boat gas at Stephen Foster State Park in the Okefenokee.

Tents, of course, were necessary as protection against insects, although as it developed bugs were no problem. It is possible to use a sleeping bag and a ground cloth during the warm nights if there are no bugs, but a tent is more comfortable particularly if it rains. You camp on sand bars, and with the river at normal height, have no trouble locating them. However, if the river is high you must pitch your tents on the higher banks. It is advisable to start looking early for a suitable campsite. It's no fun trying to pitch a camp in the dark, let alone find a place.

Our provisions were planned for 6 days, and we didn't go hungry. Food is never a problem, for there are stores at all of the refueling points. We carried drinking water, although it is possible to use river water with a

purification system. It seemed simpler to replace our drinking water at each gas stop.

Leaving the Waycross side of the swamp the camper plunges into one of the nation's unique natural attractions. The Okefenokee Swamp is not a true swamp, but actually a watershed draining south. The Swamp is 128 feet above sea level on the northeast side, and 103 feet on the southwest where the waters leave the Okefenokee via the Sill. Even in the twisting, prairie boat trails, you notice the current moving southward, particularly if you happen to be running northward roaming the swamp. By starting from Waycross, you take advantage of the current during the entire trip, and at times the current is strong.

The Okefenokee deserves its title, "land of the trembling earth," as the Indians named it. The land does just that. There's floating land that trembles when you walk on it. There's also land that won't hold your weight. The term "swamp" confuses many. It's not a dense, dismal, dark jungle, and it's not all trees, for there are some 60,000 acres of prairie, often studded with colorful flowers.

Breaking out of the thick cypress strand a few miles south of the Okefenokee Swamp Park, the route winds through cypress strands, around cypress heads, and twists across broad, colorful prairies. Acres and acres of pristine white water lilies stretch off to a horizon of cypress, gum, and bay festooned with Spanish moss.

Purple pickerel weed and pitcher plants dot the treeless areas, while purple bladderwort peeks shyly from the base of cypress trees.

Like the old swampers who named Dinner Pond, you can arrive at the rain shelter for lunch. It's a welcome break. In push-boat days, swampers reached Dinner Pond for the midday meal (dinner to them) if they started poling at daylight. We can cover the distance in much less time with boats and motors.

Leaving Dinner Pond, boaters encounter the roughest terrain enroute to Big Water. The "Dinner Pond Thick" is just that—darned thick! You can't help but marvel at the early swampers who crossed The Thick in push boats. It was plain hard work, and it's still work even with mechanical horsepower. Underbrush blocks the seldom used boat trail, and it is necessary to pole repeatedly or to carry the boat over cypress knees. It's only about a mile through the strand, but it takes at least an hour to fight your way past.

Beyond The Thick, the going is easier, although there's still plenty of pushing, because of stumps left from logging days and debris from ancient fires. The blackened trees have largely vanished, often showing up in the boat trails. It's a relief to reach Big Water, the beautiful lake in the heart of the swamp. This placid mirror is surrounded by towering cypress trees from which startled birds spring at the sudden intrusion of visitors.

Cruising from Big Water to the narrow, cathedral-like trail leading to Minnies Lake and Billys Lake is smooth and easy. These lakes, easily reached from the south, are two of the Swamp's most popular fishing areas. Late in the afternoon you arrive at Stephen Fos-

Dinner Pond Thick is the toughest portion of the camping trip. It lies across the Okefenokee Swamp like the scene from a Tarzan movie.

Beginning the Swamp part of the cruise. The sign is a challenge and tells the truth. You can get lost.

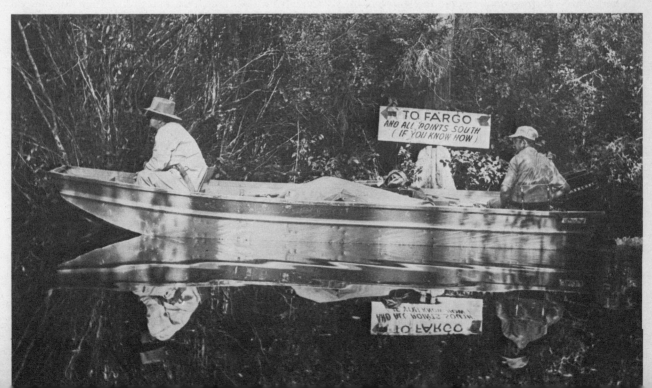

There are places in the Okefenokee where our 5-foot wide johnboats were too wide to go between cypress knees. The only thing to do was to carry our craft as Johnny Seldeon (left) and Jimmy Walker demonstrate.

ter State Park in the swamp for your overnight camp. One must reach the park for camping is not permitted in the Refuge. Besides you'd be hard pressed to find a dry campsite. There are rental, air-conditioned cabins available here.

The Sill, the earthen dam erected in 1960 to control the flow of water from the Okefenokee during drouths and to prevent erosion, is crossed next day. In order to cross the Sill it's necessary to obtain a free permit from the U.S. Fish and Wildlife Service. All that is required is a letter advising the Refuge Manager of your plans and your date for crossing the Sill. The permit system controls the hauling of boats over the dike which could be damaged with too much traffic. Contact the Manager, Okefenokee National Wildlife Refuge, P.O. Box 117, Waycross, GA, 31501 for permit details and regulations of the refuge.

It's a twisting cruise through the River Narrows to the Sill. There's ample water but a route a snake would shun. Then begins the work of portaging boats and gear across the earthen dam. There is no other way to get into the river. Beyond the dike the Suwannee is still ill-formed, meandering through a picturesque tupelo swamp, only gradually developing a definite channel. It flows 18 miles to Fargo, the first refueling stop. Leaving Fargo, it's a good idea to begin looking for a campsite.

The Suwannee develops steep banks now and the camping possibilities are limited. But they can be found depending upon the river's height.

Passing the Florida state line, the river's character changes again. This time sheer rock banks, some 10 to 12 feet high, line the shore. Cruise past this area and look for a camping site near where Florida Highway 6 crosses the river. By now everyone's accustomed to sleeping in tents, but before dropping off to sleep, listen to the river. It has a different lullaby than does the Swamp.

There are bad rapids—as we unfortunately discovered—several miles north of White Springs and on the third day be alert for them. Half way there we rounded a bend and suddenly encountered the worst water of the trip—white water and exposed rocks. We'd been expecting to portage, but instead found trouble. Johnny Hickox and Kit in the lead boat moved closer to investigate. Turning to come back, their motor hit a rock, breaking the motor mount. Powerless, they were swept broadside upon a huge partly exposed rock on the edge of the first falls.

Johnny Seldeon and I tried to land on the left bank, but near shore the current was too powerful for our heavily ladened, underpowered johnboat. We had to shoot the rapids. Keeping the bow straight and lifting the motor, we bounced over the three falls, each about 3 feet high, in seconds, finally stopping in the quiet backwater below the rapids. We were safe but Johnny and Kit were in real trouble.

Beaching our boat, Johnny and I scrambled back upriver with two lengths of rope brought along for emergencies. Securing the longest (100 feet) to a tree, Johnny carefully waded out in the shallow but fast moving water and fastened the line to the stranded johnboat. With this improvised lifeline and the boat temporarily secured, Kit and Johnny Hickox inched their way to safety on foot. Johnny made two more trips fastening the second line to the boat and bringing out cameras and other personal gear.

Initially we intended to unload and then pull the boat down over the rapids. But the footing was too tricky and the current too swift. Instead we decided to pull it over still loaded regardless of the risk of losing our gear. The boat appeared in momentary danger of sliding over the first falls but it was firmly lodged. Three of us hauling on the line couldn't budge it. Finally, by shifting the two ropes downstream to utilize the current's power, we managed to work the boat loose and over the first falls and into shore. Because of its beam it did not upset. Unloading, we eased the empty boat down the last two rapids with a rope on the bow and one on the stern then reloaded and gratefully chugged toward White Springs. We towed the disabled vessel. It was a long, slow ride interspersed with rain squalls. Finally at 7 PM we reached our destination. It seemed like midnight. With a new motor we resumed our cruise the next day.

One of the problems of planning this cruise is that there's little current information available. It is known that there are numerous shoals and rapids in the vicinity of White Springs, but the height of the river governs whether or not they're problems. There is one night's shore camping between White Springs and Branford. The Suwannee is a wide navigable river below Branford. Once stern wheelers plied its waters from the Gulf to Branford hauling cargoes of cotton, peanuts, lumber, tobacco and naval stores. The golden age of the Suwannee river boats was from 1886 until 1914. The steamboat era ended in 1923 when the City of Hawkinsville, last of the stern wheelers, sank.

The river is wide and deep, still the same dark color it was when it left the Okefenokee. From Branford to the Gulf the Suwannee's character remains the same, dense woodland, sometimes high banks and lush vegetation. Unfortunately, weekend retreats ranging from shanties to old railroad cars, sub-division signs, and more and more private docks are seen.

The last camping night is in the vicinity of Fanin Springs. Another half day's cruise ends at the little hamlet of Suwannee at the river's mouth. Seeing the broad Gulf of Mexico at the mouth of the Suwannee, you know you've completed a rare camping trip. Camping and boating the Okefenokee Swamp and the famous Suwannee River is indeed an unusual experience. Too bad Stephen Foster missed it.

The watery route meanders through the Okefenokee Swamp, twisting like a drunken snake.

After manhandling our disabled johnboat from its perilous position in midstream to the shore, we had to unload it before attempting to lower it past the remaining rapids. Johnny Hickox shown in boat, Max Hunn (author) in middle and Johnny Seldeon, the rescuer, on shore.

by ERWIN A. BAUER

RECENTLY in western Canada, a newspaper reporter compared the daily weather predictions, which are gathered scientifically from satellite sensors, with the predictions made by a very old Indian woman who lived in a lonely log cabin without even a radio. Day in and day out the lady's hunches proved more accurate, and for purely local weather predictions, she was astoundingly correct. The reporter asked the secret of her success.

"I tell by the stiffness in my joints," she answered.

That may or may not be true. But in the absence of local prophets, any camper's best bet for foretelling weather is still the news media. Knowing the approach or end of a storm can make all the difference in planning a trip. It can even tell an outdoorsman where and how to camp. But of course up-to-date weather forecasts are not always available in the woods. Still any camper can predict weather on his own, with considerable accuracy, even without stiffness in his joints. Often it is possible to foresee major *changes* in the weather if you can read some of the clues and signs all around you.

Almost anywhere during fair weather in America the air becomes more and more laden either with dust particles or with moisture (humidity), depending on the particular region. A light haze seems to hover above the land and at dusk this develops into the beautiful, salmon-colored sunsets which campers enjoy. Mountains in the distance seem far away and indistinct. It's a lazy, pleasant time to be outdoors.

But suddenly the sky may become clearer and those peaks in the distance are more distinct and may even seem closer. All at once the air has a fresher scent to it; at least your sense of smell seems more keen. As every bass fisherman knows, this is a good time to be on the water because bass will go on the prowl. But it is also a time to drive tent stakes deeper, zip up the flaps and put camping gear under cover because a storm front is approaching. Your campsite may not exactly be in its path, but a wise camper gets ready for wind and rain or snow.

There are many, many more indicators of weather change. You may notice, for example, that your sense of smell is working overtime, that coffee brewing on a camp stove has a more delicious odor. The scent of pine or spruce is stronger and so is the sweet aroma of wild flowers. Nor is it an illusion if you happen to be hearing better. The rush of a nearby stream will be louder and the first thunder you hear may not be quite as far away as it seems.

But keep in mind that wildlife is even more sensitive to changes in atmospheric pressure than is man. When a storm front is approaching, most birds and animals detect it well in advance and react in different ways. For one thing all are likely to be more active, or at least more restless. Gregarious animals, wild and domestic, tend to group together more, but also to be more irritable. Watch for the whitetail deer (or Jersey cow) licking or pushing another. I noticed once that the chipmunks and whiskey jacks which had been freeloading around my campsite became more bold before a major weather change. Such insects as mosquitoes really do become troublesome. If you are on a pack trip using horses or mules—and you have a harder time than usual catching them in the morning—look for an atmospheric change,

A long period of dry weather which is so common in the Southwest allows particles of dust to remain in the air and the landscapes in the near distance appear hazy as here. But storms can come up anywhere and the wise camper will batten the hatches when the air suddenly clears and those vague shapes become distinct.

How to Predict the Weather

probably for the worse. Many riding horses are more nervous, more spooky when weather will be unsettled.

Usually clouds are the first visible signs of impending change. Especially in the mountains, faint whisps of high cirrus clouds appear very high up and they may be so thin that the sun shines right through as before. You can ignore these lofty cirrus clouds unless a solid sheet of angry, gray cirrostratus clouds follow close behind because that combination means trouble. The leading edge of the cirrostratus forms a ring around the sun or moon and when it does, dig out the raincoats and prepare for a spell of wet weather. The larger this halo, which is often beautifully multicolored, the more severe the rainstorm which is following.

Bob Bauer ignored nature's warnings and tries to warm himself in the smoke of a smoldering campfire while the rain threatens to extinguish the few burning sticks of wood.

Campers in wide open plains country often can clearly see major storm fronts approaching in the form of threatening, unbroken banks of clouds on the horizon, maybe as far as 50 miles away. But in hilly or mountain country where visibility is limited, a camper must depend on more subtle signs. One of these is cloud caps building over peaks (often obscuring them) and spilling downward. If the caps increase in size during the day, there is plenty of moisture on the way. If the caps become smaller, there will be no serious storm.

The smoke from your own campfire or cabin chimney might be your most accurate weather barometer. A smoke plume rising high and straight indicates a high barometer and promises fair weather—or at least dry weather. If smoke does not rise and instead dissipates close to the ground, the prospects are for unsettled weather and possibly a storm. Depending somewhat on wind currents, indoor fireplaces draw better on a high barometer. If you suddenly detect a change in draft, if wood burns more slowly, you can also figure on a change in the weather.

Even many common plants offer clues about approaching weather. Long ago American Indians depended on watching familiar vegetation to tell them what to expect. The sudden appearance of many mushrooms or toadstools was a sign of rain to come—and probably in quantity very soon. Many different kinds of flowers begin to close up whenever a storm or rain is imminent. Often I have watched dandelions, one of the most widespread plants of all today, close up long before I ever heard the first distant rolls of thunder. Some other native wildflowers are even more sensitive and the stems noticeably droop with the onset of rain. But the same flowers perk up again just before the storm passes. Most of us have heard the old saying which goes: "Red sky in the morning, sailor take warning; red sky before night, sailor's delight." While this may be fairly accurate at sea, it doesn't work too well for campers inland. But a heavy *gray* sky in the evening is definitely a warning of precipitation to come within the next 24 hours, probably by next morning.

Of course it is easy to miss or misinterpret signs, especially when camping in a completely unfamiliar region. But a little experience and observation can cure that. Especially in mid-winter, visible signs are fewer and may be harder to understand, but they still are present. Very cold, still, mornings when trees and bare shrubs are covered with heavy hoar frost are practically guaranteed to continue fair, at least until nightfall. And a clear windless sky at night, illuminated by stars will probably be followed by another frosty morning.

Lower than normal temperatures for any region of North America usually are a promise of fair weather to

Wherever You Go Camping

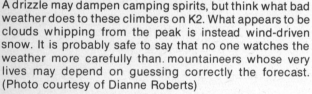

A drizzle may dampen camping spirits, but think what bad weather does to these climbers on K2. What appears to be clouds whipping from the peak is instead wind-driven snow. It is probably safe to say that no one watches the weather more carefully than. mountaineers whose very lives may depend on guessing correctly the forecast. (Photo courtesy of Dianne Roberts)

A low bank of fog as seen here at the base of Mt. Moran in Grand Teton National Park is a common morning phenomenon. The whispy cirrus cloud in the sky is probably meaningless, but should it become larger or darker it would be a prudent thing to postpone a mountain hike. Pay particular attention if the sky has been completely clear preceding this.

remain, although there have been a few dramatic exceptions to this in the eastern United States during recent winters. But sudden warming trends are likely to mean trouble in the form of heavy snowfalls—or rainfall in more southern latitudes.

The early explorers of America, especially the mountain men who trapped beavers and otherwise matched wits with nature in the Rocky Mountains, monitored the weather without really realizing it. If they noted that pintails were flushing reluctantly from beaver ponds, or if they felt especially clammy on an otherwise dry day inside their homemade buckskin jackets, they automatically found a more sheltered spot to spend the night. If sweat evaporated readily and ducks flew high, they could sleep anywhere on open ground, rolled up in a buffalo hide, figuring it wouldn't rain.

Even though we are less attuned, much less sensitive to our environment today, we still can get a better night's sleep under canvas if we have some idea about the impending weather. During favorable dry weather you might very well pitch your tent where a steady

crosswind for ventilation is the first consideration. But with a storm expected, you should consider moving it to a more protected area. Or you just might face it in a slightly different direction so that the full brunt of the wind is not against the entrance. A quick, short shift in position could make all the difference in keeping dry.

If you are depending on firewood for fuel, the period just before bad weather breaks is the time to collect it. Stack the wood, cover it with a waterproof cloth held in place against wind with rope or stones. Be certain also that your tent—in fact your whole campsite—is not in the shadow of dead trees which are likely to be toppled by high winds.

Every year without fail, too many campers lose all their gear (and occasionally their own lives) by being trapped in dangerous, low-lying areas by sudden storms, cloudbursts or (during mid-winter in deep snow regions) by avalanches. This is especially true in dry canyon areas of the southwest which suddenly become torrents right after a sudden hard rain. All of these tragedies can be avoided by proper campsite selection and more carefully watching the weather.

Camping with two tents, although one is technically large enough for the family, makes for needed privacy and space and better dispositions.

How to Survive Your Children's Summer Vacation

by LORI NELSON

IF YOU as a parent dread the arrival of George Washington's birthday because the kids will have the day off from school, and it may rain . . . and they'll all be inside . . . with friends . . . for lunch . . . Or if you secretly like *Mondays* when it's quiet, and you can get something DONE—read on. You will need all the help you can get this summer.

Let's assume you already own or will rent some sort of camping vehicle in which the family will vacation. Now if you are the sort of parent described above you will need to do a lot of advance planning to have enough grit left to wave the little ones off on the first day of school. If you don't panic quite that easily, plan ahead anyway. It will pay off handsomely.

Probably the most important thing you and your spouse can do to insure a vacation with the fewest possible traumatic experiences is to practice. No great athlete or musician just starts out cold and expects to turn in a good performance. What does he do? He warms up first. So—plan at least one and preferably

more weekends away with the kids before the main event.

It is vital that all RV systems are working properly and that they are well understood by at least the adults in the group. I have heard it suggested, and I think the idea is a good one, that older children each be assigned an "area of competence." George Jr. might be in charge of water, for instance. He sees to it that the tanks are clean and filled before departure day. He understands where waste water goes, and how and also when that may be disposed of. He concerns himself with supply and demand, too. His responsibility extends through the entire operation—to emptying the system at the end of the trip to insure the survival of the RV during its period of inactivity. This is usually winter, and often in a climate where accumulated water will freeze and cause costly and probably unseen (until later!) damage. Other responsible children may be assigned other areas. Of course, it's important that the complexity and difficulty of the task be carefully geared

97

Children who have briefed themselves on the up-coming vacation will better appreciate the majesty of the scenes they will see. Allowing them to photograph special areas will enhance their worth, too.

to the individual child.

Even before the preview run, a family conference on chores is in order. Have some sort of tentative list in mind or on paper of what jobs have to be done. Washing dishes was never a favorite job anywhere, and it won't be while vacationing either, but that's the chore that tops most lists. Try rotating this task among the able-bodied children. At least in the beginning dishwashing is less onerous if the dishes in the RV are a different set from those used in the kitchen at home. I'm not suggesting you buy an entire new set so the job will be done more cheerfully, but if you decide that unbreakable plastic will, in the long run, be more practical than the usual china, you may as well purchase it now.

Bed making can be "sleeping bag rolling" or "blanket smoothing" and each member of the family should do his own. I was told as a child that "you should never make a warm bed," but as I got old and bold (about 30, I think) I discovered that, in fact, no infirmity ensued after making a bed immediately upon arising. Actually this practice works very well.

Other tasks on the list should include sweeping the RV, cleaning the bathroom, taking the laundry to the laundromat and helping plan meals. Nothing festive here. Nothing likely to fire young enthusiasms. That's just why everyone should reach an understanding about who does what and when before you set out. Make a chart. It avoids future arguments and the familiar, "Why do *I* always get stuck with . . . " and "But I did that last time—don't you remember?" (and you don't).

Another thing to be checked out before the dry run should be sleeping arrangements. If the family is small there is little to decide. But as the number of children increases, the number of possibilities increase, too. You cannot assume that because Ellen and Kathleen got along so well last summer that the same will hold true this year. Maybe yes, maybe no. You may want to try the Kathleen/Sue combination. It is certainly obvious that interests and affinities among the kids change over a year's time and the sudden maturity of your adolescent may have promoted him/her right out of the share-a-bunk category. If you find yourself with more children, sexes and bedtimes than available sleeping space, consider using an auxiliary tent. Many larger families find that this extra bedroom makes all the difference. Again—try out this arrangement ahead of time. Those in charge of setting it up should be proficient before ever leaving home. You (or they) may find that spreading a sheet of heavy plastic on the floor the instant it's erect is worth the extra effort. This saves trying to sweep out the inevitable grit and general debris before dismantling. Just empty the tent and pick up the plastic, four corners together and high, and shake outside.

There are a couple of points we would like to make here that you may not have thought of, and may not agree with when you do. We think that parents may

Thinking ahead and careful planning including assembling all necessary camping items is important to vacation enjoyment with the kids.

have a feeling, deep beneath the surface that after all, this is the kids' vacation too and maybe they shouldn't have to take such a large hand in the operational nitty-gritty. It is our strong opinion that young people, like the rest of us, thrive on being needed, having a job to do and the satisfaction of doing it well. Idle, bored children are of no benefit to themselves or anyone else.

The second point is much more broad-based than the first. This may be the first time the young ones have really been involved in the basic running of the family unit and it is likely that the attitudes learned here will last well into adult life. We feel it is vital that the kids learn and practice conservation in all areas of living. With an increasing number of us competing for a decreasing amount of the world's goods we can no longer afford the wasteful practices we have fallen into. No paper plates which we use once and then burn or leave for someone else to burn. There are now too many of us to allow indiscriminate cutting and burning of wood. We may take only the allowable number of fish from the lake. Another group will soon be using the camping place we are now occupying. The rains and winds and seasonal changes which would once have obliterated signs of our presence will have no time to work their magic. We'll have to do the job ourselves. We must re-learn what thrifty grandmothers used to teach, "Use it up; wear it out; make it do or do without," and imbue at least one future generation with that viewpoint.

During the shake-down trip you will undoubtedly discover all the things you have forgotten and believe me, that's the time to find out even the bitterest truths, not the second day out on a month's tour. Make notes

as you think of things so that all will go as smoothly as possible next time.

Having a pretty definite plan for your vacation is important when you're traveling as a group. It's fun and exciting to pore over maps during the planning stage—

Recognizing the great potential for family tent camping, Coleman makes this tent (and others) in three family sizes. Here the family watches rafters drift down the Snake River in Grand Teton National Park. Maybe tomorrow they will make this same journey.

Sometimes a long driving holiday can be broken up by an interval of family houseboating. Many large impoundments in the U.S. will rent one for several days at modest cost. Here's one in Florida used during the Christmas holidays; it may be a better gift than anyone ever received before.

and a good education for all. Have the children write to the travel commissions of the states you will visit for information. Have them request maps that indicate not only the roads, but historic sites, geological places of interest, terrain, etc. Tape the map to the kitchen wall with your route marked out on it. Write also to any cities you may be near. Often the calendars of coming events will govern your schedule to some extent. I'm thinking now of state fairs, Indian Pow-Wows, rodeos and other special events. Many of these are interesting and fun and free. Take advantage of them. Disneyland is great, but most of us cannot afford this kind of thing for more than a day or two. Knowing that "in 2 days we will see real Indians" helps the littles be stoic during what may be a dull interlude for them. Reading about and discussing the places you will visit makes their enjoyment greater. My little cousin, Ginny, from a Chicago suburb may have been a bit over-programmed for her visit to an Indian village. The minute the family sedan rolled to a stop she marched her 4-year-old self over to an Indian brave, solemnly raised her dimpled palm and, looking the man squarely in the eye, grunted, "How."

We think that taking things on vacation to entertain the little ones en route is best held to a minimum. Have

them instead absorb the uniqueness of the places they're seeing, even if this is only by looking out of the window at the strange vegetation and geological formations. Consider how these plus the weather would influence the architecture of a region, for instance. What role has the origin of the early settlers played? What agricultural products are locally grown and which would have to be brought from other areas? The areas of thoughtful inquiry are endless.

We do think that a small traveling library of books is worthwhile. Bring the bird guide and binoculars, a wildflower identification leaflet, the tree book. The tiny volumes put out by the Golden Nature people are inexpensive and excellent for traveling. We own almost a dozen of these and take along those which pertain to the areas we will see. There are books on fishes, families of birds, reptiles and amphibians, non-flowering plants and insects. Regional guides are also valuable, the Southwest, for example, or Mexico.

At the end of the day's travel a time of genuine put-the-roses-in-the-cheeks exercise is mandatory. If you can park the RV at a campground with a pool for the same price as one without, choose the pool. If you've brought bikes, ride! The best exercise of all might be walking, jogging or running and that's always available. For reasons which escape me exercise somehow raises spirits. Things fall into perspective (tomorrow's predicted rain isn't necessarily the end of all of us) and later sleep comes promptly and unbidden.

If the vacation has been largely one of camping in the wilderness, fishing and hiking, a day in a relatively large town might be a welcome change. But what to do in a strange town? Well, first off, there's merit in consciously recognizing that it *is* different. Compare it to home. Look at the buildings. Flat roofs, thick adobe walls and tile floors? White clapboard homes with dark green shutters? Why? Revolutionary War monuments in the town square, or historic plaques are interesting to read.

Many towns have a small museum, and these can be fascinating. Also, being small, they're not as intimidating to the young (or their parents) as the huge, pillared affairs we're accustomed to. I remember a whaling museum in Sag Harbor, New York which meant far more to the children than the entire panorama of a complete whaling village at Mystic, Connecticut. There's a small gem of a museum at Colter Bay in Grand Teton Park in Wyoming which concerns itself solely with the Indian. Many southern towns have quite complete displays of artifacts from "The War Between the States." Morristown, New Jersey boasts George Washington's headquarters, the Ford Mansion, as a national monument. Anyone interested in colonial furniture could spend days here—and at almost no cost. Try your vacation town, who knows what you may find?

You should know in advance about upcoming state and regional fairs, but it may happen that you'll come across a mini-fair or traveling carnival quite by accident. These local affairs and church bazaars are good fun and usually far less expensive than the swollen, bedazzling galas which are designed to awe and impress all comers. Hot dogs are 30¢, the ferris wheel ride a quarter, and often the Ladies' Guild fancywork booth will offer for sale beautiful things at very low prices. Where else does anyone get aprons or embroidered guest towels?

"What are we going to do with Fang while we're gone?" Well, if you'll take good advice, leave him home. Leave him with a neighbor, board him at a kennel or have Grandma take over his care, but leave him. This sounds hard hearted, but it really isn't. A dog cooped up all day in the RV, or leashed to the back door is no joy. Dogs can become ill and often do. Dogs fight with other dogs. Dogs are not allowed on trails in many parks. Dogs can foul the camping area and disturb others. Kids are flexible (more so than their pets) and will hardly even think of old Shep after the first day out. The longing to see him probably won't surface again until you're 10 miles from home on the return trip. Hang tough. Say no.

It's true what you've heard: an accident can ruin a vacation. We expect minor problems, and as a responsible parent you've brought the first-aid kit and any medicines your particular brood may need. But there should be particular thought given to special hazards you might encounter on vacation. I once saw a terrible accident happen, avoidable, as so many are. A pick-up camper was parked near ours at a lake; the occupants were an average family group—mother, father, a boy about 13 or 14 and a younger girl, maybe 9. The boy returned to the camper and leaned his fishing rod on the open door at the rear of the vehicle. I saw the free hook dangling in the open doorway.

An instant later the girl raced from inside to see what her brother had caught and got the treble hook imbedded in and around her right eye. My husband, Albert, who knew the area, and the father rushed the child to the hospital. I tried to calm the hysterical mother, and the brother was left alone with his guilt. He may have suffered more than anyone else. Carelessness. Don't let it happen. Running in bare feet invites deep puncture wounds. Damp stones surrounding a campfire can explode with disastrous results. Swimming alone, especially in strange water, is folly. It may take time and effort to play it safe, but Blue Cross/Blue Shield can do without your business. Let them.

We hope that by thinking ahead everyone in your family will not only survive the childrens' summer vacation, but even enjoy it. Bon voyage.

The hot sun sets, a cool breeze blows off the water and the finest steak never tasted as good as the hot dogs cooked over a beach campfire.

A Baker's Dozen New Products You Should Know About

by PEGGY BAUER

Gluematic Pen: Shaped like a large crayon, the Gluematic Pen contains metered drops of instant glue. With a bonding strength of 5,000 pounds per square inch this instant adhesive will bond any non-porous surface in seconds. It is the solution for the 1,001 little wears and tears which confront every camper. The non-clog tip makes for easy application and the glue resists water, extreme temperature and most chemicals. It can be used on metals, china, ceramics, leather, rubber and most plastics. It belongs in every backpack, sailor's locker and archer's quiver. A broken fishing rod now needn't mean a lost day at the stream. It is made by Woodhill Permatex, 18731 Cranwood Pkwy., Cleveland, Ohio 44128.

Coleman's Peak 1 Frame: This one-piece frame for a backpack may just be the best on the market today. It is lightweight yet sturdy and has far less bulk than those made of aluminum tubing or fiberglass poles. Each slot not only decreases the weight but is a possible place to insert the upper, lower and belt straps. Any body size and shape can therefore be accommodated perfectly with 2,000 variations possible. It is made in two degrees of stiffness, the more rigid for heavier loads.

Air Lift's Ultra Light Sleeping Bag/Air Mattress Combo: For the backpacker who won't carry a single extra ounce, this new duo represents the ultimate in sleeping comfort. The bag is filled with lightweight Polarguard quilting and is designed with a special pocket to hold the new "Blue Wing" superlight air mattress. (It will also

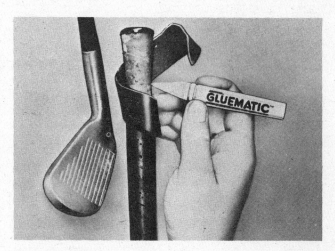

The Gluematic pen

hold any of the three other Air Lift mattresses currently on the market.) Made to use to 20 degrees F., the bag comes in two lengths, the longer weighing just over 4 pounds. The Blue Wing is the lightest Air Lift yet made, weighing only 1 pound, 3 ounces and gives a full 22x72-inch sleeping area. It packs into its own nylon stuff sack in a bundle 3½x9 inches. Like all Air Lift mattresses it is composed of 10 individual tubes enclosed side by side in a shell of nylon taffeta. One good puff inflates each tube. Some backpackers (or those using the Air Lift in a van or large family tent) prefer to inflate the outer tubes more fully than the center ones in order to get a raised side effect. Air Lift, 2217

Coleman's Peak 1 backpack frame, possibly the best on the market today for lightness and good fit.

Roosevelt Ave., Berkeley, California 94702.

Optimus Purist 1 Stove: Although this small stove closely resembles others on the market, it is an improvement over older types. First it burns white gas (or Coleman fuel) which is readily available. White gas evaporates easily when spilled and has the highest heat output (per unit of weight or volume) of any recreational stove fuel. With a full tank (about 1/3-pint) it will burn at full flame for 45 minutes. We were able to boil a quart of water on the Purist 1 in 4 minutes, slightly longer at higher elevations. The stove is small and weighs only 2 pounds fully fueled. Most stoves need to be primed before ignition, but not this one. The windscreen is not effective enough, however, and the stove should be used in a sheltered area. R.E.I., Box C-88126, Seattle, WA 98188.

Classic Backpack Tent: Although this resembles tents of older design, it is indeed new and improved. Coleman now makes it with a free-standing frame and better ventilation. The size is 7 feet, 9 inches x 5 inches with a ridge height of 42 inches. The door is plenty large enough to enter without tipping it over and there are V-shaped windows at each end. The tent roof is breathable to allow moisture to escape, and the fly is coated for good insulation in the backcountry. The Coleman Co., Inc., 250 N. St. Francis, Wichita, Kansas 67201.

Air Lift's Ultra Light is a made-for-each-other combination.

Allagash Reflector Oven: There is nothing really new about reflector ovens. They have been used since the discovery of shiny metals, but somebody put a lot of thought and experimentation into this one. Packed, it is fairly heavy and about the size and shape of a hefty Sunday newspaper. It unfolds to form an oven surface big enough for two loaves of bread, two pies or a dozen large biscuits. It is constructed of heavy aluminum sheeting. Its most convenient feature is its top reflective surface which can be lifted from behind to turn the contents to make best use of the heat. It measures 14½ inches high, 18 inches wide and the shelf is 8 inches deep. It would be a great addition to the camper's kitchen. Made by Great World, 250 Farms Village Rd., West Simsbury, CT 06092.

Rec-Pac: Here is a new multi-purpose sort of backpack made with the canoe camper in mind although it can be well used by anyone with special needs. The Rec-Pac is rigid, completely waterproof and molded of tough, polyethylene into a rectangular box shape. It has a volume of just under 2 cubic feet which means that up to 50 or 55 pounds of equipment can be carried inside or lashed to the outside. The hip belt allows the carrier to use his legs to shoulder the load, a great help when the weight is considerable. Accessory kits are available to

This is the new Classic Backpack Tent by Coleman.

attach cloth pouches (also waterproof) on the outside and there are D-rings to accommodate long items such as tent poles, fishing rods or a tripod which will not fit inside. There are handles on each end for easier lifting in and out of the canoe or boat. In camp the Rec-Pac is a sturdy seat, small table or work surface. When sealed the contents are nearly varmint proof (a bear, however, would have no trouble opening his prize). From Waters Inc., 111 E. Sheridan St., Ely, MN 55731.

The Last Light: This flashlight may indeed be the last you will ever have to buy. The makers have taken each of the problem areas in ordinary flashlights and overcome them. First, it is tough. Drop it, run over it with

Allagash Reflector Oven uses an old principle updated for today's needs.

The Last Light. Not much larger than a hot dog, this flashlight ensures light any time, any place.

104

the pickup, soak it with water, and it still lights. There is no switch at all. It is activated by twisting the head so battery contact is made and turned off by untwisting. The lens is unbreakable and it uses two AA Alkaline Batteries which will give four hours of illumination. The bulb will last twice that long. The whole thing weighs about 3 ounces. The light is not very bright, but will allow finding a track in the dark, repairing a faulty auto engine, locating a lost item in the duffle or it will hang from a string tied through a slot in the end. It is only 5½ inches long and about as big around as a quarter. It should be in every tackle box, fly-fishing vest and glove compartment as well as each backpack. Available from Early Winters, 110 Prefontaine S., Seattle, WA 98104.

Redi-Smok Bar-B-Que Cooker: Any camper, especially if he also happens to be a hunter or fisherman would welcome this portable smoker in camp or anywhere there is a 110-volt plug-in socket. The Redi-Smok is a cylindrical, upright steel oven. It slowly, evenly cooks or smokes almost anything using wood chips or shavings for a smoky flavor. The fact that the heat is electric rather than, say, charcoal makes the heat even and

The GO Insulated Parka has a two-way heavy-duty zipper plus two easy-access patch pockets.

Moistness and a deep smoky flavor enhance anything the cook prepares using the Redi-Smok.

steady with far less concern about wind velocity and temperature although these must be taken into consideration to some extent. The food is placed above the heat on a removable grill rack. A porcelain drip pan between the food and the heat catches the juices which are evaporated to circulate within the cooker. No wonder there is such a delicious smell when the lid is raised. Game meats like moose, venison and elk which generally tend to dryness emerge moist and flavorful. Upland birds the same. Smoked whitefish are a favorite and even make welcome gifts for friends. Vegetables can cook right along with the meat or fish as can baked apples, etc. Bill Carney's Cook Book comes with the cooker and has dozens of delicious ideas presented in a down-home accent. Most are for things you would cook any time, but others are exotic. Want to cook armadillo? Mexican cornbread with jalapenos? Coon or 'possom? The Redi-Smok comes in two sizes. From Redi-Smok Inc., Box 12505, Houston TX 77017. Tell Ole Bill Carney the Bauers sentcha.

Go Parka: Duck hunting is, by necessity, often done in the most unpleasant weather of the year. Early fogs and mists often merge into a drizzle and the unprotected gunner is often soaked and shivering in the blind. Now there is a parka just made for the purpose, Red Ball's GO parka. It is made of a polymer coated exterior in a brown or green camouflage pattern or solid dark green. The lining is a smooth knit and the insulation between is polyester fiberfill. The seams are permanently bonded

Cyalume lightsticks provide no-flame, no-heat illumination for hours.

and the arms have the batwing design which allow plenty of freedom for a good swing at an incoming flock of birds. The parka includes an attached hood and take-up snaps on the cuffs. Any camper anticipating inclement weather conditions would do well to bring along such a garment. For information on where to buy it write: Uniroyal Inc., World Headquarters, Middlebury, CT 06749.

Cyalume Light Stick: At first this lightweight (1-ounce) plastic tube seemed like a novelty item. The claims and description seemed impossible, a trick. Not so. The light stick is about the size of a large cigar and is activated by smartly bending it in the middle. Two chemicals are thus blended and the stick immediately glows with a rather bright greenish light. There is no flame, no heat at all, just a glow. It provides enough illumination to pitch a tent, change bass lures or read a compass in the dark. The stick gives about 3 hours of useful working light and then continues to glow for another 8-9 hours and can be seen for some distance. Once finished it must be thrown out. It would be a fine emergency light for most situations and good to mark a trail or a campsite. It also keeps the boogies from the kids in their tent. Available in sporting goods stores or from American Cyanamid Co., Chemical Light Dept., Bound Brook, N.J. 08805.

Backpacker Poncho: Any camper should own a multi-use poncho. It may be the only piece of foul weather gear a fairweather outdoorsman will need. This particular poncho is better than most in that it protects both the camper and anything (like a backpack) he's wearing or carrying. It works well when paddling a canoe or trail-riding on horseback, too. It will protect a sleeping bag or whatever gear is tied behind the saddle. At 52x118 inches this one-piece sheet makes an ideal groundcloth or cover for outdoor gear in case of a passing squall. We even built an acceptable lean-to with it. The drawstring fastens the hood snugly around the face and rust-proof snaps on both sides form a waterproof cape around the body. There are no seams over the shoulders to leak which makes all the difference in a determined downpour. Available from Outdoors Products, 530 E. Main St., Los Angeles CA 90013.

Flyweight Wader: Red Ball's new Flyweight Wader is possibly the best thing to come out of waders since their inception. Here at last is a tough lightweight fabric which resists abrasion which might result when climbing through brush. They have a drawstring at the top

The Backpacker Poncho from Outdoor Products comes in five sizes from child to deluxe long and serves many camping purposes.

and an air chamber around the top too which is inflated quickly and helps keep the water from rushing in as well as keeping the wearer afloat. These remarkable waders have a stocking foot and are worn with Bama Sokkets (which are included in the package) and ankle high sneakers (which are not included). They come in men's, women's and children's sizes. For more information write Bonnie Ackley, Uniroyal Inc., World Headquarters, Middlebury, CT 06749.

The best waders yet are the Flyweights which are tough but lightweight. These sockfoot waders are worn with Bama Sokkets which come with them and wading shoes which do not.

Cartop Canoe or Boat

a Camper's Secret Weapon

by CHARLES NANSEN

THE POND which covered only a few acres was barely visible through a damp and clinging morning fog. But soon after daybreak John Morgan and I followed an old cowpath to a low bluff overlooking the pond and there unlashed the canoe on top of my 4X4. We carried the canoe the 50 yards or so to water's edge, getting wet to the waist as we walked through the tall grass. A bullfrog plopped into the pond ahead of us.

"I'll give 10 to one," John said, "that no one else has fished here yet this spring."

We needed several moments to knot plugs to lines and then eased the canoe through a thick band of cattails which almost completely encircled the pond and which made casting from the bank nearly impossible. As soon as we reached open water, we began to cast.

I tossed a popping plug toward a huge sycamore which had been killed when the pond was impounded and which had eventually toppled into the water. The lure fell somewhat off target—tight up against the trunk—but that didn't make any difference. There was a heavy bulge in the water right beside it and when I popped the plug softly, the bass struck.

Not really ready for such immediate action, I had trouble catching the reel handles. When I did, the bass catapulted out of the water and then disappeared down

under the sycamore. The hooks pulled out and I reeled in nothing.

"What a way to start a morning," I said. One of the things I have learned in nearly 40 years of fishing is that lightning—or in this case bass—sometimes does strike twice in the same spot. My second cast fell in almost exactly the same place as the first and after a long pause and a pop, a second bass inhaled it. And this one was bigger than the first.

All in the same motion I set the hooks and held the rod high while horsing the fish away from the tree. That produced a beautiful jump, a wild run, and another jump. John had grabbed a paddle and was moving us toward the center of the pond and to more open water. Now I just held on while the bass surged toward the bottom.

"Just take your time now," John said.

In a few more minutes it was over. I slowly worked the fish to the top where it managed another half-jump, wallowed, and quickly I had it by the lower jaw. It was a 4-pounder and went on the first snap of the stringer.

What followed that early morning in May was a bass fishing session we wouldn't soon forget. By the time a warm sun had burned away the fog and action had dwindled, the stringer was nearly full with eight good bass. The smallest was 1½ pounds and we had released several smaller than that. It would be hard to find bass fishing better than that—anywhere.

But perhaps more amazing than the fishing was the pond itself. No remote wilderness water, it was instead a farm pond in a well-developed part of central Ohio and not far from a million human beings. It is close enough to a busy highway that we could hear faintly the sounds of traffic as we fished. Although it is not a public lake, the landowner does permit most people who ask him to fish. And in the past there has been a good deal of angling pressure.

Then how did we have the pond to ourselves? And what secret weapon or technique did we use to catch the bass? The answer to both questions is the same—the cartop canoe. Because of the cattails and other shoreline vegetation, fishing from the bank became more and more difficult and finally almost impossible. So local fishermen stopped asking permission to fish until nobody at all bothered anymore. But the light canoe which could be carried either on the cartop or on our shoulders made all the difference. It was the secret weapon.

To tell the truth, a light cartop craft can be almost any angler's secret weapon. It can be as important to more successful fishing and to happier fishing trips afield as the very tackle the angler uses. In other words it can catch more fish because it can take him into places where only other cartoppers can go.

The uses of cartop boats are numerous. Carry one along on a vacation and it provides instant transportation on any fishing water you care to sample. En route it is a good container or cover for any camping gear also carried on the cartop. Lash the craft to the pontoon of a float plane and fly it into isolated lakes. Explore swamps and bayous, oxbows, and other forgotten waters which fellow fishermen pass up. A cartopper owner is independent and does not have to rely on rental boats to fish strange places. But exactly what is a cartop boat?

Any craft which is not too heavy or unwieldy for one or two men to lift up onto carrier brackets on an automobile can be considered a cartopper. But some kinds are much more suitable for the job than others.

A 100-pounder is about all an average man can conveniently load and unload alone. A husky man might handle a slightly heavier craft and two men can usually cope with a 200-pound cartop model. Boats up to 300 pounds or slightly more are at times carried on the roofs of cars, but four men or mechanical loading devices (which are now available on the market) are needed to handle them. Keep in mind that very heavy boats can damage the carrying vehicle and if the weight is much beyond 200 pounds, a boat trailer offers much safer transportation and easier launching.

Thirteen feet is just about the length limit for a cartop boat. Beyond that, they are easily twisted by airfoil pressures when driving at high speeds and this makes for unstable, dangerous driving. Overhang of a boat can also interfere with the driver's vision.

The ideal cartop model, then, is shorter than 13 feet, light with shallow draft to get in tight places, of either aluminum or canvas-covered lightweight wood construction. Flat bottom boats are better than V-bottoms because of the lower silhouettes. Unless it is a very small craft, fiberglass boats are usually too heavy. Some inflatable rubber rafts are adequate cartop craft, but they are too easily buffeted by winds and not always a pleasure to handle on the water. Punctures are problems, too.

Of course canoes approach the ideal for cartop use. They are light and maneuverable, easy to propel, and have go-anywhere design. There is one model on the market today which weighs only 29½ pounds. However canoes are not the most stable craft available for some people.

No matter what kind of boat or square-ended canoe he has, an angler greatly increases his range and opportunities with a small outboard. By using a motor and keeping an eye on the weather, he can negotiate even large waters in a small boat.

I have seldom had more valuable use of a cartopper than during a recent week-long swing through Michigan's Upper Peninsula with Dick Kotis and John Oney. The trip was timed to hit the opening of the bass season on a couple of lakes we knew about in Schoolcraft County. But we wound up exploring farther and farther from our base and discovering some lonely little lakes in the process.

One morning Dick and John were fishing a lake near Steuben and not having much action when they noticed that it was fed by a small clear brook so overcanopied with willows that only the sound of running water betrayed its presence. Curious, John pushed his way through the willows and in 100 feet came upon a beaver dam and pond. Another 100 feet beyond that, he found a beautiful blue lake of about 25 acres without a summer cottage on its shores and no road leading to water's edge.

"Let's drag the canoe over that beaver dam," John suggested, "and see what's in that lake beyond."

It was sweaty work lugging the craft through the dense willows and at the same time swatting at a mist of mosquitoes. But it was more than worth it. The lake was full of willing, deep-green largemouths and for a bonus the pair caught several jumbo yellow perch.

"If those fish had seen any lures recently," Dick commented, "they didn't show it."

The next day John and I carried the canoe into a similar isolated pond and in this one we found nothing. It proved to be very shallow and probably any fish would be winter-killed. But in a third such carry-in lake, we found the largest pumpkinseed sunfish I have ever seen. What an extravagant fish dinner we enjoyed that evening!

When two boats travel together, one can carry the tent and the other the stove and food. This way a fishing float trip of several days duration is possible. This is a small stream in central Ohio impossible to reach any other way.

To transport any boat on the roof of a car, it is necessary to have cartop carriers. And the need for very stout, secure carriers is doubled on such a long trip as that one to Michigan. Nowadays a good many different kinds of cartop carriers are available. Most carriers consist of two rigid bars plus straps which are fastened onto the roof of the car, parallel to the car axles, and as far apart as possible. The boat rests on top of these bars, usually upside down. The rigid bars are fastened to the car by rubber suction cups, by metal clips or clamps which hook under the drain gutters, or often by both of these. Different arrangements work better with different car models and the wise cartopper will check out several before buying. It is also possible to install permanent carriers directly into the car's framework if the boat is to be used a great deal. Some cartoppers do keep their boats topside the year around—and never take them off except when they're ready to put them in the water.

However most owners will need some kind of between-fishing-trips storage facility and probably the simplest and least expensive is a pair of wooden sawhorses in the garage or backyard. Just set the boat on these upside down.

A better indoor storage method (particularly for canvas-covered boats) is one I learned from John Morgan who suspends his boat from the garage ceiling by four pulley ropes. To start a trip, John just drives under the boat and lowers it onto the carriers, and vice versa when he returns. When not in use, the craft hangs high and out of the way.

Considerable care should be given to securing any boat onto the carriers. I never depend on the webbed straps (which come with most carriers) alone. Instead I also use rope tie-downs from the car bumpers to bow and stern of the boat. I also use extra rope to lash my canoe to the carrier bars—this in addition to the straps. It's good insurance to frequently check all ropes, straps, and buckles for any signs of wear.

Over a good portion of eastern America, the best fishing which still remains is in the smaller rivers which have so far escaped pollution or channeling and are beyond easy walking distance of the bridges. The best and sometimes the only way to fish these sections of rivers is by float-tripping, and cartoppers were made for that. In fact if by size, weight or draft a boat isn't suitable for cartop use, neither is it the best for float trips.

The two-car system where one takes the canoe-campers to the launch point and several days later another picks them up far down stream is one of the best ways to fish. Overnight camping spots can be as picturesque as this in Wyoming.

The best technique for float tripping is to use two cars with carriers and to station one at the take-out point, probably by a convenient bridge. The other car carries the boat to the launching site, usually another bridge far upstream. I carry my own boat or canoe on a a 4-wheel-drive station wagon, and this does not confine me to bridge launchings. I can drive to many places other cars cannot.

Float trips can be of any length—a day, several days, a few hours—as much time as anyone can spare. It's possible to travel much farther, but I figure on averaging 6 to 8 miles a day. That allows plenty of time to stop and do a thorough job on the good holes. It also allows time, if the day is very hot, to take a refreshing swim and to cool off.

Float tripping does present a few unique problems to cartoppers. First it's necessary to check water levels —to be certain there is enough water in the stream before starting out. Spring is normally the best time to go because of the higher water, but spring is also the period when water is most likely to be roily. There is not much use in launching the boat when there is little chance of catching fish. Murky waters also increase the chances of damaging a boat because rocks and snags are not so easily visible.

Low water can be very rough on boats, unless the boat is carefully carried over very shallow places. Aluminum and cloth covered craft are especially vulnerable to puncturing and tearing—so it is always a good idea to carry a repair kit, just in case.

Planning a float is very important, and often one trial trip is necessary to "learn" the river. The Kokosing River in central Ohio is one of my favorite float trip rivers and there is one stretch not far from Mt. Vernon which is perfect for a 1-day trip. I've learned that by starting at daybreak I can quickly be in good smallmouth and rock bass fishing water where I spend plenty of time. During the middle of the day, I beach the canoe and find a cool place to relax in the shade. If it is early in the season, I can hunt mushrooms or collect a hatful of spring greens. Then finally I plan to hit another very productive stretch of water when it is in shadow late in the afternoon. It's interesting to note that in many trips spanning several summers, I have seen only one other angler casting this stretch of water. And he had also reached it by a small cartop pram. As I said before, the cartopper can be any angler's extra special weapon.

111

A Camping Bonus: the High Adventure of Daypacking

by ERWIN A. BAUER

EARLY ONE morning last spring we left our tent at the Watchman Campground in a grove of giant cottonwoods in Utah's Zion National Park. From there we drove a few miles to the Weeping Rock Parking Area. Close by, a weathered wooden sign pointed to the beginning of the East Rim Trail. With light rucksacks on our backs, my wife and I started slowly to follow that trail.

It was steep going every foot of the way up Echo Canyon, but it wasn't really difficult or dangerous. For the first mile the switchbacks were carefully graded and by starting early we were avoiding the crowds as well as the midday heat. In fact we climbed almost entirely in deep blue morning shadows. Early morning is the best time to find birds anywhere, and we paused often to watch hummingbirds and blue-gray gnat catchers. Higher up where the trail skirted sheer Navajo sandstone walls we heard the liquid note of a canyon wren. Just beyond that we startled a pair of gray foxes. Almost everywhere columbines and shooting stars, the first wild flowers of the season, bordered the edge of the trail and with increasing elevation the scenes of the Virgin River Valley far below us became more and more stupendous.

That East Rim Trail is not a new one. Prehistoric men—diminutive cliff dwellers—traveled it first. In 1896, a pioneer named John Winder somehow drove cattle over it. Ten years later an entrepreneur, David Flanigan, lowered 200,000 board feet of Ponderosa pine down the steep slope with the aid of cables. Today it belongs to anyone who relishes the outdoors and great natural beauty.

There is no need to return to civilization for lunch when the hiker carries a daypack into the wilderness. It carries bird guides and binoculars for the birdwatcher; paints, charcoal and sketch pad for the artist or almost anything else that might be wanted during a day-long excursion into the backcountry.

A small, easy-to-tote daypack is the belt pack (or fanny pack). It can be worn in front as here or in the rear. It carries a surprisingly large load in either of two compartments and is secured by adjustable overlapping Velcro bands topped by a wide webbed belt which is also adjustable for perfect fit. This leaves the wearer's hands, shoulders and back completely free.

(Below right) This conventional daypack by Alpine Designs has two compartments, a hanging strap and felt lined wide leather straps. It can carry all the items seen here and more. The fishing rod cylinder can be attached to the leather patch on the bag.

Well before noon we reached trail's end which is over 3 miles from the parking lot and almost ½-mile higher. From an observation point, air-conditioned by a dry wind, we enjoyed lunch with Zion Canyon yawning below us. It is one of the most magnificent panoramas in the entire U.S. National Park system, a scene which continually changes as the sun shifts from east to west. So not until the canyon was in deep shadow again and the Virgin River only a metallic ribbon below did we return to the bottom, arriving at cool dusk. It had been an extraordinary day.

Still, in another way it wasn't especially unusual. We often make such day-long hikes, short holidays which are possible almost anywhere in America and often the year around, when camping anywhere in parks or lonely wildernesses. Age or superb physical condition are not important, any number can participate and anyone can afford to go daypacking. The only ticket is a rucksack or daypack, plus a pair of comfortable, well-broken-in walking shoes.

But exactly what is a daypack anyway? It is a light cloth carrier or bag which is worn on the shoulders. A daypack is the means for toting just the things you will need to spend a day—and no more—exploring or vagabonding. In it you might carry a lunch, a camera, sunglasses and a foldup rain jacket. Depending on your special interest, you might also carry some kind of field guide, ultra-light fishing tackle, insect repellent, suntan lotion, a sweater, binoculars, note- or sketch-book. If wandering off the beaten tracks, figure on taking appropriate maps, a compass, waterproof matches, a knife and survival rations.

Daypacking differs greatly from backpacking. In the latter the hiker carries a whole camp on his back and

plans to be self-sufficient for at least one overnight, usually longer. For this he lugs a large load of at least 25 pounds and maybe twice that. Next to that a daypack, its 1-cubic-foot of space completely filled, weighs almost nothing.

A bewildering variety of daypacks are available in sporting goods and department stores nowadays. They range from military surplus bags for a couple of dollars apiece to those designed especially for mountain climbers which sell for around $40 and beyond. Somewhere in between is the now typical daypack with a $20 to $30 price tag. It will easily last a lifetime of normal use. One company even offers daypack home sewing kits. With only a sewing machine, you can manufacture your own for about half the price of a ready-made.

The typical handy daypack is a water repellent cotton canvas or nylon bag, zippered, with two compartments. It has shoulder straps and maybe a waist strap, all of webbing material. The two compartments are not necessary, but do help keep items inside separated and spaced out. When selecting a daypack, it is wise to check a number of points since there may be little difference in cost between good ones and poor ones.

First, carefully check the stitching around all seams and edges, especially where straps are attached to the cloth bag. Zippers should be of nylon rather than metal because the latter may corrode with dampness or sweat. When closed, zippers should have a cloth covering and not be exposed. If pack straps are not (at

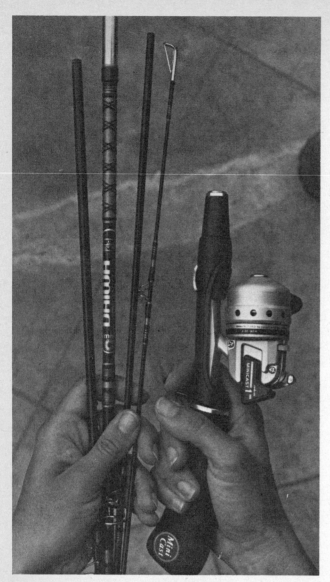

A small portable rod and reel like this from Daiwa can, with lures and lunch, be tucked into a daypack for an enjoyable day of remote lakes fishing.

The Sierra Day Pack from Outdoor Products (530 So. Main St., Los Angeles, CA 90013) is designed in the teardrop shape with a leather bottom for extra ruggedness. Shoulder straps combined with a belly band keep it from swaying too much. Small items which might be needed along the trail such as sunburn cream or insect repellant can be carried in the small outer pocket. Both zippers are double-pull for convenience.

The loaf-of-bread sized package shown here actually unfolds into a tiny shelter for the day hiker who may just decide to spend the night out, or who may be forced to do so due to weather. It will fit into a daypack with other emergency items. This is the Pocket Hotel by Early Winters (Seattle). It is made of Gore-Tex.

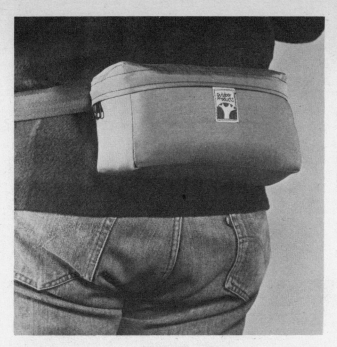

A smaller fanny pack is this #117 from Outdoor Products (530 So. Main St., Los Angeles, CA 90013). It weighs only 6.5 ounces, is made of waterproof Curdura nylon and is closed by a zipper which opens from either end. Great for carrying things otherwise in a ladies' handbag, or for children to take their own lunch, or to carry empty to fill later with seashells, pine cones or small rock samples.

least) 1-inch to 1½ inches wide, they should have thick felt or foam padding in the shoulder area for comfort. The straps should also be adjustable to fit different physiques, for either light or heavy clothing underneath and to compensate for different contents. Before making a final selection, try on several different types to see which fits best. Be certain each pack is filled with whatever you intend to carry.

There is one alternative to the rucksack type of daypack well worth mentioning. It is the zippered, contoured belt bag or belt pack which has been popularized by skiers. These can be worn anywhere around the waist, but most conveniently in front or back. While the bag's capacity is less than that of the smallest shoulder bag, its cost is also less.

Daypacks have unlimited uses. As professional wildlife, nature and travel photographers, we find the packs are indispensable for lugging our equipment. Peggy and I also are incurable anglers, for which the daypacks are again worth their weight in gold. With lunch and light tackle on our backs, we are able to hike that extra distance to waters where the fishing pressure is minimal.

A daypack is a means to more productive rockhounding (for carrying samples, ores) and enjoying the summertime spectacular of wild flowers anywhere in the land. For birdwatchers a light pack can be as im-

portant as a copy of Roger Tory Peterson's *Field Guide to the Birds*. Artists can use it for carrying pencils, paint brushes, pads or crayons.

There are a number of occasions every springtime when we head outward on the steep trails near our mountain home in Wyoming with the daypacks nearly empty except for lunch and cameras. This way we can return with packs full of fresh mushrooms, watercress or other wild edibles of the season. Later in the year we gather blueberries and the sweetest strawberries on earth. During autumn, in other places, we fill the daypacks to bulging with walnuts, hickories, paw-paws and hazelnuts, even ripe persimmons. What other pastime is so totally free and unrestricted?

Daypacking isn't only a wilderness game. Last summer we spent several happy days in San Francisco, a city where parking spots are not always easy to find—at least not exactly where you want them. But no matter, we simply slung on our daypacks (which are always kept in the station wagon) and explored Fisherman's Wharf. Later we used the same means to wander about Seattle and Salt Lake City.

Then there are those delicious daypack lunches. Forget sandwiches or any lunch counter kind of fare. Instead, carry fruit and cheeses, cold fried chicken or venison chops, jerky or smoked fish, or gorp. The latter is a fine mixture of dried fruit, chopped nuts, honey and chocolate. It's nutritious and perhaps too loaded with calories, but then a serious daypacker can stand them.

Daypacks have long been popular in Europe where escape from the ordinary has not been as easy as in America. Now daypacking is also catching on here and that isn't any wonder. Short holidays can make life a whole lot happier.

A steep ascent, a long trail and new boots can mean frequent rest stops for the daypacker. The light weight of the rucksack adds nothing to the discomfort and can indeed carry solace in the form of a refreshing handful of gorp.

A New Concept in Van Campers: the Diamond GT

by BYRON W. DALRYMPLE

This is a rearend view of the Diamond GT. It is a virtually perfect aerodynamic roof and side design, and all top heaviness is eliminated. The builder says: "People don't really need all that side-roof space. They just use the center headroom."

ONCE YOU'RE bitten by the RV bug, the resultant fever becomes chronic. You walk into a new camper, van conversion or mini-motorhome on a sales lot, and already you can feel the wheels turning. Something urges you to go, go, go. Here you are in what would be, in a house, a cramped little space not even large enough to make an over-sized closet, and it feels good. Somehow there is an appeal to these compact interiors that outshines that of the spaciousness of your own home.

I was thinking about all this recently, not on a sales lot but in my own yard, where a brand new van-type camper, a kind of cross between a van conversion and a miniature motorhome, sat ready and willing, urging me on. Here we had, at our place in the country, a big house with all the comforts, a large acreage chiefly woods, with our own ponds on it, virtually a perfect wilderness "campground" that belonged to us, a small forest flooded with solitude. And yet I was hurriedly packing, and my wife was doing the same. We were going on a kind of first-test trip in this new van—going camping.

Other campers of course easily understand why one must go camping, and those who've never camped and

never will, also never will understand. As a kid I camped by sleeping on the ground, rain or not, with a khaki blanket over me. Then came the vast comfort of a leaky old tent. And over the years I presume we have used for test-report purposes, and/or owned, an aggregate of 30 to 40 different RV types, from tiny trailers with the most meager conveniences to plush, lumbering 5-miles-to-the-gallon motorhomes with so many conveniences it took two long trips just to discover and learn to operate them all.

The old urge was still as strong as ever as I cranked up the Diamond GT Minihome—the GT short for "Grand Touring"—but on this trip there was an added appeal. This new unit, I had decided, was a kind of new frontier in the field of RVs. In a basic way it was a forecast of the future. That future, as all campers who go the RV route are going to have to learn, is certain to swiftly change from the appearance and the roominess of the all-home-comforts situation that we have today.

Notwithstanding the confusion of the present energy mess, the fact is that we *do* have a shortage, it will get worse, and probably never will we be able to return to

116

the profligacy of the days we have known. Campers who dote on various types of RVs may not have to give them up entirely. But the units are definitely going to have to change. Weight must be drastically shaved. Plush accommodations must in the process become ever more spartan. The RV of tomorrow will be the one that *really* can be used to replace the family car, to serve as camping unit and family car in one. To be sure, many are already so advertised, but few come close. Most of them are still lumbering giants.

This new frontier is what the unusually-styled Diamond GT van-motorhome cross is all about. It is definitely a construction and design breakthrough. No question, for the long run there may be still further changes. But this vehicle is the first of its kind in the entire RV field, a prototype that, it can be predicted, will be widely copied in concept within coming months. The fundamental news, you see, is that the material from which the body is made—excepting of course the hood and cab which is part of the automotive van chassis—weighs only 17 ounces to the square foot, compared to the average weight of conventional RV body construction of 2¼ pounds.

The GT Diamond Minihome is 20 feet long. As I drove it on our first run, to a Texas state park in the general area where we live, and later on several longer tours, I had the feeling I was simply driving my own personal vehicle, except that the smoothness of the ride was a whole lot better. That comparison is interesting. I use a Chevy Suburban with 4-wheel-drive. The 20-foot GT with all its basic equipment for live-in comforts weighs only 400 pounds more than my Suburban. It weighs in at 5,600, my Chevy 4WD at 5,200.

The GT body is made from formed panels of what is termed "space-age fiberglass honeycomb." The outside, of course, is smooth fiberglass, which is bonded to the honeycomb material several inches thick. Then the interior is finished partly in plywood paneling, and partly in a smart-looking rubbery foam. The unit we drove on these tests, and are still driving as I write this, is on a Ford chassis, and this one issued to us happened to have the big 460 engine, and of course automatic transmission. That's an abundance of power and on the steep hills for which our home region is renowned, it was a real zipperoo. Even so, I've averaged about 11 miles per gallon, overall, city, interstate and country road driving. What intrigues me is that I get just about the same—and a high sometimes up to 13—on the Chevy Suburban with its 350 motor.

Mileage I'm sure could be upped substantially on the GT by using a smaller motor, which is available, as are other makes of chassis. And, if we are to believe the EPA, mileage on all vehicles will be steadily increased anyway. This, however, is not the most important theme of the GT concept. The unusual lightness is basic. Added to that is what's inside the standard unit. By standards of all-out comforts in the average

motorhome today, it isn't much. That's what helps keep weight minimal. I would have to say frankly that at first we found some of what we didn't have somewhat inconvenient. The same goes for the space involved. But that is the punchline.

I remember all too well what it was like when our family first camped in a small and far from modern tent. The basic secret of successful tent camping is learning how to use efficiently a space much too small, how to pack, move things, keep out of each other's way, how to cook, keep reasonably clean, and still enjoy the whole experience. Nobody does it by bumbling around. You have to make a conscious effort to learn how to live well and comfortably *with what you've got*.

That's how we all used to do it, whether we started with tents or with the crude (by today's standards) little travel trailers and pickup campers of a few years ago. And, that's how we had darned well better learn to do it all over again, not to be sure without a lot of comforts those early days didn't have, but with back-to-basics vehicles that are as hassle-free as possible and that keep energy consumption down.

How well I recall when my wife and I were trailering years ago with what we thought—in the perspective of those times—was a marvelously cozy and comfortable little unit. It had so little inside! There was a bunk big enough for two at rear, a small dinette up front, a dinky two-burner gas stove, a small built-in ice box. There were two small 110-volt lights. Otherwise we used a gasoline lantern. No water tank. When in a park, however, we could hook a hose directly to the tap over the small sink. No toilet. No shower. No carpeted floor. Just linoleum. A small wardrobe. A couple of small overhead cupboards. It was an absolutely marvelous little rig—we thought then—and we hauled it some 50,000 miles before stepping up to improved innovations as those developed.

The reason I go over the equipment of that small trailer of 30 years ago, is that in some ways the Diamond GT model we've been using is reminiscent of it. And that is the whole idea—back to basics—back once more to *camping* on wheels, at least some. This model has a tiny sink, a hand-operated water pump (no hose hook-up), a small 12-gallon water tank (not one of those hugies that cart around 50 or more gallons) filled of course from outside. There is a two-burner gas stove—just like old times!

The refrigerator is about the size of that ancient ice box, but runs off one of the two 12-volt batteries with which the vehicle is equipped. Interestingly, there is no 110-volt inlet on this model. There's a 12-volt light over the galley stove and twin small 12-volt lights on either wall over the side windows. These of course run off the auxiliary battery. Frankly, we've been using an oblong plastic pan filled with ice, shoved into the bottom of the refrigerator, and not switching it on to the battery except while under motion. That way we have plenty of

Lorraine and Terry drink coffee at dinette in Diamond GT Minihome — it is on righthand side, facing cab.

ice for drinks, as well as saving pull on the battery. The second battery, I probably should note, is an excellent idea, for you take no chance on running down with lights the battery that starts the vehicle.

Above the galley area is a small double overhead cupboard. There are three small drawers below the miniature counter top, plus a small cupboard that will hold several pans and a skillet. Limited storage space dictates what you can take along—a kind of forced reduction to fundamentals. Across from the miniature galley is a wardrobe that contains a Porta-Potti. I'm sure most readers are familiar with this item, a portable toilet with its own small water tank and its own holding tank that can be removed, carried by its handle and emptied into any park dump station.

The entire floor is carpeted. There are four large sliding windows, sliding (tie-back) curtains. On one side is a couch that makes up into a bed. When both beds are made up, there's still a narrow walkway between—snug, but workable. This model has two ''captain''-type chairs deeply upholstered, up front just before the cab. These are in addition to the tall-backed bucket-type cab seats.

This model, it should be noted, with the four chairs (including cab seats) is actually slanted to some extent toward the younger crowd who will use it chiefly for short trips, football games, and quickie outings. Preferable for a small family or for a couple is the GT 3. In this the two extra chairs are deleted. The counter is extended farther forward to utilize the gained chair space, and on the other side an extra wardrobe closet is built in. This model is much more comfortable for the average camping couple and/or their small family.

Other items worth noting are the clear-plastic see-through roof vent toward the rear, and the unique large window built into the smartly designed forward part of the roof, which is slanted to present perfect air flow and cut wind resistance. There's a spare tire hidden away under one dinette seat. And, the butane bottle is slung under the chassis frame, well out of the way and with excellent clearance. It is filled on the vehicle, and has a sight gauge so one can check gas level easily.

There is a third model available, the GT 2. This one has flush-type toilet and holding tank, a sunken shower, 110 volt inlet with converter, electric demand water pump, and a host of optional extras. We've seen and

118

examined this unit. It is a stunner. However, for what we are talking about here, the back-to-basics *camping* vehicle, the spartan interiors of the other models are just right. And of course these basically equipped models are also lighter, and certainly less expensive.

Retail prices on the GTs will run, depending on where you live, what model and optionals you select, from $12,000-plus to $15,000-plus. Compared to scads

Lorraine at work in the small, compact galley at rear of minihome.

of others, and today's general automotive price structure, that's economical. My 4WD Chevy Suburban, for example, now a year old, listed with equipment I chose was only slightly less. The GT Minihome, remember, is a kind of double barreled affair—a camping wagon with all the basic comforts, and a handily maneuverable family or business vehicle as needed. Angle parking, incidentally, is easy with it, with ample vision out the side windows for backing into traffic. In traffic, city or interstate, the unit fits just like a station wagon.

Options—the younger crowd love this—include stereo speakers front and rear, radio-tape-deck combo. In fact, the unit we have is so equipped. We let one of our sons, Terry, and his wife Lorraine try it out, and they gave the speakers a thorough workout. For old hands who date back to thinking that little stripped-down trailer of 30 years ago was something, set in its time frame at any rate, a tape deck seems like a bundle of money riding the wings of a great deal of noise.

Viewed from front or rear outside, the design of the GT ushers in another step toward the future. It is narrow at the top, broad at the bottom, not bulky-square as the standard motorhome design usually is. I talked to Bud Coons, the owner of the Diamond company about why.

"In the average motorhome," he told me with a wry grin, "the only full headroom that is used by *people* is down the middle. The squared interior sides along the roof are taken up with cupboards. No one truly *needs* all that storage room. RV'ers have got to begin to break themselves of taking everything from home except the house itself. Sure, we build hundreds of motorhomes of more or less conventional design, but in the GT I'm trying to show what tomorrow is probably going to be like.

"By eliminating the upper side cupboards we can give the exterior an almost perfect aerodynamic contour, cut weight drastically. We also avoid even the slightest feeling of top-heaviness. The unit, I think you'll agree, drives about like any station wagon." I agreed.

All of which gets back to the theme stated earlier. No one has to have everything from a freezer to a TV room and a pool table in an RV. Better to still be able to go, light and basic, than not to be able to go at all—which could happen to the all-comforts large units in our energy-disturbed future. Besides, "camping" in the super-posh biggies so common today isn't even remotely related to the authentic experience.

True, vast numbers of modern campers attuned to the RV life don't really want it "the way it was." For many that's understandable. I no longer want to sleep on the ground under an old blanket in a drizzle, either. Yet there is a point of compromise, and the camping industry is going to have to meet there perhaps sooner than most of us believe. The tenters and tent-camper

Somebody has to do the cooking, and though I prefer an open ground fire, in today's parks one must abide by the rules. Learning how to live with and in this compact unit was a worthwhile schooling. I'm sure it is a prediction of the future.

owners will be ahead of the game. Almost certainly close on their heels will be those in the GTs and their many sure-to-come imitators.

The switch is really not so bad. During the time we've used this unit we've got over griping about what *isn't* in it that we had before, and learned to make do and enjoy camping trips with what *is* in it. The bathroom, for example, is snug. It sure beats the two-holers we saw plenty of years ago! The hand water-pump can be a minor nuisance, as can the small sink, getting down so low to get anything out of the refrigerator, or putting one leg ahead of the other in that narrow aisle to move front or rear when both beds are made up. Or is it simply that too many of us have forgotten that doing a little work, being a little bit inconvenienced, learning how to make do with fundamentals and adjust to your outfit is actually what camping is all about?

Indeed, our trips in the GT Minihome have been a little bit like going full circle. I for one am beginning to be immensely relieved by the simplicity. We often

chuckle—it's funny now but wasn't then—over treks we've taken in the past with big motorhomes equipped to the nines. I used to say that to own one and be happy you needed to travel with a retinue of workmen. It isn't possible to cart around that many gadgets all with complicated entrails, and not have something go awry daily—if not six times a day. I've spent the major share of many a trip just tinkering—maybe nothing serious, something loose, something not running. Fix, fix. It became a hobby. Who needed fishing? Or sitting by a lakeshore doing nothing? Busy, busy. Scores of people have lately fallen into that rut. *Camping* isn't their hobby; the machine they incessantly tinker with is.

So, along with the new design, the new lightness, the concept of what is almost sure to be mandatory for tomorrow, the tests we've made of the ingenious new Diamond GT have taught us a pair of long forgotten truisms. Simplicity is the basic ingredient and joy of the camping experience. Gadgetry too often makes you its slave.

BARBECUING SMOKE SIGNALS FROM THE PAST

BARBECUING has always been fundamental to the American way of life. The first Virginian settlers learned these cooking methods from the local Indians. Without it, it is doubtful they could have survived in their new world. British colonials took well to the culinary art and added a social dimension to it. They used the word "barbecue" to refer to gatherings centered on outdoor cookery, something we still do today.

In the 1700s, barbecues were the New Yorker trend, perhaps even part of high society. Also around this time, barbecues were so commonly used in electioneering rallies, that the words became almost synonymous. From daily food fare to social events to politics, the versatility of barbecuing was obvious.

Louisiana Acadians and Texans both claim title to introducing barbecuing into American cuisine. Acadians point out that the word barbecue comes from the French *barbe à queue,* "From whiskers to tail," as in

cooking the whole animal. They are the originators of Cajun (Acadian) cooking, the flavorful charcoal smoking cookery.

But the Texans remind us that the Spaniards were first to learn this barbecue cookery from the Carib Indians. The Indians' technique differed from today's. They smoke-dried fish, fowl and game on a green wood lattice over an open fire or heated stones. The Spaniards renamed this "*boucan*" process "*barbacoa,*" which later became the word barbecue. Whether the Texans or the Acadians deserve recognition for the charcoal barbecue, all Americans can take credit for knowing how to enjoy one.

However, Henry Ford, father of the Model T, is responsible for making barbecuing as American as apple pie. Besides being handy with cars, he was also the inventor of the charcoal briquet, by accident. In 1924, he found himself with so much leftover sawdust and wood scraps from his car industry, that he decided to burn them. What he thought was disposal of a by-product was in fact mass-production of a useful energy source, charcoal. Once he realized this, he had the powder pressed into uniform briquets for easy packing, transport and home use. Today, many companies share in the production of charcoal briquets, making it convenient for all Americans to enjoy a taste of history.

Charcoal briquets do their part for environmental balance through helping eliminate waste. They are made from natural by-products of the forest industry. A valuable and economical source of energy is captured rather than discarded. These by-products are carbonized at high temperatures, pressed into pillow-shaped briquets, dried and packaged. It's as simple and natural as that.

In the search for alternative energy sources, charcoal briquets answer some present and future needs. The Barbecue Industry Association estimates that, depending on what's served, cooking complete meals over coals can save about one-half to two-thirds of the energy required to cook the same foods on a kitchen gas range.

On a warm day, barbecuing outdoors also saves the electricity that may have been used for indoor air conditioning. Conserving energy resources by charcoal barbecuing in camp translates into preserving financial resources too. And of course, don't forget the energy the cook and cook's helpers conserve through the convenience of charcoal cookery and cleanup.

Charcoal briquets, a ready source of energy, are conveniently packaged and easily available. They are most often packed in heavy paper bags holding 5, 10, or 20 pounds. They can be found year-round in most supermarkets, gas stations, discount, hardware and garden supply stores. Some stores keep their briquet stock in storage during certain seasons, but a salesperson will gladly get some for you.

Smart Barbecuers' Guide To Selecting A Grill

Planning to buy a charcoal barbecue grill for a camping trip or use at home? Charcoal grills have become ordinary equipment for three out of four American households. No longer just warm weather cookery, barbecuing at home or away has grown into a year-round activity. And the versatility of barbecue cooking methods is matched only by the variety of charcoal grills. With a grill for all reasons and seasons you'll be sure to find one that suits your family's needs. Use this guide to help you select the charcoal grill that's right for you.

What Size?

If you usually grill for two, a hibachi or small tabletop grill is perfect. On the other hand, it you're often surrounded by a small crowd, choose a larger brazier, kettle, covered cooker, cooking wagon, or water smoker.

KETTLE GRILL

What Foods Will You Cook?

For charcoal grilled steak, hamburgers, hot dogs, cut-up chicken, turkey parts, fish kebobs, fruits and vegetables, any kind of grill is fine.

Roasts, whole chicken and turkey or game birds are great on the rotisserie. Look for a kettle, wagon or square covered cooker that comes with this attachment. You can also use a square cooker or kettle minus the spit but with the top down to achieve that mouthwatering charcoal flavor.

Smoked foods of any type can be created in a water smoker. Try turkey, chicken, ham or roast beef, whole fish, spareribs, hot dogs and even vegetables.

How Much Storage Space?

To keep your grill alive and well, keep it in a dry storage space, all covered and away from the weather. Thus, when you're considering the size of the grill you're planning to buy, remember the amount of space you have for storing it.

Where Will You Grill?

If you're looking for a grill for picnics, overnight camping or antique hunts, choose a small totable lightweight variety. A hibachi, tabletop picnic-style grill, or small brazier (with collapsible legs) are in line. If you're the backyard chef, the fancier kettles, square covered cookers, wagons, or water smoker may be just the grill for you!

122

CHARCOAL WATER SMOKER

finish or pebble-grained for easy cleaning. Many of these come with a two-sided set of controls to allow for greater temperature control versatility. Can be used with top up or down with or without the rotisserie. Almost every food can be charcoal grilled in this type of grill.

Cooking Wagons: Cooking wagons are made for backyard chefs. They can come complete with work shelves, built-in charcoal starters, warming ovens, hoods, rotisseries and storage drawers. They are mini-backyard kitchens. The hooded wagons are particularly good for keeping winds away from cooking areas.

Kettle Grills: These are great for all-year grilling. The domed cover protects the fire from dampness, wind and bad weather. They're fine for dry-heat smoking as well as conventional charcoal grilling. These also come with the pebble-type finish or durable porcelain-enamel finish.

Water Smokers: This is a heavy dome-type grill with water pan. Foods are kept moist and juicy while they're slowly cooked with charcoal briquets and hickory chips or your favorite aromatic wood. The water pan is placed over the coals (set in its own rack) so the steam will rise to the food and permeate.

The Nitty Gritty—Getting Down to Details

Grid: Be sure it's easy to clean and easily removed. It should also be coated with a long-lasting chrome plating. If you like to cook foods simultaneously over different heats, look for an adjustable tilt cooking grid. You can cook steaks rare to well at the same time. For convenience, see that charcoal may be added by raising and lowering the grid if necessary, without removing the food and grid. Oiling the grid with vegetable oil or a non-stick spray will keep foods from sticking.

Fire Pan: The fire pan holds the coals. Many are adjustable to help regulate the cooking temperature. Lining the fire pan with heavy-duty aluminum foil helps make ash clean-up easier.

Ash Catcher: This pan does just that. It may be inside or outside the grill base. It should be removable or swing out for easier cleaning. Ashes should be brushed from coals, as they burn, to help keep heat high.

Grill Finishes: The shell of a grill can be either a durable aluminum or heavy-duty steel. They may be coated with a smooth porcelain-enamel finish or paint finish for rust protection. Many grills now come with a pebble finish for longer wear and easier cleaning. If you want a portable grill make sure the material is not too heavy.

Legs: Look for sturdy, folding legs for portability and easy storage, if that is your need. Some have adjustable or detachable legs to vary the height. Grills also come with a pedestal base for easier storage.

Basic Models

Tabletop Grills: The simplest grills, these are small grid-topped models supported on folding or collapsible legs. They're light and easy-to-clean and come in 12, 14 and 18-inch sizes. Great for camping or beach picnics.

Fireplace Grills: Made especially for use in a fireplace, these grills can be folded flat for easy storage. Any small grill, such as a hibachi can also be used in a fireplace as long as there is adequate ventilation (be sure the flue is open!). Both are great for camping and picnics.

Hibachis: These oriental-inspired grills come in large and small models. They're for hors d'oeuvres and small scale complete meal barbecuing on patio, porch or campsite. Many come with stands for easier cooking and now there is a "double grill" hibachi for not-so-small meals.

Braziers: These popular shallow round grills sit on 3 or 4 legs. They can be extremely simple, with just a grid over the coals, or have half-hoods, covers, electric or battery rotisseries and wheels. Many families keep an extra on hand for feeding extra-large crowds.

Square Covered Cookers: Here is a popular new look for grills. Square cookers come in several price ranges. Outer shell may be a sturdy porcelain-enamel

TABLETOP PICNIC GRILL

BRAZIER GRILL

Hood: The hood may tilt away on a hinge, be removable or snap on.

Vent Covers: Vent covers may be top, bottom or side adjustable draft controls. Most important in a grill with a lid, you can regulate the heat of the coals by regulating the amount of oxygen you let in. When through cooking, the air can be completely shut off, preserving charcoal for future use.

Side Table, Bottom Shelf: These allow convenience in preparation. Side tables often fold for easy storage.

Heat Indicator Knobs: They assist in regulating the cookery temperature. They are not a must but add to barbecuing convenience.

Windguard: A windguard is handy on braziers or tabletop grills when cooking in a windy area. It helps maintain a hot cooking temperature.

Handles: The most protective are thermoplastic heat resistant or wooden handles.

Wagon-hoods: A full view see-through hood is convenient for checking on the food and retaining heat on colder days or for longer cooking periods.

Easy Assembly: Some grills come preassembled. All you have to do is attach the legs.

Wheels: Wheels are an asset for mobility.

Grill Frills—Assembly

Barbecuing has become a true culinary art with its own set of helpful cooking tools. Let accessories expand your cooking repertoire.

Grill Brush: Brass bristles and metal scraper make for easy cleaning.

Utensils: Look for chrome-plated or stainless steel with thermoplastic or wooden handles. Well-stocked supply should include tongs for turning delicate foods, forks and spatula.

Flat Spit Basket: Convenient for spit cooking of ribs, fish or flat roasts.

Cookout Grill Basket: The basket holds food firmly in place. Great for hamburgers.

Rotisserie: Every barbecue needs one! A simple way to cook delicious meats and poultry. Battery or electric powered ones do the turning for you. If you choose electric, make sure you have an electric outlet available. The foods are evenly cooked over a hot fire.

Tumble Basket: Provides tumbling action without

HOODED BRAZIER WITH ROTISSERIE

HOODED COOKING WAGON WITH ROTISSERIE

burning. It self-bastes cuts of meat and fowl.

Roast Rack: A roast rack holds the roast over the hot coals, allowing for even cooking and simple lifting when it's time to serve.

Warming Rack: A warming rack rests on the grid. Helps foods stay warm and adds extra cooking area.

Hot Dog Roaster Fork, Skewers: Handy holders for hot dogs and kebobs. Great for crowds and family fun.

Aluminum Drip Pans: These pans are helpful when rotissing or cooking a fatty cut of meat. By placing the drip pan under the food and over the coals, the pan will prevent flare-ups. Can also be shaped from heavy-duty aluminum foil.

Wok Pan: Some kettle grills have wok pans that fit right into them. Great for oriental cooking.

Grill Cover: Vinyl covers are fitted to the grill models. Protection of your grill from bad weather will extend your grill's life.

Hickory Chunks: Can be added to the charcoal briquets to add an extra hickory flavor to the foods you cook on the grill.

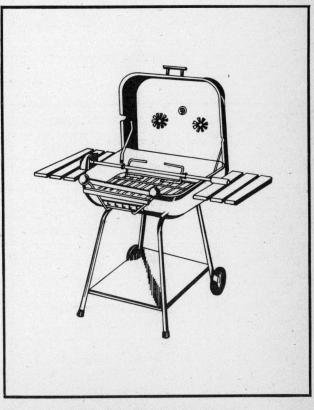

SQUARE COVERED COOKER WITH ROTISSERIE

Barbecuing Tips

Charcoal barbecuing offers tremendous versatility in preparing meals. But as each food has its individual characteristics, it requires special consideration. For your convenience, this chart is a handy reference of the best methods for barbecuing each food.

FOOD	CUT or VARIETY	KIND OF COOKING	SPECIAL NOTES
Beef	Sirloin, rib, club, porterhouse, T-bone steaks	Charcoal broil	Cook quickly on hot fire
	Flank steak	Charcoal broil	Marinate before cooking and serve rare
	Round and chuck steaks	Charcoal broil	Use meat tenderizer and/or marinate
	Hamburgers	Charcoal broil	Best served rare
	Whole tenderloin	Charcoal broil	
	Rib and sirloin roasts	Spit or covered grill	
	Round, chuck, rump roasts	Spit, covered grill or water smoker	Use meat tenderizer and/or marinate
Veal	Chops and steaks	Charcoal broil	Baste frequently
Lamb	Chops and steaks	Charcoal broil	
	Leg	Spit, covered grill or water smoker	
Ham	Slice	Charcoal broil	Use basting sauce
	Half or whole	Spit, covered grill or water smoker	Use hickory chips
Pork	Chops and steaks	Charcoal broil	Cook until well done
	Spareribs	Charcoal broil	Cook very slowly
	Loin, shoulder roasts	Spit, covered grill, or water smoker	Use hickory chips
	Fresh ham	Spit, covered grill, or water smoker	
Poultry	Whole chicken	Spit, covered grill, or water smoker	
	Chicken — halves and quarters	Charcoal broil	May marinate before cooking and baste during cooking
	Turkey — split or pieces	Charcoal broil	
	Whole turkey	Spit, covered grill, or water smoker	

FOOD	CUT or VARIETY	KIND OF COOKING	SPECIAL NOTES
Seafood	Clams	Charcoal broil	Open, half shell, baste with butter
	Fish steaks and fillets	Charcoal broil	Use a hinged wire basket for fillets and small steaks, baste frequently
		Foil-grill	Wrap in foil with wine or juice and spices and place on grill
	Shrimp	Charcoal broil	Baste with butter
	Split lobster	Charcoal broil or water smoker	
	Whole fish	Foil-grill, charcoal broil, or water smoker	Wrap head and tail in foil or oil fish and place directly on grill over medium coals
Combination Dishes	Kebobs	Charcoal broil	
	Casseroles	Grill-top	Sear meats over coals, place in covered dish and heat over medium-hot coals
	Fondues	Grill-top	Place fondue pot on grill, medium-low heat, add hickory flavoring
	Sandwiches	Foil-grill	
	Chinese dishes	Stir fry	Use wok or skillet over hot fire
	Vegetable or rice mixtures	Grill-top	In skillet or pot
Vegetables	Thick-skinned	Ember	Oil skins lightly
	Soft-skinned	Ember	Wrap in heavy-duty aluminum foil
Fruits	Bananas	Ember	Oil skin lightly
	Oranges, grapefruit, peaches, plums pineapples	Charcoal broil	Halve and cook over low fire, brush with lemon or apple juice
	Apples	Foil-grill	Low fire
	Stewed fruit	Grill-top	Reheat in pot over low fire, stirring occasionally
Breads	Hard crusted breads and rolls, breadsticks	Foil-grill	Brush with herb butter
	Soft crusted breads and rolls	Charcoal broil	Toast lightly
Cakes & Pies	Most varieties, especially fruit pies	Foil-grill	Reheat those already prepared over low fire
Soups	Any type	Grill-top	Place pot on grill

by TOM WALKER

BEAR COUNTRY. I live in it. My home is 35 air miles from the nearest road in the Alaskan bush. It's prime black and grizzly country. I am often awakened in the morning by the heavy footfalls of a bear on the porch or hear one passing beneath the windows. Yesterday when I began work on this article, a black bear visited the cabin. I saw him first by the cache, then by the workshop, sniffing around in a search for anything at all edible. He circled the house once, walking so close that I could see the mosquitoes on his face. It was a treat to watch him. He walked down the trail toward the outhouse and turning off, sauntered into the timber the way he had come.

As a wildlife photographer I have worked around bears and lived in their country most of my life. There have been remarkably few problems with them. Most encounters, which total nearly 100 each summer, end just as harmlessly as the one above. Yet each year people are mauled or worse and much valuable property is destroyed by the bruins. In 1978 in the North three people were killed by grizzlies and several others injured by bears of all kinds. Sad to say, most such attacks did NOT have to happen.

Bears rarely harm people, but the potential is always there. Most people recognize the danger of a grizzly, yet it is a fact that black bears in the western states annually do more property damage and hurt more people than all of North America's grizzlies combined. Black bears are not the harmless clowns of television fantasy, but powerful *wild* animals capable of inflicting serious injury to humans. *Any* bear should be treated with caution.

Those people most vulnerable to bear attack and depredations are the growing legions of backcountry users and roadside tent campers. In the backcountry there are no vehicles in which to seek refuge and food can't be safely "locked up" in a tent. The chances of encountering a grizzly today in the contiguous U.S. are quite small, but with black bears found in 30 of the 50 states, *anyone* who plans to camp out in a tent should know what to do to avoid trouble with bears. With a little knowledge and common sense, a camping trip into bear country can be an experience to long remember—pleasantly.

Bears are extremely powerful animals and completely unpredictable in their behavior. One professional animal handler says that a black bear that weighs only 50 pounds is *as* strong as a person. The very same bear that one time will run at the merest sign of a human being, will on another occasion vigorously defend its territory. This unpredictability is a bear's most dangerous characteristic. Most times the critters avoid humans. However, there are those times when one can be decidedly more dangerous than usual and extreme cau-

Grizzly feeding on berries. Never approach a bear for any reason. This bear was filmed from a car!

CAMPING IN

tion must be exercised by anyone confronting such an animal.

1. A sow (female) with cubs can be extremely protective and is considered by experts to be especially dangerous. Records compiled by the National Park Service indicate that in the vast majority of bear attacks, the aggressor was a sow accompanied by cubs.

2. Bears protecting food caches or actively engaged in food gathering are also a potential threat. In the case of a bear boldly walking into a camping area, the animal

Watch out! This bear is displaying threat posture. Don't imitate any bear positions or sounds.

BEAR COUNTRY

is there solely for the purpose of obtaining food and should be treated with caution.

3. The breeding season for bears is in late spring, May and June, and mated pairs can be quite aggressive. Not long ago a hiker in Alaska was seriously mauled by two adult bears the hiker inadvertently came upon while they were breeding.

4. A bear suffering from some physical debilitation, such as a broken leg or old bullet wound, is also an animal to avoid. Obviously some of these physical disabilities are not immediately apparent, but a man in

Montana was killed a few years back when he approached a bear with a broken leg.

Bears in these situations are almost always more ready to defend themselves and their territory than a lone bear feeding on a hillside grass patch. Camping and backpacking in bear country is not unduly hazardous. Crossing a street against the light is more perilous. Precautions are taken when crossing a street and commonsense precautions taken while camping can prevent most bear problems. Veteran campers and backpackers offer the following guidelines to the novice:

The first rule on every expert's list is *NEVER* knowingly approach a bear for any reason, especially a sow with cubs. Bears can defend young and territory quite dramatically.

Secondly, don't surprise a bear, and for safety's sake never hike alone. When hiking walk downwind whenever possible so that a bear can be forewarned of your approach by the sense of smell. However, don't rely on smell alone, but make plenty of noise while hiking. Tie bells to the packframe so that they constantly jingle, or shake rocks in a can, beat on a cup, or loudly talk or sing to alert bears to your approach. Avoid heavy brush where a bear might be concealed and if a route travels through brush, make plenty of noise and move slowly to give bears time to move out. The hiker in Alaska that stumbled on the breeding pair and was mauled could have avoided 6 months in the hospital by making a lot of noise while walking.

Third, never attract a bear by cooking highly scented foods, or carrying such foods into bear country. Take freeze dried meals or foods with little odor on trips. Fresh meat, sausage, bacon, cheese, and other odorous foods should be left at home. Such smelly items are a dinner invitation for bears. Also never leave food or garbage out where bears can get to it. Be sure to PACK OUT all trash and garbage, leave nothing that a bear could eat.

Avoid camping in areas of high bear density. Most people associate bears with wilderness country. Truly wild bears are the least dangerous of all for they most times run from people. On the other hand, it's the bear *most* accustomed to people that is most dangerous for they've lost their natural fear. Regularly-used campsites in the backcountry and along the road system are not necessarily safe places to camp. Some bears have learned to loot regular campsites and are accustomed to finding food there. Pick a campsite carefully. Obviously it would be ill-advised to camp near open dumps, salmon streams, heavily-used berry patches, places where bears might have been fed, or any areas of high bear use.

Lastly, never, under any circumstances, run from a bear. Almost any carnivore will chase another animal that runs. Everyone has seen a dog chase a child solely because the child ran. Bears are no different. A person that unexpectedly comes face-to-face with a bear and

A sow with cubs can be extremely dangerous and can run as fast as a whitetail deer — faster than any person!

In Alaska food is stored in caches — houses on stilts — that keep food from bears.

runs is almost asking for a mauling. A bear can run 30mph, or as fast as a whitetail deer—they obviously can not be outrun. One ranger told me that he did not know of a single case where a person who ran from a bear was not chased down and caught! The best advise is to stop and don't move. Speak softly, never yell or act threatening, and, after a few moments, slowly back away. In most cases, once the bear has overcome the initial surprise of the encounter, it'll run off. However, in the unlikely event of an actual attack, and a place of safety is not close at hand, drop to the ground and play dead, lying face down with legs together and hands clasped behind the neck. Leave your backpack on as it offers some protection. Most bear attacks are brutal, but brief, and most experts feel that a passive response minimizes injuries.

I add one additional remark to the above guidelines—especially avoid the bruin which shows no fear or concern for human activity. If a bear is observed hanging around a campsite, or other campers report such activity, *that* is a bear and a place to avoid.

The bear that came wandering around my cabin did so because it was a truly wild bear and probably had never seen a human or habitation before. He was looking for food but since he did not find any—I'm scrupulously careful to protect my food from bears and burn all garbage—he caused no trouble and soon wandered away. Secondly, I made no move to approach or alter the bear's behavior, rather I merely watched from behind windows.

Once a bear learns to get food from people—voluntarily or otherwise—that bear is on the road to becoming a serious problem. "Don't feed the bears" is a rule on every expert's list. It used to be that the rationale was that human fare was not good for a bear's

Bears actively engaged in gathering food, such as this Alaskan brown bear, should be treated with extra caution.

Grizzly claws can rip through a tent and open canned foods easily. The key to safe tent camping in bear country is to keep food away from bears and store food carefully.

A bear will vigorously defend food sources — make plenty of noise while hiking to prevent surprising a bear.

health—how true! For nowadays a bear that becomes a problem after learning to seek handouts from people meets its death by firing squad! A camper that knowingly feeds a bear or allows a bear to get food, is contributing to the eventual destruction of that animal, and/or harm to people and property.

Tent campers must take precautions to protect food. Black bears and small grizzlies can climb trees so it does no good to merely hang food in a tree. The food must be slung in a manner that gets it high enough off the ground, yet far enough out from the main trunk and limbs so that a tree-climbing bear can not get to it. Many permanent campgrounds have bear-proof lockers for food storage, and these lockers should be used religiously. When tent camping near the road all food should be locked in the trunk of the car; never in the

A tent camper puts food in a cache to prevent attracting a bear.

A black bear may look soft and friendly, but beware! Blacks are found in the majority of our states and many have learned to expect handouts from humans. Avoid the fearless bruin.

passenger section. Bears have learned to "peel" open car doors to get at food stored inside. Never cook near a tent, and never, never cook inside a tent used for sleeping.

Bears are motivated by hunger. Unlike hikers who come into bear country for "aesthetic" reasons, bears are there to live and eat. The main ingredient in successful and *safe* tent camping is careful food handling. The only serious problem I ever had with a bear is when I broke the cardinal rule and cooked in my tent. It happened this way:

I was working at a remote site building a log cabin. There were a lot of bears around the area and in 3 weeks I had no trouble with them. I carefully cooked outside away from my tent, used plain food, and hung my food *and* garbage up in a tall tree with an elaborate sling. One night after a particularly long day with the logs, and in a heavy rain, I moved inside my tent and heated a can of chili. I then compounded my error by leaving out the can and leftovers. Next morning at 4, a black bear woke me as he tried to gain entrance to my tent. Luckily I awoke in time to run him off. Unfortunately an hour later the bear was back and this time he meant business. I shot him dead *18 inches* from my sleeping bag. I was responsible for that bear's needless death, and without a firearm the injuries I might have sustained would have been justly due.

Personally, I feel that a camper or hiker can go anywhere in bear country in almost perfect safety if care is taken with food and he/she does not approach a bear.

Hikers and campers in alpine areas have a more

132

difficult time in protecting food supplies. I've camped a lot on the open tundra and have a routine worked out to lessen the worry of bear encounters. At day's end, I'll stop and cook dinner and make a leisurely meal. Then after dinner and after all the utensils are washed and cleaned, I move ½-mile or so and set up camp. I then take all my food, separate it into two halves, place each half in a double plastic bag and place each bag out of sight on the tundra a few hundred yards from my tent. That way I have nothing at the tent that would attract a bear, yet if a bear finds one of my food caches (probably one would not find both) it won't connect it to my tent.

If I'm camped in the same spot for several days, I'll still eat my meals well away from the tent. Such actions might be inconvenient, but they make life a whole lot simpler on the treeless tundra.

In conclusion, I'd like to say that I'm not trying to build up any "paranoia" regarding bears or the potential danger from them. Rather, my intent is to point out that bears *can* be dangerous, yet if a few commonsense rules are followed, the risk is minimal. Again, to use the city streets as an analogy, I'd point out that life in the city can be hazardous, but if a person walks with the lights and watches both ways, he'll cross the street safely. Being careful in the woods too, can assure pleasant and safe camping.

Finally, I've paraphrased the rules and offer these do's and don'ts to campers in bear country:

> DO burn or dispose of trash so as to not attract bears.
> DO wash all cooking utensils.
> DO store foods outside of tents and out of reach of bears.
> DO pack out all garbage and trash—think of the next guy.
> DO clean food containers to keep down odors.
> DO cook away from tent.
> DO make noise while hiking.
> DO enter thickets upwind to allow your smell to warn away bears.
> DON'T feed the bears.
> DON'T camp on bear trails or near high-use areas.
> DON'T approach bears—sows and cubs especially.
> DON'T approach a bear's food cache.
> DON'T imitate a bear's sounds or positions.
> DON'T run from a bear

(Above) Always cook away from the tent. In tundra or alpine country this is especially true for there are no trees to seek safety in or hang food from.

(Right) This grizzly met an untimely end in Alaska when it came into camp after moose meat. Properly stored food would have prevented its demise.

Camping in the Southwest

by ERWIN and PEGGY BAUER

Blistering hot during mid-summer, the best time for the camper to visit the Grand Canyon is early spring or late autumn. This spectacular view is from the North Rim.

RECENTLY during a camping trip to Utah's Canyonlands National Park, we spent several golden mornings hiking on trails which thread through that lonely, lovely land. At noon we paused in shade, near the mouth of a dry side canyon to eat the lunch in our knapsacks. But before it was unpacked, we noticed a set of strange, three-toed tracks engraved across the ancient Kayenta sandstone eroded at our feet. Each toe alone had left an imprint as large as one of our own Vibram-soled boots.

Sasquatch? Bigfoot? No, it was neither of these. But we had indeed found the footprints made in soft earth by

a dinosaur 140 million years ago when such reptiles roamed the region. The conversation around our campfire that evening was more lively than usual because of our remarkable discovery.

Still the experience wasn't all that unusual. We have spent a good bit of time camping—vagabonding, really—not only in Canyonlands, but widely throughout the American Southwest. The result has been one rich experience blended into another. No matter whether spring or summer, autumn or winter, by recreational vehicle or backpacking under canvas, we have found no more pleasant region to go camping than in this dry and spectacular part of America.

Let's return to Utah and the Canyonlands for a moment. This 500-square-mile park is one vast and extraordinary natural wonder. Much of the multicolored real estate overlooks two great rivers, the Green and Colorado, which join within park boundaries. No matter from which point you hike or drive to look down upon them, the scene below is absolutely awesome. But it is

A daypacker heads into the red rock country for a day of hiking the well marked trails.

The jutting sandstone backdrops of Zion National Park dwarf a large camper in the Beehive State of Utah.

just as awesome if you float and camp the rivers (which certainly is possible) and look upward instead.

The Canyonlands camping picture is excellent. Inside the park is a campground at Squaw Flat for tent, pickup or trailer. Or you can backpack to primitive campsites in the Island in the Sky section. Closeby are state park campgrounds at Indian Creek and Dead Horse Point, with still others in Manti-La Sal National Forest.

But before leaving Utah, where there are more fine camping opportunities along most highways than we could list, we should reveal one more favorite, Dinosaur National Monument, which remains relatively undiscovered. At Dinosaur, where flood waters of the early spring had recently slightly altered the course of the Yampa River, instead of just dinosaur tracks we have found dinosaur bones in the river bed. But in a sheltered quarry not far from the Split Mountain Campground anyone can watch technicians chipping away at whole prehistoric skeletons imbedded in the earth. This is a rare and revealing opportunity.

But so is sleeping under cloth at Dinosaur Monument's Echo Park with the monolith Steamboat Rock looming in the background.

Camping in the Southwest can be especially exciting if the campground awaits in a setting as strange as the Valley of Fire State Park, Nevada. Here is an im-

(Above) Backpacking the dry deserts of the Southwest is a favorite early spring pastime.

(Right) Awesome Zion National Park scenes reward the backpacker as well as the day hiker or RV camper.

Endless vistas in the Southwest tempt RV campers to stop and admire the desert scenery.

Chilly desert evenings make hot biscuits done in a reflector oven a delicious treat.

possible, upside-down landscape of red, white and yellow rock, but mostly red. Sandy trails now wind where jellyfish and shrimp swam in lukewarm water 300 million years ago, and where renegade Indians hid out less than a century ago. But at sunrise and again at sunset, the grotesque sandstone cliffs seem to be aflame and burning, exactly as does downtown Las Vegas which is on the horizon just 25 miles away. Incidentally you can camp on the Las Vegas Strip as conveniently as at Valley of Fire. And for still another abrupt change of scene, you might pull up stakes and simply move your entire rig to Lake Mead National Recreation Area (less than an hour away) and to the shore of the 170-mile long lake itself.

Once the Southwest from Texas to southern California was nearly waterless with only a few large rivers, such as the Colorado, bisecting the region. But that has been radically changed by the necklaces of large reservoirs which have been built for irrigation and hydroelectric power. One happy by-product of these giant impoundments has been a new kind of camping—by boat, either a rental or your own.

At lakes Mead and Powell, you simply rent a self-contained houseboat, cruise to your own private, sheltered bay and anchor it. The houseboat is your snug summer camp wherever it is "parked." But far less expensive and more adventuresome is to load your camping gear—tent, pots and pans, the works—in your own boat and head for your own secluded campsite anywhere on the lakeshore. Most of the land around most southwestern reservoirs is public, so this kind of freestyle camping is possible.

Some may regard the Southwest—and southwestern

Perhaps the most famous of the southwestern camping destinations is the Grand Canyon seen here with the Colorado River cutting its way ever deeper.

deserts in particular—as too stark and desolate, too hot or too brittle to endure, and maybe some areas are. But most deserts also teem with life, delicate beauty and pleasant pastimes. That region around Tucson is a very good example to prove it. Drive either due east or west of town to spend a day at one of the two Saguaro National Monuments. Beside the splendid campground which is adjacent to the west unit, is the Arizona-Sonora Desert Museum, a fascinating and completely natural celebration of desert plants and wildlife from boojum trees to Gila monsters. Campers frequently come to spend an overnight here, but end up staying a weekend or a week. Convenient nearby is Old Tucson, a boisterous Wild West theme park. Also look for many higher and cooler camping areas to the northeast of Tucson (the Santa Catalina Mountains), as well as lovely Madera Canyon in the Santa Ritas to the southeast.

Year in and year out, no corner of America offers more predictable weather for campers the year around. Indeed the Southwest heats up and simmers in summertime and frosts (even snows on high slopes) are not unknown in winter. But the weather is dependably dry and bright. Retreat to the shade during summer mid-days and sleep late every morning in winter. But feel free to live 14 days every week when camping in spring and autumn when the low humidity is invigorating.

Some campers like plenty of company and others do not. If in the first category you will find one of the KOA or other widespread commercial chains on the edge of each and every southwestern town. But if in the other group, you just might want to aim your rig south and or west toward Texas. For trekking and backpacking into a virgin wilderness, Guadalupe Mountains National Park should be your destination. Guadalupe, which is midway between El Paso and Carlsbad, New Mexico, may be the Park Service's (as well as a serious backpacker's) best kept secret. It is an undeveloped and so far unexploited park of silent canyons and high forests where a camper is unlikely to meet anyone else.

Deeper into Texas along the Rio Grande is Big Bend National Park and a camping destination which only a relative few campers have discovered. Blistering hot in its lower elevations during midsummer, its climate is especially attractive the rest of the year, with emphasis on the Chisos Mountains right in the heart of the park.

138

There are many prehistoric drawings on hidden sandstone walls such as these. Care must be taken to protect them from vandals or thieves as they are frequently entirely exposed and at risk.

There are trails to hike, awesome canyons of the Rio Grande to run by boat, ghost towns and forgotten mines to explore, with Old Mexico just across the border.

The vincinity of Carlsbad is another we would not willingly pass without camping for a few days. The Carlsbad Caverns National Park is open year around and here visitors can tramp through the largest, most exquisite caves on this continent. Just north is the Zoological Botanical Garden of the Southwest, also well worth pitching a tent or parking a camper nearby.

Most Southwest camping nowadays is done within easy reach, if not actually within sight and sound of busy roads and facilities. So camping here is no different, no more troublesome or hazardous than anywhere else. You keep your gear in good operable shape and keep in mind that traveling in large RVs is a little more cumbersome than driving passenger cars. But if you do venture far from the busy highways and into the deserts of the Southwest, there are a few additional rules of the road and of the campground. The first concerns water; you may need to carry a sufficient supply along. The next most important items are fuel (not always available in remotest places) and spare parts. Be certain you have enough of both.

Fortunately some of the Southwest's finest camping opportunities are also some of the most accessible. Interstate 10 passes just south of Joshua Tree National Monument in southern California and just north of San Bernardino National Forest and the San Jacinto Wilderness near Palm Springs. Interstate 8 leads from San Diego to the numerous campgrounds of Cleveland National Forest and Anza-Borrego Desert State Park. There are even good campground facilities near the several San Diego County lakes where today some of the largest freshwater bass in the world are being taken.

No matter how you view it, camping in the Southwest nowadays is one of travel's greatest, happiest bargains. Why not make the most of it?

Sculptured sandstone monoliths tower over a varied collection of camping vehicles.

139

Scenes like this are far too common in many of our camp-grounds. Catching the culprits in the act is the hard part in the enforcement of anti-litter regulations. (Karl Maslowski photo)

TROUBLE IN CAMP
by CHARLES J. FARMER

A GENTLE but persistent rain accompanied us all the way from Point Arena to Rockport as our VW streamed its way over the magnificent course of California's Pacific Coast Highway 1. Low, billowy clouds drooped from a vague sky and furious breakers took their wrath out on rocky shoreline hulks. The day was tailored for dreamers—muffled, misty and soft. At the point northeast of Rockport, where Highway 1 juts inland and marries Highway 101 to the north, the sullen veil gave way to scattered patches of blue. By the time we reached Humboldt Redwood State Park, the giant redwoods, though still dripping, were glistening with the radiance of fresh, unshrouded sunshine. With car windows rolled down, welcome doses of pure, after-rain air filled our lungs. All signs pointed to a delightful overnight camp after a long, stuffy day.

It was March, and plenty of good spots were available for pitching our family tent. Only a scattering of other campers were present and although Humboldt is a developed campground with extra comforts, we tucked ourselves away in the back corner of Area C and enjoyed a degree of campfire solitude which resembled

more remote backwoods camps. Nestled in a canopy of 200-foot high redwoods, some of which have been shielded from logger's blades since 1850, our coastal camp offered many natural rewards. With our 2-year-old daughter Brittany already asleep in the tent, Kathy and I snuggled by the fire, each of us sipping a cup of California Chablis. The awesome redwood silhouettes humbled us, and we felt good with nature. Our sleeping bags beckoned before a final cup of wine could be poured. We joined our daughter who failed to stir in spite of our shuffling. We agreed we had been fortunate in our selection of this overnight camp. Falling asleep was easy.

The first rumblings of nearby visitors did not exactly set me straight up in bed. No doubt my mind and body had been fighting the noise for some time. For the awakening process was stubborn and I secretly cursed those who broke the peaceful silence. I hoped the clatter would disappear and for a minute, or several, I sank back into a welcome sleep, a slumber of extremely short tenure.

A bottle broke somewhere outside the canvas walls

and the explosion of glass and the string of obscenities which followed had me grasping for the alarm clock. It was 11:20—a time when campers are pitched and settled, but partiers, an ever increasing and alarming number of them, begin invading forest retreats where law enforcement is virtually impossible and nonexistent. Alcohol and drug abuse are common. Ear busting stereo tapes plugged into fancy vans drown out the most persistent of whippoorwills. Litter, vandalism, theft, mugging, assault and battery occur with sickening frequency. One ranger, on duty at a state campground in northern California said it might be safer for a family to walk the streets of downtown Los Angeles at night than to camp at some state parks.

For the remainder of the night and well into the next morning (4:20 AM to be exact) the neighbors next-door staged a continuous barrage of wild antics which kept Kathy and me sitting up on our elbows with our .22 caliber pistol, still in its holster, nudging our sleeping bags. I hated the necessity of even thinking about such protection, but after judging that four or five adult men, high on whiskey and pot, were building themselves up to a frenzied pitch about 30 yards away, I knew that real trouble could break out without much warning. In my mind I planned what I must do if an advance were made toward our tent. The thought of possible embarrassment or injury to Kathy and Brittany underlined my readiness. My nerves, frayed from the sudden intrusion and frightful tones of the wild men outside, prevented any rest.

I had some thoughts about going outside and trying to quiet the men with reasonable words but the tone of the group, the nearly constant bickering and fighting among themselves, quickly dispelled any hope of negotiations. It was far better, though much more anxiety provoking, to lie and wait in readiness. Our little girl, breathing in deep restful sighs, was not even slightly aware of the powder keg. And as time dragged on, Kathy dozed periodically.

For those men, the darkness ended with the smashing of several bottles, the destruction of a picnic table because they ran out of firewood, and a sickening din of moaning and vomiting. They no doubt fell into a deep, tumultuous stupor before sleep overtook me. I lay there, deeply angered, as the final waffs of dried smouldering leaves filtered through the porous walls of our tent. As a single bird somewhere in the giant redwoods chirped to pre-dawn I too, eased into sleep.

Our earlier plan to fish a crystal stream a couple of miles above the spot where it met with the Pacific was foiled by exhaustion the next morning. I wanted to pack up our gear and leave the Humboldt nightmare behind and Kathy agreed. In the process of breaking camp, we studied the now-quiet site next to ours. We counted two pup tents, a pair of late model pickup trucks, a smouldering fire with a half burned board from the picnic table, full and empty whiskey bottles (whole and

Patrolling public campgrounds by water is a system used by the Missouri Water Patrol. Radio contact with campground attendants is maintained.

More and more persons use public campgrounds for partying.

141

Forms of vandalism range from simple pranks to property destruction.

Kathy and me. However, as full-time writers and photographers specializing in outdoor adventure, we camp by tent and RV all over the country. Some of our camps are pitched in remote wilderness areas, others in state and national parks within a half a day's drive of large cities. We have discovered that any public campground readily accessible by vehicle is a potential hideout for persons who turn to mischief and crime, rather than nature's gifts. No area is immune.

- While camping in the Sinks Canyon area near Lander, Wyoming in an Apache camp trailer, youths pelted our camper, and the tents and RVs of other campers with empty beer cans and bottles, shouting obscenities, sounding horns and screeching tires until the entire camping community was awakened.
- While camping Colter Bay campground, in Grand Teton National Park, Wyoming, several van campers, loaded with teenagers, blared stereo tapes from dark until dawn until all campers were awakened.
- Near Chamberlain, South Dakota at a Missouri River campground youths drag raced up and down

Complaints should be registered with rangers. Most are not available at night when most problems occur.

broken) and a scattering of beer cans. I wanted desperately to clang on the trash can until every last body was stirring, and I might have done just that when a park ranger drove up to collect our $3 camping fee. We told him our troubles in an angered tone, and he listened sympathetically. He left to inspect the area around their camp.

When the ranger returned he said he had enough evidence to hold the men until the county sheriff arrived on the scene. Along with the vandalized park table, a partially chopped live redwood tree and a heap of litter, evidence of marijuana was discovered and even without our testimony the offenders were in for trouble. The ranger suggested we quietly pack up camp and head down the road. After we left he would wait for the sheriff and the men would be placed under arrest. We drove from the campsite, feeling weary and at odds with mankind in general, but confident that the ranger and the sheriff had a good case. While most campground bandits get away, those men would soon experience a rude awakening and punishment for their behavior.

I wish I could report that the California experience back in 1977 was the first and only one of its kind for

Most campers are the friendliest people in the world.

Private campgrounds, for the highway traveler, offer more in-camp security.

the campsite access road shooting M-80 firecrackers and throwing rocks at RVs.

- At a Grand Canyon, Arizona campground, teenagers blocked access to heated men's and women's restrooms. Morning investigations by park rangers turned up marijuana, cocaine, broken toilets and mirrors and clogged sinks.

- All wooden U.S. Forest Service information signs near the Kern River in Sequoia National Forest, in California, were chopped to the ground by vandals. Other state and national parks, where wooden signs are erected, have been likewise subject to frequent destruction.

- Concrete camp tables and benches in Shoshone National Forest near Lander, Wyoming were broken with sledge hammers.

- A vandal in Missouri, according to the State Forestry Division, smears human feces over campground entrance booths, signs, restrooms and tables every year in the Mark Twain National Forest.

- Six gas lanterns were stolen during the night in White River National Forest, near Aspen, Colorado.

- A 9-year-old boy was assaulted in the men's restroom by teenagers at a campground at Grand Canyon National Park.

Modern highway access and proximity to large towns means no campground is immune from trouble.

Records of complaints and arrests at public campgrounds are continually increasing. Law enforcement, at such areas, is difficult.

In addition to those incidents, research field trips with park rangers, game wardens, campground managers and water patrol officers, have produced drug busts with such alarming frequency that law enforcement personnel now consider public campgrounds to be major breeding grounds for drug sales and addiction. And as one officer states, "The money for drugs often comes from handy and easily fenced items like camp stoves, lanterns, fishing tackle, portable radios and TVs, boat motors and wallets left unattended in camp."

Not too long ago items left in camp were considered safe by an unwritten but highly regarded rule (among true campers). Most genuine outdoor persons consider a camp thief on the same plane as a salted slug. However the once-honored rule is slowly dying except in some remote locations. Even tents, most of which now cost between $200 and $300 for a good one, are subject to theft and increasing numbers of campers are returning to camp only to discover that even their stakes have been pulled.

Why the Increase of Trouble in Camp?

1. The drug culture. The remote locations of public recreation and camping areas make ideal out-of-the-way but accessible meeting places. Such areas are usually at the far reaches of law enforcement jurisdictions.
2. Alcohol abuse. In some teenage and young adult groups the very fact that camping grounds are distant

144

The more remote camps, away from heavily used areas, are usually free from people problems.

from the usual constraints leads to overindulgence. Where wild parties might be snuffed in suburban or urban environments by telephone complaints to police, the campground community is not protected.

3. The ever-increasing cost of organized entertainment has put more of a burden on public campgrounds where young people can entertain themselves with the aid of drinking and drugs.

4. The back-to-nature, me-first syndrome has captured many immature imaginations. The result is an easily upset balance between the urban youth and his new-found wilderness setting.

5. The proof of guilt or disturbances in relatively remote camping areas makes enforcement of laws and prosecutions difficult. Law enforcement personnel concentrate on high crime areas in or near towns and cities where they are most needed. Finding evidence in the woods usually at night with witnesses reluctant to become involved on their vacations, presents special problems. Most campground attendants are not trained in law enforcement. The majority of park rangers are unavailable for assistance at night when most problems occur.

Campground Danger Signs

Some public campgrounds have more problems than others, usually the result of one or more contributing factors. In pre-planning camping trips or choosing a last-minute spot for the night, campers should consider the following guidelines for trouble-free camping.

1. Campgrounds near dense population centers, say within 30-minute driving distances, have more trouble than those less accessible.

Closely patrolled recreation areas are best bet for campers. In many areas, wooden signs as shown, are chopped down by vandals.

2. Campgrounds near state colleges and military installations are apt to attract party goers rather than true campers.

3. Campgrounds without live-on attendants, closing hours, camping fees and number limitations are trouble-prone.

Keeping one or more people at camp discourages theft and vandalism.

4. Campgrounds whose grounds are littered, have dirty restrooms, broken tables, grills and unattended trash cans should be avoided.

5. Loud music in the afternoon, unleashed dogs and large groups of sub-adults or teenagers perhaps using alcohol or drugs are trouble signs.

Solutions—Preventative and Otherwise

1. Private campgrounds, such as KOA, are fine for the highway traveler and overnight stops. They offer a greater degree of in-camp security than public campgrounds.

2. Some public campgrounds have public phones available. First, make sure such phones are in working order. Emergency phone numbers are provided at *good* sites. Take down the number and know who to call in case of trouble.

3. If in doubt about a campground, move on to another location or even a motel.

4. Try to set camp early enough in the day so a selection of sites are available. Remember, trouble makers like remote sections of campgrounds, but not for the same reason you might. Good campers and neighbors are obvious by their pride in outdoor skills. Camping families ordinarily make the best neighbors.

5. Self-protection. If you are 6-foot 4 inches and weigh 240, self-protection may come easy and your stature a deterrent to possible troublemakers. Most problems however, arise at night, and groups, rather than one or two persons, are behind the mischief. Tools used for personal protection are a matter of choice. Some individuals and families who elected not to rely on weapons of any kind, have many times found themselves at the mercy of individuals who have little regard for life or property.

6. Secure valuables. At night before retiring, and especially in a crowded campground, it is smart to lock stove, radio, fishing tackle, camera gear in the vehicle out of sight rather than leave it out in full view. Some equipment can be stored in the tent. Wallets or purses should never be left unattended on camp tables or inside tents. Outboard motors should be bolted and locked to boat transoms. If possible leave someone in attendance at camp. During daylight hours lock valuables in the car and close tent flaps and windows.

You will, for the most part, come in contact with some of the finest people in the outdoors when camping. But the more you camp, the greater your chances of running into some bad ones too. Use common sense, because you are dealing with groups which have lost theirs. Be selective. Try to choose your neighbors and report violations. It is easy to turn one's head at a campground, but we all have a responsibility to nature and each other, too.

A New Trail in a New Park Lures Both Canadian and U.S. Citizens

by TONY SLOAN

Unexpected water sources make good places to refill canteens, cool trail-warmed feet or take a refreshing impromptu shower.

CAMPING backpackers and hikers who have heard exciting news about the new Coastal Hiking Trail along the north shore of Lake Superior have heard true tidings. If you are partial to rugged Canadian Shield country trekking, this is indeed the trail of trails.

The Coastal Trail, still under development incidentally, is already the established premier attraction in the newly created Pukaskwa National Park. It is in every way a notable addition to such other well-known hikes as the Bruce and Rideau Trails in the southeasterly end of the province.

The remote, rugged north shore terrain has everything—crescent beaches along cobalt blue bays separated by lofty forested headlands; huge causeway-like rocks negotiated by hand and toeholds; rushing rivers or placid streams that can be waded, paddled or spanned by footbridges; and campsites that only the magic of the lonely and beautiful Precambrian Shield can provide.

We overnighted at the pleasant Pic Motel in Marathon, Ontario before setting out by van for the mouth of the Pic River, 27km south of town. Here we boarded a motorized launch for the 48km run south along the coast to our starting point at Oiseau Creek. The boat ride is a nice sightseeing opportunity to view the island-studded coastline and is a pleasant prelude to what one can expect in the way of scenery on the hike back north.

Oiseau Bay is the kind of spot where you'd like to build a cabin someday. We lit a small fire for tea and lunch and then hiked up Oiseau Creek looking for likely looking fishing holes. We spotted the odd rainbow

Backpackers on the new Coastal Hiking Trail in Pukaskwa Park in Canada should try to keep the pack light. A tent this size can provide shelter for three or four if they don't mind a little crowding. It is absolutely spacious for two.

trout, but nobody scored, so we returned to the lakeshore and started back north along the coast.

Park naturalist, Norm Ruttan, as leader of the outing, manned a cached canoe and proceeded to ferry our party of five hikers across Oiseau Creek. This stream could most likely be waded with little effort later in the season.

Our first test was a few kilometers of bushwhacking as the actual trail had only been completed as far as the next cove. It was a relief to emerge from the heavy going in the virgin bush and splash our faces in Superior's cool water.

After traversing the beach, we re-entered the woods at the actual start of the freshly cut trail and moved along easily among a boreal forest mix of birch, hemlock, balsam fir, white and black spruce and a few jack pine. It was ascertained that the area had been burned over in 1936. The forest, now regrown halfway to maturity, appeals to the eye of the appreciative hiker. Frequent windfalls (downed trees) lay across the trail and were attributed to a particularly devastating storm the previous November.

The late autumn or November storms that assault the north shore of Lake Superior are almost legendary, being recounted in song (Gordon Lightfoot's, "Wreck of the Edmund Fitzgerald") and story. Evidence of these fierce gales is easily noted all along the Coastal Trail. Sticks of pulpwood for example were observed high up in the narrow rocky defile leading down to Morrison Harbour. The wood, presumed to be deposited there by high waves or ice, was estimated to be 10 meters or more above the present level of the lake.

The heat and dense woods had a few of us nipping at our water bottles so we paused to refill and dunk our heads upon reaching Ahdik Lake. "Ahdik" is the Ojibway word for woodland caribou and a small herd is indigenous to Pukaskwa Park.

As the day wore on, such names as Cave, Fish and Morrison Harbours were recalled as intervals of sun, sand and a cooling breeze blowing in from the limitless expanse of the great lake.

We camped at Shotwatch Cove. The scenic beauty of this spot is not to be discounted, but the name "Shotwatch Cove" warrants a note of explanation. A trapper once lived here and his deserted cabin still stands with door ajar back in the shelter of the woods. A few rusted artifacts are found within, depicting the lonely life of the erstwhile resident. A curious item was discovered by park personnel when they inspected the cabin upon their arrival on the site a few years ago. It was a pocket watch with a bullet hole exactly in the center. What prompted this lonely trapper to shoot his watch? Did the inexorable passage of time in his solitary state weigh heavily upon his mind? Did he sense the fires of youth draining away and to forestall the weariness of age, attempt to kill the passage of time? What spectres beset the introverted silence of the isolated bush-dweller? Thoughts to ponder should you ever camp at Shotwatch Cove.

The intriguing Pukaskwa pits were encountered the following morning. Believed to have been constructed more than 2,000 years ago, these curious man-made depressions or excavations, in the boulder-strewn shoreline, remain a subject for speculation among archaeologists today. Did they have some religous significance or did they merely serve as shoreline shelters, perhaps with a covering of hides, to protect ancient Indian fishermen from the fierce late season storms? Fascinating region, this Pukaskwa country.

We next topped a lofty bluff and after photographing the shimmering offshore islands, proceeded to pick our way through great blocks of wave-washed rocks where the trail is marked by cairns.

The rugged rocky terrain eventually gave way to shady wooded draws leading up to treed ridges and occasional rock outcroppings frequently affording fine views of the coast. Steeper gullies followed where sparkling streams treated the thirsty hikers to refreshing draughts of clear, cold water.

We crossed the swift flowing and silted Willow River by canoe (a raft and cable are proposed for subsequent public use) and stopped for lunch where the river mouth forms a wide sand duned beach on the lakeshore. You then walk 1km of beach before the trail traverses another high headland. This is a very pretty stretch of mixed forest, where deep green moss and lichen-covered rocks vie with frequent springs, adding sparkle to the sun-dappled forest floor.

The garden-like path led down to a beaver meadow, where a pair of ring-necked ducks whistled off and a tiny marsh wren did a close-up appraisal, before flitting away into the willows. The route then climbed abruptly in stepped ascents toward the crest of a high ridge of exposed rock. The mid-afternoon heat plus the heft of my trail pack slowed my pace to a plodding climb. The crispy rock tripe (lichens) crunched under my boots and little rivulets of sweat streaked my glasses and stung my eyes.

Once atop the ridge, it was time to pause and drain the last drops from my water bottle. You get about 2km to the liter when you climb open terrain in hot weather. Again the trail became an easy stroll along an undulating forest pathway following the spine of the mountain with open and lofty vantage points to view the mountains beyond. A spring-fed stream replenished my water supply, even before the trail descended to skirt the shore of three separate little lakes. Then the roar of the upper falls on the White River was heard.

The spectacular White is crossed by a suitably terrifying suspension-type footbridge erected in 1977. Suspended an estimated 70 meters above the river, the bridge is located at the head of a sheer-sided canyon and offers a fascinating view of the longest stretch of the wildest water I have ever seen. Great pictures are to be had from the midpoint of the bridge, either up or down river, but unless you have a very stable tummy, it's no place to switch lenses or change film.

We camped that night on a pleasant little island already occupied by a flightless but nimble-footed Canada goose. After fishing away the morning hours in the swirls and rapids of the White River, we were picked up at noon and boated back to Pic River and the end of the road.

In retrospect, a quote from the Parks Canada brochure on Pukaskwa Park seems to say it all: "A remote and unyielding wilderness where man is and forever will be only a visitor."

Park Superintendent, Al Fisk expected the trail extension to be completed from Oiseau Creek to White Gravel River in 1979. The overall distance from White Gravel back to the Pic River would be 57km or 4 days of hiking taking time out to sniff the flora and wait for wildlife.

The new section, (Oiseau Creek to White Gravel River) according to Superintendent Fisk, is even more spectacular and physically demanding than the section described herein and hiked by our party. Access to the trail head is still by boat from the Pic River which is in turn accessible by car from the nearby Trans-Canada Highway (Hwy. 17) or via train to Marathon. Contact Bruce McQuaig of Heron Bay Marina, Heron Bay, Ontario or call (807) 229-0605 to reserve boat passage. The craft is almost 12 meters long and can carry from 20 to 25 passengers depending on quantity of gear. The boat trip from Pic to White Gravel River takes about 3½ hours. The per day rate is around $250 for the trip. Detailed information may be obtained by contacting Superintendent, Pukaskwa National Park, P.O. Box 550, Marathon, Ontario, POT 2EO. For general information on Canada as a travel destination, contact the Canadian Government Office of Tourism, Ottawa, Canada KIA OH6.

Alpine scenery tempts hikers and backpackers into the backcountry. This is the trail of trails for rugged Canadian Shield country trekking.

RV-ing Hawaii's Big Island

by JAMES TALLON

A LOT OF Pacific waves have lapped at the shores of Kealakekua Bay since Captain James Cook, the first European to see the Hawaiian Islands, died there in 1779. Controversy cloaks his death. Some say he was a good man. Others say not so good. His mistake was letting the Hawaiians believe he was Lono, their god of harvest, returned. They stuck a spear into him and were dismayed to find he was not immortal after all. Pleasure-craft dot the bay now. Some of the romance is gone. But Hawaii is very much alive and well, nonetheless.

Unlike Cook, we arrived by air—by Pan Am jumbo and Hawaiian based short-hoppers. We were castaway a week on Oahu, the melting pot of the Pacific. We walked a palm-fringed beach, devoid of other humans, on Molokai. We climbed the cloudy, silversword stairways of Haleakala, the 10,000-foot-plus extinct volcano of Maui. But, found, as the locals put it, "Big Island, mo' bettah."

The island of Hawaii is sometimes called "The Orchid Island" or "The Volcano Island," but most often, "The Big Island." These are attempts to be specific, to avoid confusing the mainlander. For most citizens of the Aloha State, the term "Hawaii" means *all* the islands.

The Big Island is twice the size of all the major islands combined, 4,038 square miles, and it has less than 10 percent of the state's total population, about 70,000. Hilo, with 30,000 people, is the only bona fide city on the island.

For a month we researched how to handle the Hawaiian Islands. The island paradises have a reputation as greenback-gobblers and we wanted as much as possible for those we had to spend. Rockefeller's Mauna Kea Beach Hotel near Kawaihae gets $205 per day for a family of three. That's on the low side. Pass. On the other hand, the Manago Hotel at Captain Cook will rent a room for three for $10 a night. Pass again. We paid $35 a day for our motel and got wheels with it. We are avid campers and our mainland van conversion with 108,000 miles helps confirm it. Why not go one of the ways we knew best?

Before departing Phoenix we corresponded with two camper companies: Beach Boy and Holo-Holo. (A third, Aloha Campers, has since come into existence.) Beach Boy was indifferent to our needs. Holo-Holo, the opposite. Gordon Morse, the owner-operator, either meets, or sends someone to meet, all his customers who land at Hilo airport. Our mini-motorhome was mechanically sound but showed mistreatment by previous drivers. Morse explained that repairing every little nick and dent would necessitate an increase in rental fees.

Hilo was like a step back into the 1940's and '50's. A quiet town with no traffic congestion. Strains of Hawaiian music filtered from cafes, taverns, shops and markets. The air was heady with the sweet scent of flowers—plumeria, the blossom so often used for leis, hau, a yellow member of the hibiscus family, bird of paradise, ginger and countless more. The Big Island also has 22,000 varieties of orchids. Some are wild, most tame.

150

"The harbor area of the town has been flattened a couple of times by tsunamic waves," said Hilo friend, Gene Wilhelm. "The bad ones were in 1946 and 1960. Parking meters were bent flat to the pavement. It could happen again. Now we have a breakwater in the bay and keep a tidal wave watch."

Actually, more than 50 tidal waves have connected with Hilo in the past half-century. The 1960 wave ripped in at 440 miles per hour.

Before campers leave Hilo, there are two stops to make. One, the Department of Parks and Recreation and, two, the supermarket. Camping on the Big Island is by permit only, but the DPR issues them free. And you have to eat. The best prices are in Hilo.

In Hawaii, eating is sheer joy. The restaurants offer tremendous variety; the supermarkets even more. And for good reason. In addition to 260,000 Caucasians, the Islands also support 210,000 Japanese, 61,000 Filipinos, 30,000 Chinese, 125,000 part Hawaiian (only about 8,000, or 1 percent, pure Hawaiians are left), and 86,000 of numerous other races. Thus, even mom-and-pop food stores cater to this wide diversity. Grocery shopping is pure adventure.

Until now we had made no hard, fast plans to explore the Big Island. Morse gave us a map and some suggestions. We added a copy of Hawaii Recreation Guide ($1). In it are listed 24 surfing areas, 34 quick-look highlights such as coffee mills and painted churches, 13 parks, including state and national, and 23 beach parks. Only Volcanoes National Park charges a camp fee. The rest are free. Some have such facilities as lighted pavilions, electricity, barbeques, picnic tables, modern toilets and showers.

Since it was late in the day, Harry K. Brown Beach Park, about 35 miles from Hilo, seemed like a sensible destination. It is centered in an area of considerable interest. Dinner was simple—hamburgers topped with long-stemmed mushrooms (new to us), fried potatoes

RV-ing Hawaii is the way to go. The late afternoon sun silhouettes swaying palms and a mini-motorhome.

Out-rigger canoe off the Kona Coast of the Big Island of Hawaii. They're made of fiberglass now, but popularity is even greater than in early-day Hawaii.

and a small salad. During the meal we discovered a stowaway, a mouse. Six-year-old Rachel is a mouseatic and has three of her own for pets. Attempts at capture failed and after the first evening we saw our visitor no more. Harry K. Brown Beach Park sits in a hole in the jungle. Dark green lushness. Uncrowded. Only three other families camped here. The surf lulls you to sleep.

Shortly after dawn we vaulted out and walked along Kaimu's Black Sand Beach (Hawaii also has brown, white and green sand beaches.) Surfers were already on the waves despite warnings of dangerous currents. Undulating, long-stemmed palms completed the South Seas look. I expected to see Tyrone Power and Gene Tierney (stars of the epic *Son of Fury*) come running by, holding hands.

Next we took in Wahaula Heiau—"heiau" is Hawaiian for temple. The story goes that here about 1250 A.D. a Tahitian priest named Paao introduced taboos and human sacrifice.

Southeasterly, the highway beyond Wahaula disappears under a lava flow. Just about everyone knows that the Hawaiian Islands were born of volcanoes. And I feel redundant mentioning that you're more likely to see an eruption on the Big Island than anywhere else in America. But maybe you don't know that the Big Island is made up of five volcanoes. Combined they form, counting what lies beneath the sea, the highest mountain in the world, the top being Mauna Kea at 13,796 feet. Adding in the sub-surface, make that more than 30,000 feet.

Kilauea Caldera, on the southern flanks of Mauna Loa, is the volcanic hot-spot. Where the action is. A few years back it spouted off, pouring lava into the Pacific. Everyone in Hawaii turns out for a big event like that, including Honolulu friends Ken and Joan Brown. They boated over to see it. "The water was so hot," Joan said, "that the boat's engine started to overheat. We had to move well out to sea to keep it cool. Absolutely nothing is more awesome than a volcano erupting." (Just 2 weeks after we returned to the mainland, Kilauea kicked off again.)

During lunch, which included fresh, chilled pineapple spears, we scanned our maps. There was no way to see the Big Island intimately in our allotted 3½-days. We would have to make another trip, one specially-tailored to the Big Island. Our plan was to circle-the-island, but we could dilly-dally at only a few prime places.

With this in mind, we backtracked along Route 130 to Keaau, caught Route 11 and drove up to Volcanoes National Park headquarters for a first-hand look at Kilauea, which native Hawaiians say is manipulated by the goddess Pele.

The caldera is scary-impressive, spanning 2 miles and sunk into the mountain several hundred feet. Steam and gasses hiss threateningly from fissures below. A

Beachcombing on the Big Island's black sand beach at Kaimu.

layman gets the impression Kilauea can go off at any instant. In this part of the park lava beds and roads are new. The old roads, like down at Wahaula, are underneath. Along with a Park Service vehicle.

We aimed the mini-motorhome downhill, through a prickly pear cactus landscape that reminded us of our home state, Arizona. ":Lovely Hula Hands" came over the radio. We hummed along. There were temptations to turn off Route 11 at Punaluu Black Sand Beach and at Ka Lee, or South Cape, the southernmost point in the United States. The road curved gradually until we were going almost due north. We sped along volcanic slopes a thousand feet above the sea. Mauna Loa's last lava flow. Now the road drifted downward again. This was the famous Kona Coast.

"I can't stand passing all these interesting looking places," Vicki said. "Let's take a quick look at Hookene Beach."

The road in was no wider than a one-car driveway on

Enjoying a remote sandy beach on the Big Island of Hawaii.

the mainland. Rock walls bordered it. We dealt in inches. No wonder our motorhome showed scrapes and dents. Even an experienced driver who lets his eyes rove for a second could be redesigning the RV. Squeezes like this are plentiful on the Big Island.

Hookena was a step back in time, too. Old Hawaii. Mutiny-on-the-Bounty-ish. Back on the highway again. But another left in just a few miles, a scheduled stop and one of the most interesting on the Big Island, the City of Refuge.

The City of Refuge may come closest to the way mainlanders expect Hawaii to look beyond Waikai. The National Park Service has brought it to that aesthetic level through restoration. Under a canopy of coconut palms there are grass huts and outrigger canoes and carved, wooden gods and Hawaiians doing village work. A cocoa-skinned lady teaches the hula with movements and interpretive dialogue you don't get on TV. The serenity is misleading. Originally, the City of Refuge was synonymous with drama. It offered sanctuary to lawbreakers and other transgressors. That is, if they could outrun or outswim their pursuers. Once in this haven they were safe and after a period of "purification" by refuge priests, released into Hawaiian society once more. Forgiven. Accepted. Free from retaliation.

From the refuge we took a short-cut, Route 16, to Napoopoo Beach Park. Typical of short-cuts, it had more chuckholes than the Oregon Trail during the 1880's. Pots and pans rattled. Flatware clattered. Napoopoo came into sight. The late afternoon sun sidelighted the park. It sparkled on the sea, and on pop and beer cans. A mess. A disgrace to Hawaii. But it was too late to look for a new campsite. We endured and picked up some of the litter. It was here that I mused over Captain Cook, the Hawaiians and his fate. Without a boat this is the only practical place to see the Cook Monument. An important historic place. Shouldn't it be policed?

The next morning we drove back to the main highway, motored through Kona coffee-lands and into my favorite town on the Big Island—Kailua-Kona. That fondness is directly tied in with 2 super weeks of photo journalistically covering the Hawaiian International Billfish Tournament. The event centers here because of the incredible fishing waters just a few yards off shore. Billfish weighing several hundred pounds have nailed lures at the edge of Kailua-Kona's tiny harbor.

In this town I knew where to go and we spent most of the day there. For lunch it was a Japanese feast at the Kona Tei. Vicki and Rachel chopsticked sashimi like it was going out of style. "But it doesn't *taste* like raw fish," Vicki said. From our balcony table we watched glass-bottom boats range over the reefs and that became our next objective. Then it was shops for Vicki while Rachel and I sat on the seawall dodging spray and nibbling at Macadamia-nut ice cream.

From here we stepped up our pace. Late afternoon found us at Samuel M. Spencer Beach Park. This one had all the modern conveniences and shallow, safe seas for swimming. Exotic and uncrowded. We turned in early that evening and before 9 AM the next day, Waimea (or Kamuela) and the 200,000-acre, 50,000-head Parker Ranch showed in the windshield. Vicki is a Parker, a relative born too late to be included in the Parker Family Book. Ranch employees were unimpressed. "Everyone says they're related to the Parkers," said one. Adulation of ranch owners seemed to be the order of the day. *We* were unimpressed.

Now it was down the mountain to Honokaa and the northeast coast, through forest and jungle, pasture and taro farms and sugar-cane fields, across deep canyons and steep slopes. A 4 PM airline departure pressed. Time for just one more stop. That was Akaka Falls State Park and worth it just to walk through the multi-flowered, 66-acre arboretum. The falls, a feathery veil, drops 420 feet; 227 more than Niagara's American Falls.

The jet airline banked across the north end of the Big Island of Hawaii. Visions flood. Nice memories and we're not even out of sight of the island. We congratulated ourselves on the wisdom of RV-ing the Big Island. Some items were priced higher than we were used to and some lower. Overall, about 10 percent higher than in Phoenix. Careful spending kept costs down to that of a vacation anywhere, and cheaper than some we've taken. In the final tally, we guess-timated that we spent one-third to one-half what the average person would taking the conventional Hawaiian tourist route. Next time, with our new knowledge, it might be even less.

But wait. Something troubled me. In our haste I could not remember something I wanted to try. Must not have been important. Then a flight attendant said, "We're offering complimentary Kona coffee." Kona coffee. That was it. An incredible coincidence. And just like the movies, we sailed—er, flew into the sunset.

"No frills camping" is cheaper than staying at home.

CHEAPER THAN STAYING AT HOME

by CHARLEY DICKEY

The Chateau Tent (Holubar) has a large entrance which makes it easy to enter and leave. During rainy spells Dick, Katie and little Matt plus all their gear can fit inside.

MOST YOUNG married couples in college have skinny budgets. With the inflationary costs of higher learning, there's little cash left for recreation. But getting away from the classrooms and laboratories is important for a change of pace.

Dr. Dick Sayre, a post-doctoral research associate in molecular biophysics, beats the budget crunch by taking inexpensive camping trips with his wife Katie and son Matt, 2½ years old. When he can grab a day or two away from his laboratory work at Florida State University in Tallahassee, the family heads for the boondocks.

They travel light. If the gasoline situation becomes too critical, they're geared up to go by bicycle rather than stationwagon. From Tallahassee, they're only 20 minutes from the 550,000-acre Apalachicola National Forest. In 30 minutes they can be to the Gulf of Mexico or in a remote area of the St. Marks National Wildlife Refuge.

By the time you read this, Dick and his family will be at the University of Kentucky in Lexington, where Dick is doing more post-doctoral research. Their camping gear will have first priority on the move. It won't take them long to find new wilderness areas. They're both from California, and his academic career has got them used to moving.

Katie, who has the look of Ireland on her friendly face, says, "The only extra expense we have on a camping trip is for gasoline going and coming. If we make short trips, that cost is held down. We don't spend any more for food on a weekend camping trip than we would if we stayed at home. And in the woods we're not using utilities. Maybe camping is cheaper than staying home."

Dick usually takes fishing tackle on their camping trips—the 18-inch shorty Zebco rod with a spincast reel and a longer breakdown rod fitting the bill for compactness. These rods are easy to carry on half-day hikes or all-day packs from base camp. When he catches a stringer of bluegills or bass, it's a free dinner. Money saved this way helps make more trips possible.

Their camping is kept simple. The less time they spend with gear, the more time they have for hiking, swimming, fishing and general nature observing. Dick and Katie have been married 5 years, after meeting at the University of California at Riverside. They've been camping together ever since. Until young Matthew came along, they didn't even bother with a tent but waited out rainstorms with ponchos.

Actually, they've accumulated some excellent equipment. They bought it a piece at a time as they could afford it, and the gear has increased in value; that is, it would cost a lot more now to replace it. They use a Holubar Chateau tent with a high front arch. There's a tunnel vent at the arch backed by mosquito netting and two large window vents on each side. The high arch makes entrance and exit easy, especially when you're moving sleeping bags in and out. If it rains, the Chateau

155

(Above) Although there is plenty of wood for a fire in the area, the Sayres find it easier to use their little backpacking stove.

(Below) There are old boats, shore birds, fiddler crabs and a variety of plants and wildlife for the Sayre family to see on remote stretches of Florida's Gulf Coast.

tent has enough room for Dick, Katie, Matt and all of their gear. They can even add another person. Steve Theg, a doctoral candidate at FSU, sometimes camps with them.

The tent can be put up in about 5 minutes. The sectional tent poles are made of aluminum tubing. There are 14 stakes. The entire tent, including stakes, weighs only 10¼ pounds. The tent floor fabric is urethane-coated nylon and it extends up the sides. A heavy rain may make you feel like you're in a water bed but you stay dry.

Oddly enough, the Sayres seldom build a campfire although there's plenty of dead trees in Florida's panhandle. In fact, the U.S. Forest Service not only encourages the burning of fallen trees but, when camping in the Apalachicola National Forest, with a free permit you can chop it up and take it home for your fireplace. The Sayres have done so much western camping, where firewood was at a premium, that they cook with a Svea Model 123 camp stove. It measures only 5 inches by 3¾ inches and weighs just 16 ounces. The handy little stove, with brass construction, burns white gasoline or Coleman fuel. It's a backpacking

(Above) Dick Sayre, left, with backpack and Steve Theg, right, with day pack plan a day's hike from base camp.

(Below) Alert campers in Florida often see shy deer and other wildlife. Many areas are a bird watcher's delight and cost nothing.

stove but is all Katie needs when cooking a family meal.

Dick began camping as a boy, but Katie did not take it up until she went to college. Despite having to watch their nickles, they've camped in the Sierras, Tetons, Mt. Whitney area and spent a summer on a university expedition collecting plants near Durango, Mexico, where Katie's Spanish major came in handy. They camped in the snow in Yosemite and have enjoyed cross-country skiing in several mountainous areas. Dick took a 1,000-mile bike trip one summer from San Francisco to Mt. Ranier in Washington. They've learned the shortcuts to simple camping.

They have one Eddie Bauer sleeping bag and a Holubar Ultimate Signature. This is not exactly inexpensive gear, but it will hold up for years. They bought the bags when camping in the high Sierras. In Florida, they slept on top of them. Both use Ensolite pads under the bags. Their other gear includes backpacks by Kelty and Camp Trails plus a day pack by North Face. Three backpacking pots and pans, a few items such as mosquito lotion, clothing and food make up the rest of their equipment. They can break camp and move in a few minutes. The rucksack and backpacks come in

Favorite rods for the Florida wilds are the short Zebco which Dick (right) carries and a two-piece rod that Steve brought along. The large tackle box is left in camp, only a small plastic box of specific lures is brought along.

handy for long daily hikes, especially if they're picking blackberries, wild onions or catching fish for dinner.

Dick says, "Once you get your basic equipment, camping is the most inexpensive recreation I know. With our backpacking gear, we can go to remote areas or we can set up in a designated camping area near other campers. We stay light and portable and it gives us a choice. Even if the country goes to gas rationing, I hope we'll have enough gas to get us out of town. If we don't, then we can use our bikes."

New campers, according to Katie, either take so much equipment they spend all of their time fooling with gear or they don't have the right equipment. She says, "Our camp is a place to stay so that we can explore, swim and fish. The key is to be reasonably comfortable with a minimum amount of equipment."

Some campers and hikers go to extremes. She laughs about the backpacker who cut off his toothbrush handle to save weight. "Wives new to camping," she says,

"usually take too many clothes. One change, in case you get wet, is enough for a week. Some girls going out for a weekend take enough clothes for a semester in college."

The Sayres don't really go out into the boondocks just to eat. They take enough food for balanced meals, but the food is to sustain them—not an end in itself. Even with their stationwagon parked nearby, they don't take food that requires long preparation. On any outing, Katie is as anxious to get a break from household duties as Dick is to get away from his test tubes. Because their budget is limited, they don't buy dehydrated foods from specialty stores. It may be light for backpacking, but it's expensive. Katie says she learned the hard way that the best place to shop for budgeted camping is at a supermarket. Lipton dried dinners, with a small pot of rice, are one of her favorites for a fast meal at night. The supermarket food weighs a little more than special dehydrated foods but the weight is not critical

Largemouth bass are often found in brackish water, though generally overlooked by most anglers. When the tide is out the fish are concentrated in small pools.

Fish brought back to camp for dinner are not only delicious, but also save on the food bill.

on a 3- or 4-day trip. She usually takes a carton of eggs with a few eggs removed to make room for a stick of butter.

She buys high energy food such as salami and cheese. If they want to leave base camp and explore for the day, that's all they need for lunch. They forget about mustard, mayonnaise and bread. Sesame bars also provide a lot of energy at moderate prices. An inexpensive but nutritious food for camping is dried fruit. It can be eaten "as is" on the trail or cooked when at camp. Dried peaches and apricots are ideal. They're not likely to spoil no matter how hot the temperature. Anything not eaten at camp is taken back home.

Since Matt came along, the Sayres are limited to how far they can hike and explore in a day. But he doesn't curtail their overall activity. They just have rest breaks between hikes and swims.

They usually take two or three canteens of water from home. Although Florida is loaded with freshwater

(Left) A critical item on exploration trips is fresh water. It's the best thirst quencher of all but sometimes hard to find in the salty marshes and flats.

(Below left) Instead of a cold wind from a gas-hungry air conditioner; instead of a V-8 engine, how about biking in the breeze you stir up yourself?

(Below) Inexpensive campgrounds like this (St. Andrews State Park on Panama City Beach) attract budget-conscious people who like to swim, fish or go boating.

lakes and springs, some remote areas, such as the coastal flatlands, do not have handy water supplies. When they're in doubt about using water from a lake, they quickly boil it on their Svea camp stove or use a purification tablet.

One of the keys to successful camping Dick says, is to hit a happy medium. Too many newcomers overdo. They walk too far the first day and become exhausted. They lie in the sun too long and get blistered. They forget their insect repellent and get chewed on. It's hard to get them to try a second trip, especially wives.

Dick suggests moderation for all things when starting camping and backpacking. It isn't necessary to buy expensive equipment to begin with. Army surplus stores provide the basics at reasonable prices. In fact, camping has become so popular at many universities that they rent complete camping gear at nominal fees.

Katie, who will have another little camper by the time you read this, says the new baby won't slow them for long. Perhaps the best thing low-budget camping has given them is a chance to see a lot of backcountry together.

Dick says, "You know, too many students today at large universities never see anything but the campus. It's not that way with us and never will be. We want to see everything an area has to offer and that includes the mountains, lakes, woods and streams. So far, we haven't missed a thing—low budget or not!"

You may drive the Big Rig to the campground, but riding a bicycle built for two once there is a balm to both the change purse and cramped muscles.

BAJA CALIFORNIA

Desert Camping With

JUTTING stiffly downward from our own southern California, Baja California remains stubbornly unlike its thriving brother to the north. While the lower end of our Golden State throbs with growth and innovation, Mexico's peninsula is a seemingly useless appendage, a dry barren stick where no endeavor of man has ever really succeeded. Mineral ores are of poor quality, the pearl producing oysters around LaPaz died of an unknown disease, and unlike the Mayans and Aztecs of the mainland, the natives wandered unclothed and hungry from oasis to oasis. This inhospitable land forced even the indomitable priestly orders to retreat in defeat.

Indeed, Baja California would not ordinarily appear high on anyone's list of desirable camping areas. But surprisingly, it should. It is one of the most unique and wildly beautiful areas in the hemisphere. The slim 900-mile long cane is washed on the west by the waters of the Pacific Ocean, its backbone is a ridge of purple mountains and the eastern shore is separated from the Mexican mainland by a deep trench, the incredibly blue and fertile Sea of Cortez (or Gulf of California). And with the recent completion of Highway 1, all of Baja, from Tijuana at the northern terminus to Cabo San Lucas at the southern tip is open to a camper with an ordinary vehicle and some determination. Countless side roads leading to the cactus studded deserts of the backcountry and deserted azure coves can be negotiated by 4WD vehicles. Organized campgrounds, some with hookups, are found at the larger towns, or campers can decline group living and set up a campsite far from lights and plumbing.

One remote and awesome camping area is the Parque de San Pedro de Martir in the mountains of the northern part of the peninsula. From one high peak it is possible to see both the rolling Pacific to the west and the sparkling blue of the Sea of Cortez to the east. The roads here can be impassable at times (check with local police or park wardens), and there are no facilities of any kind nor are there any trails. But for the backpacker who relishes remarkable scenery in complete solitude this area is perfect. For a detailed map showing the location of Mexico's parks write for the "Mapa Turisco de Carreteras" from the Mexican National Tourist Council, 405 Park Ave., N.Y., NY 10022.

Most campers will reach Baja via Highway 1 which is only a two lane strip in some places, stretching for 1,058 miles down the 900-mile long finger of land. All vehicles must be in top condition before leaving the states to negotiate this roadway. Tires must be able to survive a terrible beating both on the tread and on the sidewalls. Bring along a spare or two and a repair kit. Mexican mechanics are often excellent but service stations can be few and far between so a working knowledge of your car's engine and a boxful of spare parts will add to the camper's peace of mind.

Other things that will be needed at the border for the long trip are jerry cans of drinking water, extra gasoline and any kerosene or white gas that will be needed. Butane and propane are sold in large towns. The authorities will require proof of citizenship and proof of ownership of the vehicle at the check station. Tourist cards can then be issued. U.S. auto insurance is not valid in Mexico, but short term Mexican policies are reasonably priced, and we recommend you buy one at any of the convenient places near the border.

While supplies of gasoline are problematical here in the U.S., it appears that the Mexicans will have no such worries. All gasoline in Mexico is sold at government owned Pemex stations which are no farther than 50 miles apart. However it is advisable to stay at least half full since pumps are occasionally empty. Unleaded gas comes from the silver pump (called Extra) and regular from the blue. The true octane rating is lower than that marked on the pump but we have never had any problems with it. Some high compression engines will need an adjustment to retard the spark for best performance. Air-cooled engines should be regulated to avoid pinging which ruins pistons in a short time. Payment for gasoline is in pesos, not dollars, and the camper will be happy to see that (at least at the time of this printing) prices are low compared to those in the U.S.

The Mexican government, anxious for tourism from the U.S., has made travel on Highway 1 more attractive by having the Green Angels patrol the road. Pairs of mechanics dressed in green constantly search the highway seeking out stranded motorists they can help. They carry spare parts, water, gas and oil and their services are very low cost or even free. One of the pair can speak English.

Caution should always be exercised while driving the Highway but especially on a 400-mile stretch of 20-foot wide paving between El Rosario and San Ignasio, generally the middle third of Baja. This narrow section has no shoulders. Not only can an accident ruin your vacation, but even minor ones are viewed with gravity by Mexican officials. Should there "be blood" both the vehicle and its driver are impounded immediately. Ex-

a Mexican Accent by PEGGY BAUER

(Above) This Old Man of the Sea proudly shows off his enormous white sea bass.

(Right) Casting from a small boat for groupers, snappers etc., is great sport for the camper who brings his own boat.

planations come later and usually through an attorney. In Spanish, of course. In case of accident do not surrender your insurance policy and pay no one.

We advise anyone venturing into Baja for the first time to carry along a small valuable book, *The Baja Book II* by Tom Millar and Elmar Baxter, Baja Trail Publications, Inc., Box 6088, Huntington Beach, CA 92646. This is a complete guide with maps and information and even helps with the Spanish language. Another caution is never to drive at night. There are no street lights to speak of and the hazards include free-roaming livestock and resident motorists.

On secondary routes there are small shrines erected by the faithful (and fearful) at the top of what will be a steep and difficult descent. These are small box-like enclosures containing a plaster statue of a saint or the Virgin Mary and perhaps a few plastic flowers. Some have remanants of novena candles lit in memory of those whose vehicles took them to their death at the bottom of the canyon. Several we saw contained a few pesos and one had a penciled note signed "Your friend, Amos."

It may well have been fishermen who were the first tourists to Baja California for the waters surrounding this land are incredibly rich in both variety and numbers of fish. Wealthy anglers have for a quarter century flown into a few well appointed camps to haul in fish

California sealions can be seen on many of the islands which dot the waters surrounding Baja. These are on Espiritu Sanctu.

until their arms were too sore to continue. Baja waters run from cool, up-welling areas such as those found off central California to tropical areas where the temperatures range from 70-90 degrees F. in late summer. Great tidal currents mix in the upper reaches of the Sea of Cortez resulting in the distribution of nutrients and a bountiful mass of sealife, one species feeding on another.

Many fishing campers bring their own boats to Baja to sample the great opportunities here. Should you join this group, be sure your insurance will cover your boat on a Mexican trip before leaving home and bring along proof of ownership to be shown at the border. Often the car-top or trailed boat will just be waved across the border by the officials. But the law dictates that the Republic of Mexico charge about $5 per month for a boat license plus 13¢ for each ton of weight. This is always enforced on the mainland, sometimes on Baja.

Most boat-carrying rigs can negotiate the main highway with little or no trouble. The closest fishing areas in Baja are Ensenada on the west coast and San Felipe at the head of the Sea of Cortez. Ensenada was once noted for what was thought to be an inexhaustible supply of yellowtail, halibut and white seabass, but uncontrolled commercial fishing has diminished the stock drastically. There is still sportfishing here however with 25 open party and charter boats operating. With a local guide you can fish the bays at San Quintin and Guerrero Negro or fish from shore at high tides. The in-shore species are perch, croaker, corbina, and opaleye.

The flats around San Felipe are subject to hot winds from the desert. Sharks and corvina thrive in the warm waters during the summer while other species retreat. White seabass can be caught in winter and spring and sierras in fall and spring. San Felipe was once known mainly for giant totuavas weighing up to 300 pounds. But again the Mexican government failed to act to protect this resource and commercial overharvesting and the destruction of spawning areas have brought them to the brink of extinction. There are a number of informal camping areas here on the beach plus a well organized camp, "Camp Nuevo Mazatlan" with water and toilets.

Probably the best fishing is found in the Sea of Cortez from Cabo San Lucas at the southern tip, past La Paz and northward to the Midriff Islands. Here are sandy coves and rocky inlets with outstanding beauty just off the main road. The camper can erect his tent in a deserted area or within sight of the huge tourist hotels dominating the higher headlands. He can fish the same productive waters. Marlin and sailfish invade these waters in summer plus schools of dolphin and tuna. Roosterfish, amberjack and yellowtail can also be found. The surfline fisherman might also hook into a sierra, pompano, barilette or bonito. Something is always biting somewhere.

An American fishing from his own boat will need a standard Mexican fishing license. At this printing the costs are around 37 pesos for a week, 50 pesos for 30 days or 100 pesos for a calendar year. Possession of some species including shellfish is forbidden, and there are limits to certain other fish. Check for current regulations. Fishing licences may be obtained by mailing a check to Oficina de Pesca Office, 233 "A" Street, Suite 3, San Pedro, CA 90731. They are also available in some tackle stores in Southern California.

Many of the islands off the shores of Baja are nearly as interesting for their wildlife as the Galapagos—and so much closer. Some can easily be reached in a small fishing boat and others require chartering a larger craft.

Abandoned missions dot the Baja California peninsula. Some are preserved and restored, others like this are allowed to fall into decay. Many missions are easy to find, others turn up at distant, unexpected locales.

A campground can be wherever nightfalls finds you. Deserted areas with indigenous elephant trees will be long remembered.

The second largest island in the Sea of Cortez is Isla Angel de la Guardia; it is indeed the guardian angel for the town of Bahia Los Angeles which it protects from strong easterly winds. The island is 42 miles long and rises to over 4,000 feet. While on a trip to this area last May we landed at Punta Estanque on the southern end to find nesting western gulls and fish-eating bats under the rocks. We chased fin back whales and could easily see their double nostril, mouth and white underparts. Strange desert plants dotted the U-shaped valley on the north and tiny lizards appeared as the sun lowered. An osprey pair was nesting on a pinnacle, and there we found two young birds already banded. We hurriedly left under the insistent low swoops of the parent birds.

We also inspected a neighboring island, Granito, and found several colonies of sea lions on the rocky shores and on two sandy beaches. The females must just have arrived as only one pup was seen, but the beachmaster bulls were defending their territory. Cardon cactus jutted up to the sun and black chuckwallas (lizards) which inhabit the island warmed themselves on rocks only to dive into their burrows at our approach.

The western shore of Baja has a climate different from the hot, dry desert conditions which prevail on the east. Here during the summer there are warm days and cool nights and often fog rolls in. The tiny amount of annual rainfall occurs from December to April.

It was a windy, foggy and cool day when we approached Isla Cedros, almost directly west of Angel de la Guardia in the gray Pacific. Both elephant seals and California sea lions lazed on the rocky beaches. Mating time finished, all the elephant seal bulls had left for life

There are many coves where the camper can decide to spend the night, the week or his whole vacation.

at sea while the females and their new calves remained. Young bulls spared with each other on land and then cruised the coastline. They would depart with the cows and calves later in the season.

Black shining sea lion pups were younger, many just born, and gulls, both Western and California, patrolled the area for edibles. A walk up a dry wash took us past agave, barrel cactus and several species of sedum, one with a flattened round berry called lemonade berry. The elephant trees on this forever windy island were bent to earth, each leaning eastward in the face of the continual westerly blow. After a long hike we reached the head of a small stream to find scores of inch-long bright green frogs leaping and swimming in the clear water. There are many other wildlife islands around the peninsula. Some have little of interest left due to feral goats, nest-robbing and settlement, but others remain nearly untouched. Most are accessible by boat; a few are protected by the government.

Spain and the Spanish Roman Catholic missionaries spent most of the 15th century on the Mexican mainland, and it wasn't until 1696 that the Jesuits first came to Baja. They and the Franciscans and the Dominicans all built missions and attempted to convert the nearly 50,000 natives to the faith. Their attempts resulted in no benefits to either the Spanish crown or the church and left the surviving Indians numbering fewer than 6,000. The priests retired to greener lands leaving well over 30 missions on the peninsula today in various states of decay, restoration or original condition. Many are in the larger towns such as Loreto and Mulege, but there are also some in out of the way places where the wandering camper may explore these deserted bastions of the faith. Mission San Francisco de Borja, 20 miles northeast of Rosarito on a dirt road, is now one of the best restored in the area. It once served nearly 300 converts after its completion in 1762, but when it finally closed in 1818 only 100 converts remained. When we were there, there was no restoration going on, and we found the area completely deserted. Swallows swopped over the alter where an alter cloth was fouled by their droppings. A tiny baptismal gown was neatly folded on the front. There were long structural cracks in the ceiling and the better pieces of carved stonework were missing.

The nearby small buildings seemed to have been abandoned with great speed, too. In one we found a shoemaker's wooden last and in another a branding iron neatly hung by the door. The inside walls were entirely "papered" with slick magazine advertisements for digital watches, stereo sets and transistor radios. It is important that the old missions be preserved because vandals often take away precious old items such as looming carved and decorative iron work to sell. They can often be seen as part of the homes of wealthy Mexicans.

Camping the Baja peninsula today is much like what camping in our own Southwest must have been a half century ago, with both its good and bad aspects. Things which should be protected are not, and travel is often difficult. But there are areas still to be discovered, shores and mountains to be enjoyed and explored without the intrusion of too many others. The adventurous camper may well find Baja his favorite campground.

Grass River Provincial Park is located 46 miles (74 km) northwest of The Pas. This park wilderness is perfect for the person seeking a camping experience in an area untouched by over-development. (Photos courtesy of Manitoba Government Travel)

Camping in Manitoba Today

by MONA MARSHALL

IF YOU'VE been planning a vacation for a long time and are tired of coping with high prices and gas shortages, a camping trip in Manitoba may be just what you need. The open spaces stretch for miles with small towns located in between, linked by well-kept but sparse roads. The drive is half the fun because of the variety of scenic beauty that Manitoba has to offer. If your favorite fishing lake is over-taxed, the 12 provincial parks scattered throughout the province have a wealth of fish in numerous crystal clear lakes.

With three-fifths of the province consisting of verdant forests and clear lakes, few people could fail to recognize the tremendous camping potential available. There are over 60 campgrounds with more than 5,000 campsites run by the province; another 5,000 are provided by the private sector. Manitoba's Provincial Campgrounds provide convenience and pleasure with facilities ranging from near wilderness (for those who enjoy "roughing it" away from other campers), to fully serviced campgrounds, for those who prefer the conveniences of home. Fees for an unserviced site are around $4 to $5 for those with electrical hook-ups and about $6 for fully serviced sites with sewer, water and electricity. The admission fee to any provincial park is around $1.50 per day, or $8 for the season. (All prices in Canadian dollars.)

Nothing is as relaxing as soaking up the sun on a sandy beach, taking a hike through the woods or fishing on a still lake nestled somewhere in a dense forest. You can do all this in Whiteshell Provincial Park, located adjacent to the Ontario border. It has more than 200 lakes inhabited by walleye, northern pike, and smallmouth bass; lots of opportunities for you to catch that "Big One." For a non-resident, the price of a 3-day fishing license is around $6 or $11 for the season.

Take advantage of these lakes and go boating, water-skiing, or canoeing in the wilderness. The park has 13 campgrounds with more than 2,000 tent and trailer sites, as well as motels and cabins. Falcon Lake has an 18-hole golf course, a marina, tennis courts, bowling greens and riding stables.

An excellent retreat for city dwellers is Birds Hill Provincial Park, located just 14 miles north of Winnipeg. The large campground features 355 unserviced, 104 electrical hook-ups and 45 fully serviced sites. There's lots to do in this suburban park with its 80-acre man-made lake, riding stables and walking trails through otherwise unbroken land.

Highlighting Grand Beach Provincial Park, located 57 miles north of Winnipeg, is the long expanse of fine, sandy beach. Perfect for water and sun lovers, the campground has 300 unserviced and 110 electrical hook-up sites. Lake Winnipeg features unlimited boating and sailing potential, the east beach is laced with trails, and tennis and volleyball courts are available.

The more northerly parks in Manitoba have re-

Great family fun awaits when staying at any one of Manitoba's campgrounds. Twelve provincial parks, seven provincial forests and one national park promise an escape from frantic city life.

mained close to their natural state and are therefore the best places to go for a real wilderness camping experience. Twelve miles north of The Pas, Clearwater Provincial Park features three campgrounds with mainly unserviced sites around the lake. The chief attraction here is the first-class fishing for lake trout in this crystal clear lake.

An ideal vacation area is Duck Mountain Provincial Park, 60 miles northwest of Dauphin, located on the Manitoba Escarpment. Four campgrounds can be found at various lakes; all are unserviced except for Wellman Lake campground, which has 10 electrical hook-ups. The fishing is great and the rolling landscape offers hikers unique opportunities to explore nature trails.

For a truly rugged adventure in outdoor camping, the province's northernmost park should be ideal. Grass River Provincial Park, 46 miles northwest of The Pas,

(Right) Formed during the Glacial Age, Wellmar Lake attracts vacation seekers with its good fishing and modern campgrounds as well as its natural beauty. Wellman Lake is 22 miles (35.5 km) south of Minitonas on Highway 366, situated in Duck Mountain Provincial Park.

With 100,000 lakes, streams and rivers to choose from, the Manitoba wilderness is an ideal area for canoeing. Many resorts offer canoe rentals for exploring the great outdoors.

has remained almost entirely wild, and campgrounds at Gyles Park, Tskwasum and Reed Lake have unserviced sites only. There are 150 lakes with great fishing and wilderness canoeing opportunities.

Manitoba's only national park offers ample opportunity for camping enthusiasts. Riding Mountain National Park preserves 1,150 square miles of a diverse landscape of forests, prairies, rolling hills and clear lakes. Wasagaming, located at Clear Lake, has facilities for golfing, swimming, tennis, boating, sailing and some excellent trout fishing. The park entrance fee is about $1 per day, $2 for 4 days or $10 for the season. Camping fees are around $3 for an unserviced site, $5 for electrical hookup and $6 for a fully serviced site. Five campgrounds are located at various areas around the park, from fully serviced sites at Wasagaming to unserviced sites farther inside the forest areas.

If you'd like to combine a modern resort area with untouched wilderness, camping at Hecla Provincial Park can give you all that and more. Hecla Island is the largest island on Lake Winnipeg and teems with wildlife and beautiful scenery to provide visitors with a spectacular vacation land. The campground at Gull Harbor has 113 unserviced campsites, along with an 18-hole golf course, beach, tennis courts and an amphitheatre.

Right on the Manitoba/North Dakota border is a delightful sight—the International Peace Garden. Here in Turtle Mountain Provincial Park you can camp around three lakes containing 85 campsites and enjoy the variety of wildlife, trees and shrubs, fish for trout or tour the beautiful Peace Garden.

Other parks that offer relief from crowded city living are Spruce Woods Provincial Nature Park, where camping facilities have been set up near the desert-like Bald Head Hills, allowing you to observe the unique flora and fauna of this sandy region; and Manitoba's newest provincial park, Nopiming, meaning "into the wilderness." Located on the Canadian Shield, Nopiming features rocky shorelines, sparkling waters and abundant wildlife. Camping, wilderness canoeing and fishing are great reasons to head up to this park, 130 miles northeast of Winnipeg, for a vacation in nature.

In a deep valley near the Saskatchewan border, Asessippi Provincial Park features a campground near the man-made Lake of the Prairies. The most popular attraction in the park is the Shellmouth Dam, built on the Assiniboine River. The lake is equipped with excellent boating facilities and features an extensive beach area.

Just about every town in Manitoba is equipped with a camping area for overnight stops and there are numerous campgrounds dotted along provincial highways, set into cool treed areas where visitors are made welcome anytime.

A camper's paradise can be found in any of the provincial parks amidst Manitoba's clean air, natural beauty and wide open spaces.

Running the Geikie River

Camping Saskatchewan's Unknown

by TONY SLOAN

THE BEAVER aircraft droned on and on, north of the setting sun, and over the green trees and blue water country of northern Saskatchewan, in north-central Canada. It seemed like a very long time since we took off from the little town of Missinipe and headed north toward the headwaters of the Geikie River.

There's a mighty big stretch of evergreen and trackless wilderness up here and after an hour of watching it drift by below, you start getting lonely just looking at it. If canoeing a wild river in a remote and beautiful wilderness is what turns you on, then northern Saskatchewan is the place for you.

Eventually we landed safely on the east end of Big

Sand Lake and taxied carefully onto a sand beach. We were able to land the canoe and gear directly from the plane's pontoon to shore without even getting our feet wet. Then the Beaver roared away, lifted off into the wind and was soon backgrounded by a dark rain cloud to the east. Sun dogs and dark clouds heralded rain, maybe a storm front moving in from the west.

Here was our situation. One hundred and sixty kilometers (100 miles) of wilderness river flowed between us and the nearest road. We were strictly on our own. Quickly my partner, Doug Elsasser of Regina, Saskatchewan, and I moved our gear inland out of the wind and made camp in dense jack pines up on a nearby

172

(Above) The Saskatchewan government offers canoeing information for many different trips in the province. In many cases the advice is to portage around particularly wild rapids. In this remote area it is wise to follow the admonition. (Opposite page) Natural campsites atop the high eskers along the Geikie River in northern Saskatchewan add to the pleasure of canoe travel in this wild country. (Credit: Canadian Govt. Off. of Tourism)

ridge. Saskatchewan's Department of Tourism has published individual booklets on 55 separate canoe trips throughout the province and tomorrow we would begin one of them. Based on individual canoeing surveys, the literature is the most detailed and comprehensive ever produced by a governmental agency in Canada and is positive proof of the government's new interest in the outdoor recreational potential of the rivers and lakes in the vast northern forests. Geikie River is number 38 in the canoe trips series and the introduction reads, "This is a far northern trip—between latitude 57 and 58—and is one which is extremely isolated from help in the event of an emergency. This is definitely not a trip for beginners. There are many long and dangerous rapids. Portage trails are poor or non-existent which forces canoeists to shoot tricky rapids and to do a lot of strenuous wading and portaging." Once on the river, that introduction was more sobering than when we read it the first time. I slept uneasily that first night.

We were totally outfitted by Churchill River Canoe Outfitters in Missinipe and our traditional first night steaks were done rare. Churchill River Outfitters are obviously convinced that deep wilderness voyageurs should be well provisioned and have extra food in the event of delays and emergencies. Sound reasoning, but we seemed to have enough food for an entire brigade, not just a single canoe. Maybe they expected us to succumb to the spell of this lonely and beautiful land and stay over winter. It did cross our minds.

All squared away in the morning, we proceeded to cruise down the easterly shore of Big Sandy Lake. It was breezy enough when crossing the mouth of the wide bays, but it was a quartering wind, and we logged about 16km (10 miles) before stopping for lunch. That is very good time, especially for a first day out. We spotted an old abandoned canoe tied up on an island with a trail leading inland, which would indicate a trapper's cabin. We pulled in to have lunch and explore.

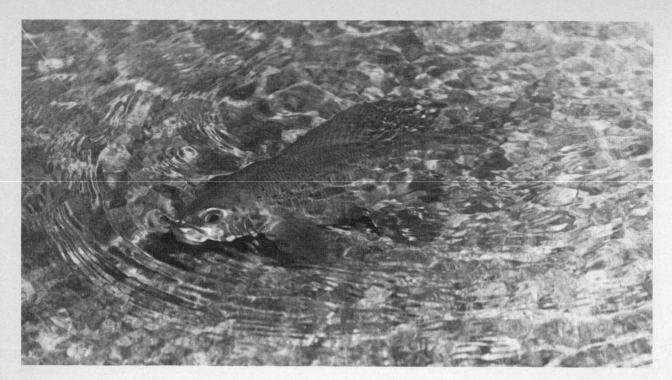

In some areas we had to fight off northern pike in order to bring in a grayling like this.

The tiny low buildings, two of them plus a lean-to for firewood, were located about 100 yards from the shore. It was an attractive spot except for an unsightly pile of bones from fur-bearing animals piled up a few strides from the front door. Since the trap lines are only worked in wintertime the proprietor is not around in summer when the weather gets hot and the bones smelly. Suddenly Doug was startled when he heard what sounded like marching feet. The mystery was resolved when he spotted a porcupine backing down a nearby tree.

By mid-afternoon we reached the end of the lake and immediately negotiated a fast, shallow ripple. It was our first taste of the Geikie and that was only a mild beginning. We moved downstream cautiously through some class 2-pushing-class-3 waters and then the roar of rapids became really heavy from around a blind bend. We pulled in to eyeball the situation from shore.

We found a portage trail after a few minutes of bushwacking and observed that the river stepped down over a small falls and then converged into a high speed, heavy water chute hemmed in by canyon walls. It was as beautiful a spot as one could desire, so we portaged all gear and camped right there atop the gorge for the night. Our tent was a light, two-man model with a fly over the top. Doug, the ever-ready angler, got down in the tail of the fast water to try his luck for arctic grayling. The grayling was there and he actually landed a couple between strikes by big and powerful northern pike.

Every time a pike hit, it would clean off Doug's light grayling gear, and he would have to re-rig. After he was stripped three times, he called it a day. The rush of the river pouring through the gorge is a soothing sound. We slept far more soundly than during our first night.

We had to launch in fast water below the chute the following morning so all gear, particularly cameras, were carefully stowed in watertight bags. Directly following the fast water came a tiny island and Doug's quick eye and keen ear detected a moose on it. We heard the moose hit the water on the opposite side of the island and strike out wading for the mainland. By paddling quickly around we had an excellent opportunity to photograph a swimming moose at close range except, as luck would have it, our cameras were not accessible on such short notice. Once again we were frustrated by that age old dilemma of white water canoeists: how do you keep your cameras dry, but instantly available at the same time.

Soon after the moose encounter we were confronted with a typical wilderness river rapids, and this is where the isolation introduces factors that are minimized on less remote and more frequently traveled rivers. First the rapids have to be carefully scouted from shore and this means a good deal of bushwhacking as there is no portage trail. Ever present game trails are utilized if they are located close enough for an unobstructed view of the river but, for the most part, the going is rough and in some instances almost impassable.

There is a constant temptation to skip a section of rapids because of a stretch of almost impenetrable shore line growth but it is far wiser to look at every meter of the wild water. Surprises lead to accidents, and

174

a river such as the Geikie does not condone trial and error. This rapids, approximately 500 yards long, would involve several course changes to avoid large souse holes and one particularly dangerous rock garden with a high volume (class 3) of very fast water.

Should we run it or line it? That was the question.

If you run, it is with full gear so an upset can be quite serious. Should you have the misfortune to "horseshoe" your canoe (wrap it around a rock) in this powerful river, you are in very serious trouble indeed. If you're lucky, you're able to walk out. So we took more than an hour to stumble and hack our way down and back but when we returned to the canoe, our course through this tricky stretch was well set in our minds. *IF* we did everything right, there would be no problems.

A few trappers live along the Geikie during the winter, but when we beached our canoe we found only old bones to indicate their business. In summer the trappers find employment elsewhere.

Eventually we *did* do everything right but the element of uncertainty is what makes wilderness river running the fascinating sport it is.

Upon congratulating each other on a successful run, we noted with a touch of concern that this somewhat formidable test wasn't even marked on our map. So we couldn't rely on that entirely. From here on, the map did indicate long rapids every few kilometers. This would be a day to remember. We scouted and ran three major sets of rapids, some a kilometer long; we hung up twice but escaped unscathed in both instances. The state of excitement maintained during these prolonged periods of frantic paddling and decision-making on a hell-for-leather river, such as the Geikie, puts a heavy drain on the adrenalin. By 4:30 PM, we were ready to make camp again. I was glad to drive that last tent stake.

Most canoeists are familiar with the rock outcroppings and rugged grandeur of the Canadian (Precambrian) Shield farther south, but this was esker country we were crossing. Eskers are made up of the accumulated sediments deposited by sub-glacial rivers and are high elongated mounds running parallel to or, at this location, actually forming the high banks of the present river. Our campsite was halfway up the spine of a high esker and just off to the side of the ever present game trail that leads like a garden pathway through the jack pines. Except for the steep climb from the river, to the top of the eskers, these high ridges, with their beautiful views of the countryside, are among the most beautiful and natural campsites a wilderness paddler is likely to find. A breeze helps to keep insects at bay. The towering shoreline eskers compressed the river here to form a fast, heavy water approach to a class 3 rapids that carried around a blind bend before widening out into a difficult, rock-strewn shallows. It would be a real metal-tester for our first run in the morning. It gave us something to think about as we listened to the roar of the river during the night.

That run got my day off to the fastest start in many years as we rounded the bend like an arrow shot from a bow. But we were on line and the dangers were soon past. The canoe did hang momentarily away down near the end shallows but the current had slowed by then so all was well.

The reward for such skill and valor appeared shortly when we were obliged to make a short portage around a two-step falls where the river was divided into three channels by high rock outcroppings. It was frustrating not to be able to photograph this beauty spot to better advantage but the best angles were inaccessible from the shore. We would have tarried here except for the expected rough going we could spot directly ahead. No river run is ever complete without at least one long, agonizing portage to talk about when you get back home. Our trial by land was now at hand. We paddled past the head of the unmarked portage trail and only discovered it while scouting the rapids from the woods. The very existence of a trail indicates that nomadic Indians traveled this river long ago and also that the rapids were too dangerous to be run.

This was indeed confirmed. We soon encountered class 6 waters that extended a long way and eventually converged into the wildest chutes and falls. We backtracked, located the start of the trail, marked it more clearly for future voyageurs and began the long carry of 2 kilometers during a pouring rain. Windfalls had to be cut and cleared for the canoe or in many instances detoured around. We completed the portage trail weary and soaked but then the sun luckily reappeared to dry us out. It was a great, golden feeling.

Two more major rapids were scouted and run, sandwiched between an almost continuous parade of fast water slicks and ripples. Nearly exhausted, we climbed to the spine of a high esker and camped for the night. It had been one heck of a day. I was asleep before my sleeping bag was zipped.

My good old buddy, Elsasser, not one to rest on his laurels for a minute, the next day guessed that the foot of a long rapids to be ideal walleye waters. Since it was my turn as camp cook, he hastily erected the tent and then paddled back up river to try his luck. Two hours later he returned with three 5-pounders; more than enough fillets for the day's meals, plus leftovers to nibble on cold during the following day. Successive thunderstorms during the night gave us a good excuse the following morning to gorge ourselves on walleye, while we relaxed and waited for our gear to dry out. We studied a bald eagles' nest which occupied a tall jack pine within a dozen yards of our tent site. But no birds were in sight.

The 21 miles of Middleton Lake which came next provided us a change of pace in paddling, but a steady tailwind made the point-to-point crossings on this big water pass quickly. Once clear of the lake, we were back into the wild stuff which involved some lining down, frantic paddling and at least one near upset. It was a long rapid and toward the end, we missed our course and became blind-ended in a rock garden. We back-paddled furiously but still slammed hard enough for both of us to almost lose our paddles. We were able to lift off and complete the run without swamping but it was a very close call. This was followed by still another hairy run through a creek channel on the near side of an island. When we camped that night, atop another lofty esker, the discussions revolved around the notorious "Long-Mile Rapids," said to be the worst of all, which we would encounter on the morrow.

Our confidence was buoyed up the next morning by a well-executed run on a demanding little frother that called for precise course changes and coordinated paddling. I figured we were ready for the Long-Mile. At this point the Geikie is about 50 yards wide and the rapids are estimated to be 2 miles long with a consistent gradient throughout. The degree of difficulty ranges from class 2 and 3 to areas of class 4 that can be avoided by careful scouting and course plotting. We walked the difficult shoreline for an estimated two-thirds of the overall distance and decided to attempt the run and pull in at that point.

The unusual length of this rapids combined with a consistent degree of difficulty and heavy water volume makes the Long Mile a risky run in an open canoe. You can only maintain a state of responsive super-alertness for so long before you start losing your edge. Although plenty hectic, we maintained line, executed our course changes right on cue and threaded the needle when rocks converged to narrow the channels. We were doing so well and were so chock-full of self-confidence that we decided to do something stupid to make the experience more memorable. Having completed the scouted portion of the rapids, we continued on without stopping and attempted to run the rest of it blind. It was a mistake.

A few minutes later we found ourselves in the inevitable rock garden with no place to go. The canoe hung up between rocks and took water but quick work by the voyageurs got it free without swamping. We spotted a grass-capped gravel bar and swung in to dump out. It was a very welcome break. Then another 5 minutes of furious paddling to dodge rocks down in the end shallows and we were home free . . . the Long Mile had been run. We camped that night at the last rapids. Tomorrow it would be a 10-mile paddle on flat water down to the bridge and Saskatchewan Highway 105. We both felt we had had enough thrills to last perhaps until next year's vacation.

It is possible to drive to this end-of-the-route bridge by car by taking Highway 2 north from Prince Albert to LaRonge and Missinipe. Full outfitting services (Churchill River Canoe) and air transport (Nipiwin Air Services) are available at Missinipe. Prior arrangements can be made for canoes, tents, specially packed foods, and all associated camping gear in addition to topo maps and advice on water levels on various river routes. Or you can bring your own camping equipment. If you are Geikie River bound, you would be well advised, after being outfitted in Missinipe, to drive north on Highway 102 and 105 to the Geikie River bridge, having arranged for air services to fly you up river from there. A government operated campground, right at the bridge, serves as an excellent campsite and for parking a vehicle during the canoe trip.

For information on some of the finest wilderness canoeing and sportfishing to be enjoyed in North America, contact Churchill River Canoe Outfitters, Box 26, LaRonge, Saskatchewan, Canada after May 15, or 913-10th Street, East, Saskatoon, Saskatchewan after September. For general information on Canada as a travel destination, contact the Canadian Government Office of Tourism, Ottawa, Canada K1A OH6.

Isle Royale

A Camper's Paradise in the Great Lakes

by DAVID RICHEY

Many Isle Royale areas afford good fishing from the rocks or by trolling. This angler nets a nice laker as a boat trolls by.

LITTLE HAD changed since my first camping-hiking trip to Michigan's Isle Royale 15 years ago. My head was down and I was leaning into my pack. The straps were beginning to bear down where they crossed my shoulders.

I was 30 minutes into my hike from the west end of Rock Harbor on my way to Lake Richie. My mind was preoccupied with thoughts of setting up an overnight camp with my lightweight Coleman tent, a hot meal of northern pike fillets augmented by a can of beans, when the woods seemed to explode.

A cow moose, followed closely by a yearling calf, burst from a swamp near the trail and then stood in the trail staring myopically in my direction. Moose can be dangerous at close quarters, expecially when accompanied by a young one. We played a silent game of stare-down for what seemed an hour, but was probably only 30 seconds, when the cow "whoofed" and headed down the trail and back into the bush. It took 10 minutes for my heart to settle down.

I stopped often, made enough noise as I walked, and hoped mama moose wouldn't return for another visit. It required another hour of steady hiking to reach my destination.

Within 15 minutes I had erected my tent, fired up my Primus stove, and pulled two fillets from my pack. I sprinkled them with salt and pepper, dusted them lightly with flour, and started my dinner sizzling in 2 tablespoons of Crisco. The beans were warmed in their can to eliminate extra dishes and within 30 minutes I was eating a meal that tastes good only to those people willing to exert some effort to find wild places in this overcrowded world.

Boat camping is a fun way to visit Michigan's Isle Royale.

Look for moose like this big bull in many of Isle Royale's marshy meadows or along the fringes of inland lakes.

I lingered over my second cup of coffee as a timber wolf howled at the gathering darkness. This wild sound never fails to send shivers down my spine, but it's a sound of wilderness and one I enjoy. As I rolled out my Coleman bag and doused the dregs of my coffee, another wolf howled and was soon joined by a third. I fell asleep to a wolf serenade.

Camping on Isle Royale may be somewhat different than camping-hiking trips elsewhere. This area is a National Park and rules are established by the National Park Service. It is the largest island in Lake Superior and has over 120 miles of trails. These hiking trails crisscross this roadless island from north to south and east to west. The total hiking distance from one end to the other is about 40 miles.

Scenic lakes, small streams, spruce-dotted coves and countless marshes serve as gathering places for moose, timber wolves, and a wide variety of wild birds. Large coves, similar to fjords in Norway, indent the shore-lines and it is here that campers with a bent for fishing can find action.

The heaviest fishing pressure takes place on the larger inland lakes like Siskiwit, Feldtman, Chickenbone, Richie, and Sargent, but good sport with lake trout, yellow perch, and jumbo northern pike can be had in many of the sheltered bays. The south side of the island is hit heaviest by anglers, especially in Siskiwit Bay and Rock Harbor.

My advice for any camper is to either motor across to the island from Copper Harbor, Michigan, at the tip of the Upper Peninsula, or to come across the lake from Thunder Bay, Ontario. I made the trip once in a 20-foot

This trophy pike weighed 18 pounds but fish larger than this are caught from Duncan Bay and other Isle Royale bays.

Boston Whaler powered by a single 100-horsepower Evinrude, but I wouldn't recommend it to many people. Lake Superior can turn from flat calm to treacherous rolling seas in less than 30 minutes.

A far better bet is to make arrangements to have the National Park Service boat transport your craft from Copper Harbor to the dock at Mott Island on the east end of the island facing Rock Harbor. For additional information on this method of boat transportation contact the Superintendent, Isle Royale National Park, 87 N. Ripley Street, Houghton, MI 49931. Reservations must be in early (usually in March) for the coming season.

The same boat can transport hikers and campers from mainland Michigan to the island for a nominal charge. Check in at Park Headquarters on Mott Island, obtain a detailed map of the island which shows hiking trails and the locations of overnight trail shelters, and then head out for a once-in-a-lifetime experience.

Trail shelters are conveniently placed at various points around the island. Some of these are at the head of Washington Harbor, Lake Denor, Lake Richie, Lake Sargent, and at the National Park Service headquarters area.

I've used trail shelters in the past but it's not the same as doing it yourself. My preference is to carry everything I need on my back, hike as long as I wish, and then find a clean, dry campsite on the fringe of a lake or along a high outcropping overlooking Lake Superior.

Trails are well marked, often with a metal tag at junction points, but hiking the same trails as other campers isn't my idea of getting away from it all. I prefer setting my own pace and hiking until I'm comfortably tired and then scouting out the area for a place to pitch my mini-tent. Nine times out of 10 my campsite will be located where I can cast for northern pike.

If I've motored across Lake Superior to Isle Royale or had my craft ferried over on the National Park Service boat, this frees me up to explore the rugged coastline, locate a quiet cove in the lee of the wind, and establish a boat camp. From this central location I can then hike back into the bush, explore fishing or camping possibilities in a different area, and still count on the boat for transportation back to park headquarters or to the mainland.

Whenever I hike, my equipment is limited to what I can comfortably carry on my back. This usually consists of a lightweight tent or simply a space blanket to drape over a tree limb and anchor to the ground, a lightweight sleeping bag, a Primus stove, two pans for cooking and making instant coffee, a change of cotton and wool socks, and a lightweight poncho in case it rains. My food is normally of the dehydrated variety and supplemented by whatever I catch. A compass, map of the island and a spinning outfit complete my list.

A sturdy pair of hiking boots is as essential as a good bedroll. A poorly fitting pair of boots will wear blisters on your heel before you've traveled a mile from park headquarters.

Boat camping is actually the way I prefer to work Isle Royale. Although the average camper who fishes the island will fish those bays and coves near park headquarters or troll for lake trout off the Isle Royale lighthouse on Long Island, I prefer to cast around the east

This young couple pauses for a break while hiking along one of the many well-marked trails.

lets of sparkling crystal before flipping into another dive. This run was shorter and soon I could feel the battle swinging to my side. Five minutes later I led an 18-pound northern, as lean and mean as a diamondback rattler up to the boat and the waiting net.

I unhooked the fish, held him horizontal in the water until he regained his balance and then released him into the cove with the hope he would furnish some other camping angler with the same thrills. Another swirl nearby resulted in another hooked fish on the first cast. This pike was smaller, only 8 pounds and just right for two meals the following day.

Three days were spent on that bay before I moved on in a restless search for other camping locations and more fishing action. My largest pike from Duncan's Bay was an even 20 pounds although I hooked and lost what surely must have been an even larger one. I saw it once in 10 feet of water and the pike looked to be at least 50 inches long and probably would have weighed in at 25 pounds. Maybe more.

My 3 days at Duncan's Bay were a healthy mix of relaxing and cleaning up camp, hiking southwest for a half-day visit to Mt. Franklin, and another short jaunt to Tobins Harbor where I spent some time casting from shore without success.

Some smallmouth bass are found in the inland lakes. This angler plays a jumping fish from shore.

end of the island and fish the north side in Robinson's Bay, Duncan's Bay, Stackley Bay, Five Finger Bay, McCargoe Cove, or Todd Harbor.

I'm so mindful of one fishing-camping trip I made to Isle Royale. My first destination was Duncan's Bay where I hastily set up camp on a rocky bluff overlooking good pike water. Boat camping allows one the luxury of taking more equipment. Coolers contain cold drinks, canned food, fresh lettuce, and jumbo T-bones.

My rare T-bone was just about cooked when I noticed a large swirl in the shallows near my Boston Whaler. I flipped the blood-red steak on my tin plate, scooped a spoonful of beans beside it, grabbed a slice of bread, and wolfed everything down in 5 minutes.

My rod was set up in the boat and I cast off from shore as I rigged a red-white Dardevle to the snap swivel. A jumbo northern pike gulped my spoon the instant it touched down in the vicinity of the swirl. The rod bucked in my hands as I fought to control this cold-water wolf of the weedbeds. The fish darted off on a 20-yard run, reversed direction and dove for bottom beneath the boat. I could see him twisting in 20 feet of water as he tried to shake the bite of the hooks.

It took some doing but I was finally able to raise that brute up from deep water. He lashed the water to drop-

180

Later I spent one day camping and fishing on tiny Green Island, and then another fishing the rocky shores of Amygdaloid Island where I picked up numerous lake trout. Nothing big, but gorgeous pink-fleshed fish that tasted as wonderful as they looked.

I rounded out this boat camping trip with a 2-day visit to Todd Harbor where I set up camp on a rocky bluff overlooking the bay. This is one of the most scenic areas I visited and due to its size one of the most frequented by summer visitors. A ferry runs during summer months around the entire length of Isle Royale and larger areas tend to concentrate more park visitors. Some come to fish, most camp and look the area over; and some come to get away from other people, which they cannot.

Old log cabins can serve as a spot for a break as this young lady is doing. Note her sturdy hiking boots.

My campsite was more remote but one other boat visited me just as I was preparing to leave. I'd spent about 4 hours each day casting spoons for the big pike in Todd Harbor and had been rewarded with two fish over 15 pounds each. One was kept for two meals on the trip back to park headquarters, and the other I released.

The visitors arrived about noon and talked while I cleaned up camp. They were looking for a boat campsite for the following year and asked if I planned to return. Although fishing, camping, and travel to remote places has got into my blood, I much prefer to visit an area once and then move on to other wild places. I told them that I probably wouldn't be back. They were planning a 7-day camping trip to Todd Harbor and would use this campsite. They marveled at the 15-pound northern on my stringer and that was the clincher—they would certainly be back.

Isle Royale does strange things to people. My boat camping trip was one of the best I've ever taken. It gave me the opportunity to visit one of the least visited national parks, to camp and hike at leisure and to boat some of the last remaining unpolluted waters in northern Michigan.

The lasting impression that I have of Isle Royale is not just the fantastic fishing, it is the pristine wilderness—a remote area with lasting outdoor values that is available to anyone. It is the sight of a moose feeding on pond lilies along a shadowed shoreline; the haunting cry of a loon at dusk over wilderness waters; and the howl of a wolf. It is the opportunity to be free and to hike and camp wherever the mood takes me; and best of all, it is the chance to get away from people and enjoy wild things and wild places close to home.

Come to think of it, I may change my philosophy and go back to Isle Royale. It does things like that to people.

Dave Richey hefts a brace of trophy pike from Duncan's Bay. The fish weighed 14 and 17 pounds.

How to Shoot Camping

NO MATTER whether it is only a weekend outing or a lengthy summer vacation, making a photographic record of your camping trip can at least double the pleasure. It's not difficult, expensive or time-consuming. And of course it's the best way of all to recall the trip with warmth and nostalgia on the long winter nights to follow.

Perhaps the best plan is to film any trip in the same manner as a professional photographer on assignment. In other words, you tell the story of the adventure with your camera. You record everything that happens—and often events which might have happened. But let's see exactly how this can be accomplished.

It's most important to show the locale or locales of any camping trip. If you camped on the seashore, at least some of your pictures must show the sweep of the surf or shoreline. If in the mountains you should have pictures of peaks. Whenever it's possible, your camp should be in the center of the scene—no matter whether it's a luxurious mobile unit or a colorful tent. Simply show where you were.

Although it may complicate the business of pitching camp, why not locate your camp where it will take the greatest advantage of the background and the scenery all about you? Place your tent so that canyon walls or mountains loom in the rear. Consider also the sunlight, and place the camp so that it catches the direct sunlight in either morning or evening. The trouble will surely be worth it. Remember also to shoot the scene from inside; as you see it through the tent flaps or through a camp window.

Your story—or rather your set of pictures—will not be complete without close-ups of the camp exactly as you were enjoying it. But it's easy to make mistakes here, and these are mistakes you may not notice at the time of filming. Chances are that you have seen pictures of the immaculate camp where every item of camping gear appears brand new and where each item is in perfect order. Perhaps some of the campers are sitting stiffly in the picture. On the other hand, you've also seen the camp scene in complete chaos or disarray and the camper somehow detached from the camping. Try to avoid both of these opposing situations.

The ideal camping scene is one which shows you are a good, efficient camper. A few clothes may be hanging on a line to dry and the coffee pot may be simmering on the stove. Some evidence of camping (of living, really) is good, but it should suggest order. In addition, your campers should be busy. They should be having fun or doing something productive. However pose them just enough to see happy faces instead of backsides.

Once camping was confined to summer and warm

Trips Like A Pro by KEN BOURBON

weather. But nowadays we camp the year around and that is someting to consider when filming a trip. Be certain to reveal the season. Warm jackets and trees without leaves will help to do the job. So will the colorful foliage of fall. But why not also shoot closeups of ice on the water bucket, frost on the tent ropes or the wildflowers which usually grow around springtime campsites. Show also any unique methods you may use to insulate a camp against cold weather.

Maybe you go camping alone, in which case you belong to a minority. More than likely you are with family or friends and probably quite a number of them. It should be obvious to include *all* of these companions in some pictures.

Pictures of people busily occupied are vastly better than people merely posing or doing nothing. Since camping is a succession of activities—from shaving to cooking to sweeping the tent—catch your friends engaged in all of these chores. Besides, if you keep busy enough clicking the shutter, you won't have so many chores to do yourself.

Still—you may want a group picture, too. But remember that even group pictures need not be dull. Instead of posing the campers in even rows somewhere, why not have them singing around a campfire? Or hiking in single file along a forest trail? Or divided in a tug of war with a tent rope?

No two camping trips are ever alike and this is one of the fascinations of the game. Something different happens every time—or you engage in some different activity at every campsite. You meet new people, have new problems and have great new experiences. Get all of these on film.

One activity which frequently goes with camping and which complements it is fishing. Of course, shoot fishing pictures, not just pictures of the catch. Make exposures of any guides, of launching the boat, casting while waist deep in a singing stream, the backlash in a reel, gathering bait, cleaning the fish and even cooking them. The opportunities for lively angling pictures are endless.

The same is true if you go rockhounding or bird watching, hiking or swimming, climbing mountains or searching for mushrooms. Carry the camera along on all these expeditions. But try to capture the actual doing—the high dive into the water, digging for rocks, studying the birds (with the birds in the background if possible) through binoculars, clinging to a steep cliffside.

Sometimes you may miss the exact picture of action you want. Fortunately most people are very tolerant of cameramen and will usually perform for them. So why

Occasionally the early morning riser will be lucky enough to see a timid deer to photograph. A telephoto lens brings this doe close.

This strap for the camera frees the photographer's hands while he finds new vantage points from which to film. It also hugs the camera to the body avoiding bouncing.

This single picture of a fishing trip shows many different things: The vegetation is obviously Florida; the vehicles show the transportation; and the fisherman in his boat displays his catch. Having the subject in natural, relaxed poses removes any stiff look they might have had.

Showing everyone doing something they would ordinarily do is better than posing the group standing shoulder to shoulder like a class picture. This also shows the camping area and a bit of the surroundings.

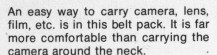

An easy way to carry camera, lens, film, etc. is in this belt pack. It is far more comfortable than carrying the camera around the neck.

not ask for a repeat? There may even be a slightly better camera viewpoint than you had the first time. Most camping trips are leisurely enough, without tight schedules to follow, so that you can spare extra time to take the best possible pictures. It's a shame not to make the most of it.

As in any other type of photography, the best and most dramatic photos are the unusual ones. The usual camp scene, for instance, is that front view shot with the camera held at either chest or eye level. But why not try to vary this old standard?

Consider the very low-angle shot in which you shoot across the campfire or maybe emphasize steaks broiling in the foreground with the tent and campers looming behind. Often it's possible to get a high-angle shot by climbing a nearby tree, a fire or water tower, or just onto the top of your station wagon. From directly above, you can get a completely fresh viewpoint on the old campground.

Most campers are also gadgeteers. A walk through any busy campground in summertime will reveal countless devices and bits of equipment designed to make camping easier or more luxurious. Consider the fun you can have in filming these gadgets—and maybe improv-

Good light, a fast shutter speed and lots of action make rodeos good places to shoot family entertainment on a camping trip.

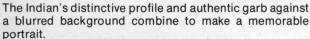

The Indian's distinctive profile and authentic garb against a blurred background combine to make a memorable portrait.

ing on them later on when you have time on your hands.

All kinds of outdoor pictures—and especially camping pictures—can be considerably brightened by a minimum of planning ahead. Convince your fellow campers that bright colored clothing will make better pictures of the trip. Carry along props—reflectors, flash units—to eliminate the heavy shadows which have a habit of invading so many camp scenes. When you pose a camp scene, make the best use of camp equipment. Light a lantern or two and place them to add a glow here and there to pictures made early and late in the day.

Many extremely fine camping photos have been lost by carelessness or the failure to take ordinary precautions with camera and film. Camping is an outdoor activity with more than normal exposure to the elements and so it's wise to take a little extra care of your equipment.

For example, keep the camera in a waterproof bag or container when you are not actually carrying it. Check the neck straps for undue wear before each trip and never leave the camera in hot sunlight very long. The heat will not hurt the camera, but it will surely ruin the film inside.

Because optical glass is much softer than other glass and because the lens coating is very thin, keep your lens covered when not in use. And keep it clean. Remove dry dust with a camel's hair brush or by blowing on it with a small ear syringe. However *never* breathe or blow on the lens element with your mouth. This leaves a coating and affects the ability to transmit light. Do not use a handerchief, cloth or facial tissue to clean a lens.

These will leave tiny scratches. Nor should you ever lubricate the moving parts of a camera. Load and unload in subdued light and be certain the film you load (and buy) is the correct type for your needs. Some of these dos and don'ts may seem very basic to experienced photographers, but they are also very common mistakes made by a lot of people.

Nor does it hurt to repeat old advice here on how to make a picture more attractive. Try to compose camping pictures so that there are no distracting influences. Eliminate the power poles, the litter, garbage cans and other unattractive backgrounds which have a way of creeping into a scene. Usually only a slightly different camera angle can create a splendid picture from a poor one. Use "frames" for scenes whenever it is possible. A frame might be a tree or the tent flaps, a doorway or the silhouette of a companion holding an axe.

Do not limit filming to bright sunlit days alone. Put your flash to use for close-ups on dreary days. And remember that early and late hours give very picturesque effects, especially on campgrounds, which are out in the open or near water. The resulting colors and the mood become very dramatic.

Although it may seem wasteful, shoot more than one exposure of all the pictures of your trip which you *really* want. In other words, figure your proper exposure and then shoot a half stop on each side of it. Film may seem expensive, but it becomes inexpensive when you figure you may never have another similar opportunity—and may never camp in that particular spot again.

Maybe the best advice of all before beginning a

Aperture, shutter speed and focus are all set and the photographer now awaits the action.

In brilliant light situations like this at Taos Pubelo, long shadows and late afternoon (or very early morning) side light makes the shapes stand out distinctly. The texture is good and note the good contrast between the building and the dark mountain behind. A midday photo would be flat and ineffective —and probably show modern day tourists which would distract from the mood of the picture. (Photo courtesy of New Mexico Dept. of Development)

The good photographer will have to think ahead for a shot like this. He should disembark some distance from the photo scene and walk downstream positioning himself in the best place for an unobstructed shot of the raft as it passes. Exposure and distance should all be calculated in advance. A motor drive would allow several shots of the great action here, but even without it quick action will permit two or three exposures. (Photo courtesy of Canadian Office of Tourism)

Little camp visitors like this chipmunk make good photo subjects.

camping trip is to copy a technique of the professional photographer starting on an assignment. Usually he prepares a shooting script—or a checklist of pictures to take. We have included a fairly comprehensive checklist which any camper might use as a guideline. Add any ideas of your own that occur.

The list is by no means complete because every camping trip is a fresh and exhilarating adventure. And each one is a fertile field for the clever camping cameraman.

Suggested Shooting Script

Campers poring over maps or charts to decide where to go. This might be done at home or in the family car, perhaps on the hood or tailgate.

Display of all gear and equipment used on the trip, spread out as an inventory. Overhead angle shows this best.

Panoramic view of the various campgrounds visited, showing as many individual camps as possible. High angle is good here, too.

Scenes of important, scenic or historical places visited on trip.

Campsites showing the specific locale or geographic region, probably by natural features in background.

Details of each campsite. Add gadgets, important

A fine scene including your fellow campers should be part of the shooting script. This is Virginia Falls in Canada's Northwest Territories. (Photo courtesy of Canadian Office of Tourism)

Having the camera's eye on a level with the subject makes an interesting shot.

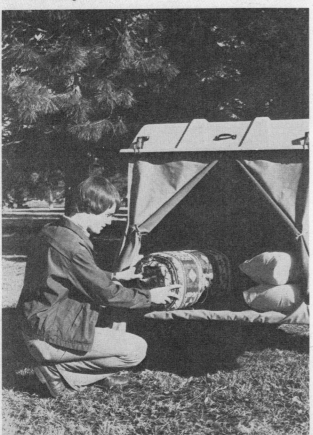

equipment here.

Pitching camp, setting up the tent, driving tent stakes.

Cooking. Get close-ups to show methods used and food cooked. Maybe the cook flipping pancakes?

Any unusual devices or gimmicks used to make camping easier or more pleasant. Examples: home-made galley to fit in a station wagon; cartop bedroom; boat overturned to provide a table; portable shower suspended from a tree limb.

Camp living. Examples: Somebody crawling from a sleeping bag in the morning; shaving outdoors and maybe using a stream as a mirror; gal putting curlers in her hair.

Camp visitors, people as well as animals (chipmunks, squirrels, birds, bears).

Views along the travel route. Camping rig parked by scenic overlooks, driving down a highway, tailgate lunch along the way, driving toward a covered bridge.

Family flag or identification marker hanging beside the camp.

Action. Campers doing all the things, and more, described elsewhere in this article. Strive for naturalness here. Huddling in a tent during storm or bad weather. If tent is blown down, film it. Try to capture any humorous situation—like junior after falling in a muddy swamp or catching a fish smaller than the bait. After dark activity. Around the campfire, brewing coffee, singing, story telling, visiting other campers.

Snow coach rides into the park during the winter months bring passengers to winter scenes like this along the Firehole River. Bright sun, deep snow and low temperatures characterize the months in the park.

by ERWIN A. BAUER

THE TWO FACES OF YELLOWSTONE

IN RECENT summers crowds have been heavy as Americans jam the roads into Yellowstone National Park. Almost all of them see only the "public" face of Yellowstone—attractions within eyesight of the 500 miles of road within the park. Old Faithful, Mammoth, the Grand Canyon and other well-known park attractions are along these crowded trails.

The second face of Yellowstone is the one beyond the roads and deep into the backcountry—a vast diverse Yellowstone that is seldom seen. Fortunately both faces can be enjoyed by almost any American, no matter what his budget. Strange as it may seem, near the season's end is the best time to see either Yellowstone. Crowds are thinning, and aspens soon will begin to turn color in the high places.

The familiar Yellowstone displays more than 10,000

thermals—geysers, mud pots, boiling hot springs—scattered throughout the park. But the majority and the most spectacular are concentrated for several miles north of Old Faithful, which surely is the best known phenomenon in any park. The Loop Road takes you close to all of these, and you can view many from your car window.

For a really fascinating look at the thermal activity, and the chance to see a geyser eruption close up, you should walk the self-guiding nature trails at Mammoth Hot Springs, Norris Geyser Basin, Fountain Paint Pots, Mud Volcano and elsewhere. But be sure you stay on designated trails and paths, because thin crusts can conceal pools of boiling water and breaking through one of these will give you a very serious burn.

The Loop Road also skirts Yellowstone Lake—the

The Grand Canyon of the Yellowstone River is a favorite spot for thousands of visitors each year. Here the Lower Falls drop 308 feet down the narrow gorge.

Charlie Lester, a fly-fishing enthusiast has fooled another wily Yellowstone cutthroat trout. This one will be returned to the water to catch again another day.

largest in the world at such lofty elevation (7,750 feet). Pelicans and swans can be seen floating on its surface. For many miles Loop Road parallels the Yellowstone River through wide Hayden Valley, brushes close to the Grand Canyon of the Yellowstone and climbs over Dunraven Pass on Mount Washburn. Probably no other road compresses so much great, contrasting beauty into such a short distance. A wise traveler will pause at each place to enjoy it more.

At Grand Canyon, short trails lead from roadside parking to Artist and Inspiration Points on the canyon rim for views of the 309-foot falls. Waterfowl and other birds are usually abundant close to shore on Yellowstone Lake. In places, you can catch cutthroat trout by casting from shore. Moose and other wildlife are usually visible throughout Hayden Valley. You can see

bighorn sheep on Mount Washburn, and in past years black bears were likely to be freeloading anywhere along the Loop highways.

Remember that these are wild animals. It is illegal and foolish to feed or harass them, and bears should be viewed from inside vehicles with windows closed.

If you're a wildlife watcher, your best opportunities invariably will come early and late in the day when animals are most active. Driving slowly also helps.

Now for the other Yellowstone . . . the lonely, spectacular wilderness beyond the pavement. More than 1,000 miles of well-marked, blazed hiking and bridle trails lead from trailheads along the Loop Road to remote portions of the park. Some of the trails permit easy, half-day hikes over gentle terrain. Others are steep, long and require backpacking gear, plus a good

boating. Canoeing is permitted on Shoshone Lake, the Lewis River and the Yellowstone Lake southern arms. All other park waters are closed to boating to protect nesting waterfowl and a fragile environment.

On vast Yellowstone Lake, boatmen must be especially cautious because sudden weather changes are not unusual at high altitudes. A soft, calm morning on the water can quickly become rough and unsafe as a violent thunderstorm develops.

A Yellowstone holiday can cost very little or be moderately expensive, depending on how you do it. The park concessionaires offer full hotel or motel ac-

The bald eagle, our national bird, is endangered and rare in most of its range, but visitors to Yellowstone can often see one along the waterways. This one returns to its nest wings outstretched to slow its speed.

bit of endurance on the part of the hiker. All take you away from the crowds gathered at the thermal features, and away from the heavy traffic along the highways during the peak period of summer.

The Yellowstone backcountry is ideal to escape to and unwind, to see awesome scenery, meadows full of wild flowers, distant waterfalls and cold streams which others miss altogether. Backpacking is the best way of all to genuinely enjoy it.

Victoria Falls and Shoshone Lake are two of the park's most beautiful attractions, but they are overlooked by the majority of tourists because they are some distance away from the Loop Road. They can be reached only by following narrow trails winding through the great pine forests.

It is also possible to penetrate the backcountry on horseback. You can hire riding horses for short trips at Canyon, Mammoth and Roosevelt lodges. For, longer pack trips into the wilderness areas, make arrangements with many guides and outfitters just outside the Park, such as those at Gardiner and Cooke City. Fire permits are required for backcountry camping, whether on foot or on horseback.

Considering the heavy pressure throughout the summer, there is much good fishing in the park. However, the best of it, by far, is in remote streams and lakes, the farther from the highway the better. Some productive water also is available to visitors who trail or cartop their own boats.

Remember, park permits are required for all types of watercraft. Only Yellowstone (excepting the three southern arms) and Lewis Lakes are open to power

commodations from mid-June until mid-September, and sometimes later. These lodgings are located at Mammoth, Canyon, Old Faithful, Lake and Roosevelt. They also rent fishing and sightseeing boats at Bridge Bay Marina on Yellowstone Lake, and offer a variety of inexpensive package park tours of various durations. Particularly during mid-summer, advance reservations are advised.

Snows come early to Yellowstone, in fact it may snow during any month of the year, but the Canadian geese remain, seeking the thermal waters and acquatic plants on which to feed.

"Half afraid I'll see one; half afraid I won't" is the way most visitors to the park think of the grizzly. Actually, even in the backcountry, chances of seeing one are remote. (See *Camping in Bear Country* elsewhere in this book.)

This tiny coyote pup seen emerging from its den will grow into a canny adaptable adult subsisting mainly on rodents, but willing to try almost anything. Where they are not trapped and hunted (as in our national parks), coyotes are often seen by visitors. Elsewhere they remain almost permanently out of sight.

Most of the park's several campgrounds are also open from mid-June to mid-September, although one or more may remain open through October. All are operated on a first-come, first-serve basis.

At least until Labor Day, all campsites at major campgrounds are normally filled by noon. The National Park Service has no alternative but to limit camping and overnight stopping in Yellowstone to designated camp areas. When these are full, you must find space outside the park (the regulation even includes visitors with self-contained recreational vehicles). Fortunately, space is available just beyond all the main gates.

Camping inside Yellowstone Park is limited to 14 days. In addition to the $2 per car entrance fee, campers must pay $3 per night for a Class A (showers, flush toilets) campsite, or $2 per night for a Class B (no showers, pit toilet) space. These rates are on a par with fees outside the park. It is essential when camping anywhere in the region to keep a clean camp and to keep food locked inside a car or trailer. Hungry bears are the reason.

Entrance and camping costs aside, the very best things in Yellowstone Park are free. Most obvious is the matchless scenery. Daily interpretive programs help you learn about the extraordinary treasure in which you are a shareholder. There are visitor centers (including a splendid new one at Old Faithful where the eruption times of the major geysers are computed so you can see them in action) which have naturalist-conducted walks and hikes, self-guiding trails, museums and nightly campfire programs. No license is necessary to fish in the park, although some waters are restricted to fly-fishing only and the daily limit of trout is a nominal three. Many conscientious anglers voluntarily release all the trout they catch so the quality of the sport will not suffer.

A lot has happened to Yellowstone since the first non-Indian to see Yellowstone Park (John Colter, a Kentuckian) came upon it. In 1806, he left the Lewis and Clark expedition in which he was a guide and trapper and wandered afoot and alone through this incredible, unknown wilderness to what is now Jackson Hole. On his return, few listeners really believed Colter's descriptions of what he had seen. But others were tempted to see for themselves, and more and more curious travelers reached the present park area. Without exception, they were enriched by the experience, just as an estimated 2 million visitors to Yellowstone will be thrilled this year.

Yellowstone today has two very different faces, but together they create the personality of a matchless national park—one every American camper should see.

Bike Packing
the Self-Propelled
Camper

by RICH LANDERS

Rich Landers is an outdoor writer who free-lances and is the outdoor editor for The Spokesman-Review in Spokane. He is a bike touring veteran of thousands of miles through the U.S. and two Canadian provinces. "I'm more worried about the price of peanut butter," says Rich, "than the cost of gasoline."

UNLESS YOU live there—and only 500 people do—there's not much reason to visit St. John, Washington. There's no motel, no tourist information, no dancing, not even a pinball machine. The bar might close at 7, 8 or 9 at night. There's no place to eat after the sun goes down.

But the secret to travel, I've found, is not just where you go, but how you go. By automobile you can expect to find amusement only where amusement is established for you. That goes even for car campers. Most people expect neatly paved driveways, picnic tables and running water when they take their camping rigs to the mountains. A naturalist's slide show can be a main attraction. On the other hand, travel by bicycle generates its own amusement. Even in towns like St. John.

The route my friend, Jean, and I took on a 50-mile tour from my back door in Spokane to St. John was a perfect spring bike ride. Traffic was a trickle, meadowlarks were vocal, hawks daring, ground squirrels fleet of foot. It's safe to say, however, we probably are among the precious few out-of-towners who rejoiced at the sign "Entering St. John." It was about 5:30 PM. We were dry and hungry.

Leaning against a fence were the town's good ol' boys who had spent the better portion of the afternoon debating the respective attributes and shortcomings of two western beers.

"You what?" one fellow asked. He turned to his buddies. "Did you guys hear that? These two here rode their bikes from Spokane. Came up just to camp out."

Another fellow said, "Get these guys a beer."

"Whaddaya want," another asked, "Oly or Heidelberg?"

"Oly," I said.

"Ya hear that, you guys? You can bet anyone who'd ride a bike 50 miles to St. John wouldn't be drinking Heidelberg."

In the next few minutes we became good friends with the locals. The bikes set us apart from anyone who might stop through in a car or on a motorcycle. RV's zipped through town on their way to more important places. Even though they slowed down, they still quickly passed through St. John. A $50,000 motorhome made a pit stop. The driver was given no more than common courtesy. Meanwhile, with our $250 bikes parked outside, we were Kings of the Road by popular vote in a St. John restaurant. Within a few hours everyone in town knew us as the bikers from Spokane.

Once you've made up your mind to go camping on a bicycle, you open an incredible selection of possibilities. You can ride from your home to a campground or small town nearby. Places too close to be adventuresome by car become fascinating day-long or overnight trips by bicycle. You can load bikes on a car and travel outside the city for a loop trip through peaceful rural country. You can take a train to a city a few hundred miles away and cycle back. Or you can take to the well-packed dirt roads that have been hacked through our forests, and virtually abandoned after the loggers and miners have done their jobs. Anyone can handle even these rugged backcountry trips. All it takes is reasonable conditioning, a sturdy bike, lightweight camping gear and the urge to get a closer look at what most people spend their lives speeding by.

Patti Randall, a 26-year-old school teacher, had

On hot days it's best to do most of your riding in the morning before temperatures rise too high.

never ridden a bike on an overnight trip when she set out with a small group on a backcountry tour through the Clearwater National Forest of Idaho. A hulk of 94 pounds, her bike, with its bulging load, weighed nearly as much as she. Pat had to carry more than the average touring cyclist since the route took them as many as 5 days from supplies.

Given a few days on the trail, shy and whispy Pat, 5-foot, 2 inches, the lightweight whose mother wouldn't let her fly a kite, was as vicious as anyone to get her share of the food supply. She'd handle the steep ups and downs as easily as any of the bigger and stronger men on the trip. Still she had the energy at the end of the day to fend off riders with her Swiss Army knife so she could scrape the last spoonful from the community pot.

You develop a philosophy about this sort of excursion, like a backpacker setting out for some alpine vista. Every ounce of sweat and every muscle throb is going to be rewarded tenfold. In a mountain tour such as this one in Idaho, the reward might be wild huckleberries. Maybe a glimpse of a black bear. Patti saw two. Or discovering a gold mine with old timers eager to teach you how to pan. Patti found one, complete with old timers, eagerness and gold.

A passage from the first few pages of *Zen and the Art of Motorcycle Maintenance,* with but minor rewriting, seems to be a nearly perfect testimonial for camping by bicycle:

"You see things touring on a bicycle in a way that is completely different from any other mode of travel. In a car, you're always in a compartment. And because you're used to it you don't realize that through the car window, everything you see is just more TV. You're a passive observer, and it's all moving by you, boringly, in a frame.

"When you're on a bike, that frame is gone; you're completely in contact with it all. You're in the scene, not just watching it, and the sense of presence is overwhelming. That

Backcountry bicycling in Clearwater National Forest of Idaho includes lots of magnificent scenery.

Patti Randall, whose mother won't let her fly kites lest they carry her off, psyches herself up for the next lap.

PRIMITIVE ROAD
NOT MAINTAINED
HAZARDOUS TO PUBLIC USE

On backcountry tours, it's important to check bikes regularly for loose screws and bolts.

Backpacking tents are easy to carry on bikepacking trips.

road whizzing inches below your pedals is the real thing, the same stuff you walk on. It's right there. You can hardly focus on it, yet you can put your foot down and touch it anytime.''

Not long ago, all you generally saw in typical American bike shops were the simple, mass-produced, balloon-tired cycles you'd buy, take home and let the kids ride the streets with cards flapping in the spokes. Now the choice has expanded.

For all practical purposes, the bike you have rusting in your garage likely would take you on a good bit of cycle camping. But good touring bikes are not toys. Consequently, for a good one that will stand up to years of abuse, you can't expect to spend dime-store prices. A bike under the $200 range probably won't hold up. And don't wince at the $500 tag on finely made bikes. A lot of stereo nuts pay more than that for crisp treble and deep bass. Car buffs spend a mint on mag wheels and chrome. RVers empty their wallets on gasoline. Boozers squander paychecks in bars. Some women blow their wad on clothes they only wear once. What's wrong with a good bike that's as much a work of art as a Charlie Russell painting? Consider it a timeless investment—transportation no energy crunch can stop. The indomitable RV.

If you're going to buy a touring bike, your number one motive should be enjoyment. I wouldn't recommend buying a 10-speed with drop down handlebars when deep down you know you're not going to like riding bent like the trap pipe under your sink. Drop bars have advantages. They allow you to grip near the gooseneck and ride high or drop your hands to the lower grips to decrease wind resistance. They force you to stretch your spine. In long-distance touring, this position will spare your vertebrae the pounding and crushing they'd have to endure stacked vertically while steering from conventional handlebars. But if you don't ride often, chances are your neck will get stiff every time you ride a bike with drop bars.

Good wheels are similarly important. It isn't my idea of enjoyment to be sitting along the road replacing broken spokes. Touring equipment should include a handlebar bag and saddlebags, or paniers. The front bag will hold such items as windbreaker, sunglasses, camera, sunscreen, valuables and toiletries. The rear rack and paniers, with the aid of stretch cords, will handle the heavier loads like tent, sleeping bag, stove, pots, extra clothes and food. Riding with a daypack is okay for short trips, but it's uncomfortable. Your hands are more likely to go numb; your shoulders are more likely to ache; your back will sweat, and cauliflower rear is almost certain. Worst of all, it can spoil your balance in quick stops, turns or emergencies. You might also look into toe clips, lights, water bottles, patch kits, tire irons and pumps. The rest of the equipment may be in your closet with your backpacking gear.

Several years ago, former Surgeon General Dr. Jesse Steinfeld said the only exercise most people get is jumping to conclusions, sidestepping responsibilities and pushing their luck. But recently the bicycle has emerged again as the great escape. Not from the horse and buggy this time, but rather from the automobile and a deplorable nation-wide slump in fitness. Bike tourists no longer have to put up with outrageous fuel bills, traffic snarls or pot bellies blobbing against the steering wheel.

Most long-distance campers prefer to ride alone. They find hospitality rampant along their routes, whether it's in Kansas or Nepal. With but little effort they find themselves guests in people's homes, and recipients of endless kindnesses. But it's hard to beat traveling with a group. It can be your family or friends or people assembled from across the country.

In 1976, an organization called Bikecentennial mapped the 4,200-mile TransAmerica Bicycle Trail and set up tours that led 4,000 cyclists on tours across the United States. For many it was their first taste of camping on a bike. The organization still runs group tours complete with trained leaders on trips ranging from the 90-day cross-country tour to week-long loops in Oregon and Virginia. Information on the tours and complete packages on bicycle touring—including maps, guidebooks and how-to pamphlets—is available by writing Bikecentennial, P.O. Box 1034, Missoula, MT 59801.

A bicycle tour with a group is full of insights, surprises, assistance, laughs and characters. It's also cheap. A group of bikers could ruin a restaurant with an all-you-can-eat special. A large pepperoni pizza is but an appetizer. Yet by pooling their money, cyclists can stay happily nourished while riding 40-80 miles a day and spend only about $3 a day per person on food. Eight bikers with four tents generally can squeeze into one campsite where fees are charged. Thus camping in a site that costs $4 works out to less than 50 cents apiece.

Admittedly, some days on a bicycle can be grueling, but there often can be salvation in a group. Take, for example, the day a friend, Marty, had his saddlebag split, strewing fuel bottles, underwear, oranges, apples, socks, tools and what have you down the pavement. We were on an 800-mile tour through the Canadian Rockies. There were nine bikers in the group.

His first emergency repair stitch coincided perfectly with a clap of thunder and the first splat of rain. He proceeded with his repair in the muck. We had continued some distance when he realized he'd forgot his sunglasses. He headed back just as another cloudburst commenced. Presently the wood support in one of his saddlebags crumbled and the bag flopped in his spokes. A major project was at hand. At this point the group intervened.

The traveler in an auto is encapsulated; he watches the passing landscape as he would a TV picture. The bike rider feels a part of his surroundings as here in the wilds of Idaho.

Abbie, who works for Altra Kits (sew-it-yourself outdoor equipment), manned the seam ripper (Swiss Army knife) and needle and thread while another fellow rustled through junk piles and found a large piece of 1/4-inch plywood. I went door to door in the little town of St. Regis, Montana, until I found someone who'd loan me a hand saw. During this time, another rider was consoling Marty. "You think you've got it bad; I grew up in Chicago." We cut the board, sewed it in the bag and Marty was in business. A combined effort that took only 1/2- hour.

No one goes on a bike tour—alone or with a group—without learning something. On the same trip to Canada, a fellow named Pat learned the value of a well-built wheel. He also learned he could use his broken spokes for tent stakes. We learned you have to get directions from at least five locals to get any sort of dependable notion of what looms ahead. A frisbee makes a nifty plate for the competitive spaghetti eater; a 1-pound liquid Parkay bottle will hold the contents of exactly 10 large eggs for transporting in packs. Buy a dozen, poke holes in both ends of the eggs and blow yoke and white into the bottle. A dozen allows you two mistakes.

After camping several nights on gravel driveways in campgrounds, we concluded that tent camping in the age of RV's is an endangered tradition. We also learned how hard it is to end a good trip.

Most of our farewells in Calgary, Alberta, were rushed as we scrambled to get bikes boxed, plane and bus reservations confirmed and as we helped each other carry gear to the terminals. We were from different points in the United States, and we had known each other for just two short, but intimate weeks.

We got a woman, Cheryl, to the airport with no time to spare. If that wasn't enough, I had to sprint with her bike to catch the wagon taking luggage to the plane; the airline had fouled up her reservation. The flight supervisor paced frantically while the confusion was ironed out. With her ticket in hand, we hugged at a trot to the gate. The rest of the passengers had been aboard for some time. We held hands as the trot broke into a run.

"We've got to get together again," I said. "Hope your husband can make it, too."

"I'm gonna miss you guys," she said.

"Miss you, too."

She let go of my hand and broke into a sprint up the ramp. She didn't have time to look back for one last wave. It never was like that on our bikes.

One-pot meals are fast and an easy way to satisfy hungry bikepackers. They're also cheap.

BIKING TIPS

To enjoy biking without unnecessary fatigue and aching muscles follow these simple rules:

* Wear layers of clothing: an undershirt, shirt, windbreaker jacket and a hat and gloves. Remove them a layer at a time as needed for comfort.

* Don't begin a long jaunt unless you are feeling fit and enthusiastic.

* Always ride on the right side of the road, so oncoming traffic is on your left. Be alert for vehicles approaching from the rear. Allow enough room so vehicles can pass each other, with plenty of room for you too. If in doubt, get off the road.

* The Bicycle Institute of America issues the following table for getting the right size bike:

HEIGHT	FRAME SIZE
under 5'6"	21" - 22"
5'6" - 5'8"	22" - 23"
5'8" to 6'	23" - 24"
over 6'	24" - 25"

Frame is measured from the center of the chain wheel axle to the top of the bolt that locks the saddle post. Following these height/frame size recommendations should make it possible for the rider with the bike with a horizontal bar to just straddle it with both feet flat on the ground.

* Make sure the seat is at the correct height when the leg is absolutely straight with the foot on the pedal at its lowest point.

* Handle bars should be at about the same height as the seat with the grips adjusted for easy reach.

* For information on bike routes and longer trips contact:
  American Youth Hostels, Inc., 132 Spring St., New York, NY 10012
  Bicentennial Guidebooks and Maps, P.O. Box 8308, Missoula, MT 59807
  League of American Wheelmen, P.O. Box 988, Baltimore, MD 21203
  Transportation Alternatives, 20 Exchange Place, New York, NY 10005

CARAVANNING IN MEXICO

by CHUCK CADIEUX

MEXICO offers more variety of attractions than any nation in the world. Climates range from the cold mountains near Puebla which are snow-clad even in June to the hot coastal jungles of Quintana Roo; topography ranges from the stark beauty of the deserts of Sonora, Baja California and Chihuahua to the impenetrable green jungles of Chiapas, Tabasco and Yucatan; the mixture of the modern and old are represented by modern cities such as Mexico City, which is now probably the biggest city in the non-Communist world, and tiny villages of thatched huts sheltering barefoot *Indios* who speak neither Spanish nor English.

But not many Americans have camped in Mexico in the past. Because Spanish is the language of this country, most of us "one language" *norteamericanos* were afraid to try it. Also, there was the threat of digestive upsets caused by lack of sanitation and impure water

Caravanas de Mexico's Piggyback tour rides the rails through the rugged scenery of the Barranca del Cobre.

systems. Even President Carter talked about the "Revenge of Montezuma."

But that has changed. No country has made greater strides in improving water supplies as has Mexico. The past 10 years have been especially good—and water supplies in big cities are now perfectly safe.

Of equal importance, there is now a simple, foolproof way to try camping in Mexico. That foolproof way is to take your recreational vehicle on a caravan tour in Mexico. For a set fee—no extras—you will join 40 or 50 other families with like interests, join forces at the border and then follow a prescribed route to pre-reserved campgrounds. You'll be led by experienced bilingual guides, with an expert mechanic bringing up the rear to make sure that no one has problems.

All fees, tour buses, insurance, border crossing technicalities, campground costs will be taken care of in advance by people who are experienced in dealing with such matters in Mexico. It's easy and carefree, because the chores and red tape are left to the wagonmaster. His knowledge of the area will make sure that you don't bypass the most interesting sights—you'll receive excellent guidance.

With 10 years of experience, Caravanas de Mexico is the largest of several tour companies offering Mexico services. Let's take a look at what they offer the RV camper. Biggest seller is the Piggyback Caravan, which leaves from El Paso, Texas, for a 19-day swing into Mexico. After they've smoothed your border crossing and your purchase of insurance from Sanborns, you'll drive at your own pace down to Chihuahua city, where you'll find your own space reserved at the Motel Nieves Campground. After touring that city via C de M buses, you'll drive a short distance west of the city to load your rig aboard railroad flatcars—on your own special chartered train!

Without buying a gallon of gasoline, without even having to steer, you'll enjoy the scenery as you go up and over the Sierra Madre Mountains, down to the bottom of the Barrance del Cobre (Mexico's Grand Canyon), and camp for several nights in the cool pines at 8,000 feet above sea level. The train moves at a comfortable 20-25 miles per hour, perfect for sightseeing as you go through tunnels and across trestles on the railroad—Ferrocarril al Pacifico—which has been called one of the seven engineering marvels of the world. There are stops for camera fans, for this is grand scenery. The train then procedes down the west slope of the Sierra Madres to Los Mochis, where you'll offload and drive to your own reserved space in a modern trailer park. C de M buses will take you on a sightseeing trip to lovely Topolobampo, a picturesque port on the Sea of Cortez.

Driving south on blacktopped highway, you go to Mazatlan, which was an important port when the Spaniards moved treasure from the Philippines across Mexico on its way to Spain. Here you'll have time to

The Piggyback Caravan—
RV's on flat cars of a private
train—winds its way into the
approaches of the Sierra
Madre Mountains.

Chuck Cadieux's Huntsman camper parked beneath a palm tree on the sunny coast of Baja California.

enjoy some of the world's best offshore fishing for marlin and sailfish, to improve your tan on the beautiful beaches, to shop in small shops for leather and silver and onyx and all of the other things which are typically Mexican. You'll also enjoy lots of delicious sea foods at prices far below ours.

From Mazatlan the caravan moves leisurely northward through the truck garden province of Sinaloa, past booming Culiacan and Navajoa. You'll visit Alamos, considered to be the most beautiful example of colonial Spanish architecture in the country. There'll be a stopover at beautiful San Carlos Bay, near Guaymas, and you'll finally end the tour by re-entering the United States at Nogales, Arizona. Total cost of that package is around $510 for a single unit not exceeding 24 feet, with two people. Longer units and additional passengers raise the ante somewhat.

The same company offers the Twin Piggyback. In addition to riding the rails on the railroad across the mountains, this Caravan extends the exploration southward to Puerto Vallarta—the beautiful port city where the movie, *Night of the Iguana,* was filmed. Then a second piggyback trip will carry your recreational vehicles across the Sea of Cortez to the fabled Baja Peninsula, riding on ocean going ferries operated by the Mexican government. Then the route goes north, up the full length of the rugged Baja to re-enter the United States in southern California. That trip will take 28 days—border to border—28 days of sunshine instead of shoveling snow and paying fuel bills up north. That tour

(Left) A typical catch of bottom dwelling fish taken from a small boat 100 yards offshore in the Sea of Cortez.

(Below) The fishing is good almost anywhere along Mexico's tremendous coast line—guaranteed wherever the coast is rocky.

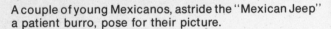

A couple of young Mexicanos, astride the "Mexican Jeep" a patient burro, pose for their picture.

is offered in November-December and again in February and March.

If you can afford even more time, there's a brand new delight in store for the adventuresome Mexico traveler. Caravanas de Mexico offers a 54-day Caravan to the Yucatan Peninsula and back! Featuring the fabulous remnants of the Mayan civilization, this tour will operate in January and February when the climate there is perfect—and the climate up north is not perfect. That tour will visit cosmopolitan Mexico City enroute, pass through the new "oil boom" states of Chiapas, Tabasco, Campeche, where you will see for yourself that Mexico has gasoline supplies running out of its ears—oil reserves which rank right up with Saudi

Arabia's. You'll soak up the surf and sun on the unspoiled white beaches of Isla Mujeres, Cancun and Cozumel Island between visits to the Mayan cities of Uxmal, Palenque, Tulum and Chichen Itza—where you'll camp almost in the shadow of the great pyramids. You'll camp in cities such as Campeche, Merida, Coatzacoalcos, as well as sleepy villages on the shores of freshwater lakes. Best of all, you'll meet the Mayas themselves—friendly, happy and polite—the remnants of a once-proud civilization which developed an accurate calendar and excelled in astronomy and built towering shrines of stone at a time when Europe was still a primitive place.

If your idea of perfect camping is to have perfect

hookups every night, the Yucatan trip isn't for you. Part of the time you'll do without hookups entirely as you "rough it" on white sand beaches shaded by swaying palm trees.

Still a fourth option is offered by Caravanas de Mexico, a summer trip to the *altiplano*—the high country—of central Mexico. It surprises most people to learn that it is cooler in Mexico City in August than it is in Chicago. Mexico has a lot of very high country, and that is where most of its people live. This trip avoids the hot coastal areas and gives you a big helping of beautiful mountain scenery, history of Cortez's conquest of Mexico, a look at the Aztec ruins at Teotihuacan, even a visit to the Ballet Nacional Folklorico in Mexico City.

RV caravanning in Mexico has come of age. Just this one company, Caravanas de Mexico, has taken more than 10,000 campers over the Piggyback Route alone! Their modern, reliable service even offers you a toll free telephone to answer your questions. Call 800-351-1685—it's free for answers to your questions. Or write to them at the address given at the end of this article.

The guidance of experienced wagonmasters is the biggest plus on a Mexican caravan. They know where the drinking water is safe and where it should be avoided. They know the best places to shop for silver, onyx, opals—for all the products of this lovely land. Their ability to handle both languages will smooth the way for your first exploration of Mexico—a real delight for RV campers!

Modern seagoing ferries, operated by the Mexican government, now transport RV's across the Sea of Cortez, making access to Baja rather easy.

For more information, write:

Caravanas de Mexico
3801-C North Piedras
El Paso, TX 79930

Old Wagonmaster Caravans (Johnny Johnson's)
10920 Brookfield Road
Chatsworth, CA 91311

Pueblos y Playas Caravans
P.O. Box 24308
San Jose, CA 95124

Points South Caravan Tours Company
5309 Garden Grove Avenue
Tarzana, CA 91356

Slow moving special train carries RV's through the pine logging country atop the Sierra Madre Mountains.

This is a Jim Whittaker, no stranger to winter camping, airing his Fiberfill II sleeping bag. Note the snowflaps at the bottom edge of the tent weighted with stones.

Tents and Sleeping Bags for Cold Weather Use

by ERWIN and PEGGY BAUER

CAMPING can be fun in any type of weather. The variety of equipment and accessories available today can keep you warm and comfortable regardless of the temperature, and dry in spite of rain or snow. Although in the past campers headed for milder climates during winter, more and more are turning toward the unique experience of snow camping. The peace and quiet of the snowy outdoors is now enjoyed by many who wake up to a fresh snowfall, eat a hearty breakfast, and begin a day of skiing or snowshoeing. No matter what the weather may be, equipment choice is always important.

And, when you're planning a winter outing, the proper tent and a warm sleeping bag can determine whether you have a safe and enjoyable trip.

Avoid going to extremes when shopping. Much of the general all-around gear you already own will serve you well in climates anywhere from 30 degrees and above if you're simply planning on spending a few days in an area where it might snow. If, however, you're going to be doing some serious wilderness camping or spending several days in below-freezing temperatures, you should be prepared for the weather.

205

Coleman makes this classic mummy bag for cold weather usage. It has a drawstring around the top which when pulled makes a snug hood and a draft tube over the zipper to stop cold breezes. It too, is filled with a synthetic filling, Hollofil II.

Basically, a true winter or high-altitude tent provides features that aren't really needed during the rest of the year, such as snow flaps and frostliners. Some extras you might want to look for include loops or cords inside at the ridgeline to use for hanging clothes, and pockets in the sidewalls for storage.

Snow flaps are skirts of tent material sewn around the edges of the tent floor and extending 8-10 inches around the entire tent. If you're camping on soft snow or frozen or rocky ground, you'll find snow flaps extremely useful. You might not be able to stake your tent securely, but you will be able to weight it down by piling rocks or snow on top of the flaps. Snow flaps also perform well in high winds by keeping the wind from getting under the tent and billowing the floor. Other good ways to secure your tent include 10- or 12-inch snow stakes of curved aluminum (thinner summer stakes often won't hold) and steel skewers which are more likely to penetrate the frozen ground. You can also anchor your tent with weights called ''dead men''—sacks stuffed and buried at the ends of guy lines, or dead branches buried horizontally and at right angles to guy lines.

A frostliner is a detachable inner canopy of light cotton or cotton/polyester blend, and can be especially important in humid climates. It takes up space inside of the tent, but it significantly improves the cold-weather comfort of your tent. First, it provides an additional layer of insulating air beneath the canopy; second, it absorbs moisture which otherwise could condense and freeze on the inside of the canopy. In the morning this liner is taken outside and the moisture shaken off.

Not surprisingly, a winter tent should be roomier than one used during milder seasons since it not only sleeps and shelters the campers but also stores gear. Bad weather may dictate an all-day stay, too. The additional roominess adds to the overall weight and makes the tent a bit bulkier. It's worth it though, to have enough space for sleeping, cleaning, dressing, reading, playing cards or whatever. Keep in mind that you spend about 8 hours each day inside your tent during the summertime—usually, you're in it only while you sleep or during the rain. In the winter, the nights are longer and if the temperatures are very low, you may wish to sleep in late until the late sun appears.

Ventilation is important in cold weather since you're constantly exhaling carbon dioxide while consuming oxygen. Ideally, the tent should provide enough ventilation—via windows that can be opened only partially and closed against snow or with vents that are easily adjustable.

If possible, place your tent out of the wind, and on the side of a hill rather than on a valley floor. Warmer air rises, especially on clear nights, and a valley can be as much as 15 degrees colder than a hillside.

Some winter tents have a second entryway located opposite the main door. This is primarily a safety factor—in case one entrance is blocked by snow or freezes up, you can usually dig your way out of the other. Many campers prefer tunneled entrances to zippered doors because they minimize heat loss and keep snow from blowing in.

Seams should be evenly stitched and reinforced at stress points. The pole structure and the tent should be solid and capable of withstanding wind pressure. Other features you should find on your winter tent are grommets or similar devices to secure the bottom end of the tent poles to the corners of the tent floor—otherwise, the tent may sink into the snow. Fiberglass poles that run through vertical sleeves on the sidewalls keep the tent walls flexed outward, providing more interior space and encouraging snow to slide off.

Choosing a sleeping bag for winter camping can be just as important as choosing a tent. Use three criteria while shopping: loft, weight, and compactability. The loft of a bag is its thickness when laid flat and fluffed up; remember, however, that a bag with a 6-inch loft will usually provide only 3 of those inches above you. Comfort range labels may provide general guidelines, but your own metabolism will also affect how warmly you sleep. Compactability is a matter of convenience—if you're backpacking, you'll want a bag that compresses into a small space for easier carrying.

The issue of whether down or synthetic fills are preferable in sleeping bags is pretty well settled. Basically, the facts are as follows. Down is still the best insulating material known. It lofts excellently and is very compactable. It's useless when wet, however, and is difficult to dry. Because demand is high, it's also soaring in price. Synthetic fills on the other hand, are somewhat heavier but can be just as warm as down and keep on insulating even when wet. Two of the best synthetic fills for winter camping are Hollofil II and PolarGuard. They're not quite as compactable as down, but they are significantly less expensive. A few winter campers swear that there's no alternative to down (they bought their bags when down was cheaper) but most others are finding that synthetic fills are also of excellent quality and keep them just as warm while costing far less.

A bag's shape also determines its efficiency and warmth. "Mummy" bags, generally considered the warmest available, are cut to conform to the shape of the body, leaving room at the shoulders and narrowing at the feet. For those who find mummies too confining, tapered bags may prove more comfortable. These contoured bags are usually warmer for the weight than rectangular ones, since they provide insulation only where you need it and conserve body heat better.

For extreme cold, many bags come equipped with hoods; if yours does, check to make sure that the closure is adjustable either across the neck or around it to allow for proper ventilation and ease of movement.

Insulation beneath you is also necessary when you're sleeping on cold or frozen ground. A closed cell foam pad is recommended as the best insulator. It's also easily rolled up and is very lightweight. While an air mattress may initially seem more comfortable than foam pads, the air inside the mattress gets cold more quickly.

If you decide winter camping is for you, you'll want to make sure that you have the proper equipment. Shop around, and don't hesitate to ask questions. The gear you choose can help make your winter camping trip one of the most unique experiences you'll ever have.

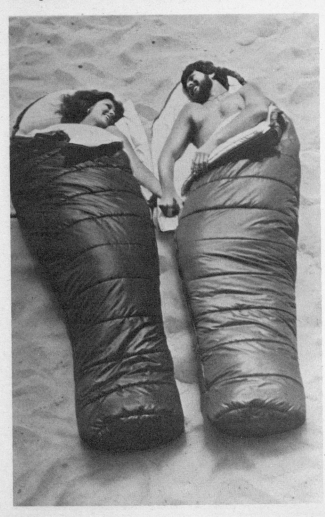

A compromise shape between the sharply tapered mummy and large rectangle is the coke-bottle which allows room for feet to wiggle. On some bags a pocket is provided to keep toes warm against the bag. This is a Polorguard® duo by Outdoor Products with no sewn through seams for warm winter camping.

Every Man Has His Favorite Camping Rig: Here's Mine

by BARNEY PETERS

THE ROAD which climbed by switchbacks over a high, lonely ridge in the Beartooths was hardly a road at all. Often we had to stop to remove large boulders which blocked the way or to fill deep potholes. A couple of ice cold creeks had to be forded. Time and again the faint track seemed to evaporate completely. In places the grade was so steep that only the 4-wheel drive and low range assured our passage. But by late afternoon we reached the relatively flat meadow which surrounded a lonely azure, alpine lake.

Judging from the lack of litter and beaten paths on shore, it wasn't a very accessible spot. Only the circle of charred rocks which was once a fisherman's fireplace revealed that anyone had been there before. We had the whole magnificent landscape to ourselves. In less than

an hour our camper trailer had been unhitched and erected, our cartop boat had been unloaded and my son Mike was casting for trout just offshore. He needed about seven casts to hook his first cutthroat. A pot of coffee brewed on the stove.

"Surely," my wife Thelma commented, "this is Paradise Found."

Paradise in this case happened to be a lake (which I will not name) on the edge of the Beartooth Primitive Area on the Montana-Wyoming border. It is only one of hundreds both within and outside of the Primitive Area. We had only to don backpacks and hiking shoes to reach other lakes, most of which contained trout. Paradise Found indeed!

But a few days later the Peters family drove into—or

Fold-out camper trailers are small enough to be erected right at water's edge. Their low profile on the road reduces drag for better fuel economy, too.

Although most camper trailer units have stoves, there's no reason not to use those provided at the campground. The awning on this one by Coleman shades campers during the hot midday hours.

rather beside—another paradise. This time we entered the Lewis Lake Campground in Yellowstone National Park and backed the trailer into a designated campsite. This time we were surrounded by other campers, but not for long. Our ticket to use the campsite was the same Golden Eagle Passport which had cost $10 and which permitted us to enter any federal recreation facility. Soon after the trailer was opened, Mike and I launched the cartopper in Lewis Lake and affixed our 5-horse outboard.

With a light tent, grub and fishing tackle aboard, we motored the few miles across the choppy lake to the mouth of the Lewis River. At this point we cached the motor in brush nearby (no motors are permitted beyond this point) and began the 1-mile paddle upstream to Shoshone Lake. Shoshone is a completely undisturbed wilderness body of water where it is difficult not to catch mackinaw trout. But it is not a particularly easy place to reach, except on foot, in which case the fishing is nearly impossible. And not many people carry along a suitable boat for such a trip.

Before last summer was finished, we discovered still other Edens, and we plan to do the same thing again and again in the future. Fortunately I feel we have the mechanical means to do it—a really versatile camping-traveling outfit. Without it, many of our paradises would not have been found. But first, my background.

I am a part-time writer-photographer. That means I write outdoor adventure stories and take plenty of pictures during all my trips. It also means I spend a good deal of time the year around traveling widely across North America; in the summertime this travel naturally includes my whole family of four. To give an example of my range, I have traveled by highway from Key West to Mt. McKinley and from home, near Chicago, to Mexico hitting all points in between. During all this wandering, I have either used or tested every manner of recreational vehicle from station wagon and tent to air-conditioned, self-contained motorhome. But it wasn't until recently that I finally assembled what I consider the ideal—absolutely ideal—outfit for my own needs. It might also prove perfect for sportsmen whose interests are similar to mine. I call it a dream outfit for vagabonds.

What I require is versatility—an outfit which will take me anywhere anytime, off and on the pavements in a great variety of situations. I have to travel often in rough or steep country, through snow, swamps or muck, in out-of-the-way places where hunting and fishing are best. But at the same time I need a combination which gets me quickly and safely from one place to another over the best interstate highways. It must be equally suitable in good and bad weather. I must be able to carry along a great deal of equipment: fishing tackle, firearms, much photographic gear and such widely assorted items as hunting dogs and saddlebags. As a result of these requirements, I did plenty of hard and thorough searching and testing before I finally settled on my dream outfit.

My basic outfit consists of a Jeep Wagoneer, a fold-out camping trailer, a Grumman Sportboat and a

Camper trailers come in a great variety of sizes with various floor plans. This Valley Forge by Coleman is a medium size and can sleep six. The sleeping alcove with large screened windows allow cool breezes to pass through from any direction.

Johnson 5-hp outboard. But as anyone will quickly realize, these are not the only specific models which would fill my needs, I have simply mentioned what I have as a matter of fact. There are other station wagons with 4-wheel drive, and there are many folding camper trailers, as well as numerous other cartop boats and canoes on the market. The selection is only a matter of personal preference or availability.

The station wagon with 4-wheel drive and low range was a necessity to take me into such places as the Beartooth Mountains, as well as to travel comfortably across country and to carry the mountain of outdoor gear. Some of the gear could be carried on the rooftop luggage carrier and under my boat. I installed fishing rod racks on the ceiling inside the Jeep for instant availability.

The trailer selection also requires explanation since I realize that other campers will naturally have other ideas. To begin, I wanted a station wagon and *some* kind of trailer, rather than a pick-up-camper-coach combination, so that I could easily park my camp and be free to wander and explore in my vehicle alone. For my own particular needs, it is a nuisance to drag the whole camp everywhere and requires too much precious fuel. And no pickup-camper yet designed can possibly take me where my Jeep alone will negotiate with ease.

I selected the fold-out trailer over the rigid sports trailer because of its lighter weight and lower silhouette. The latter is an important factor when traveling long

distances across open plains country or in high winds anywhere. It also can be towed into "tighter" places than the high silhouette campers. The trailer model I do use has built-in stove, sink, cooler and dining table—all these features being concessions to my wife. We found we could store quite a bit of gear in the trailer and that purchase of spare wheels and tires is a good investment when off-pavement travel is planned.

A boat is also an absolute necessity for me. And it must be a boat which can serve in the greatest number of possible situations. My boat fills the bill fairly well. It is really a square-ended canoe which can be rowed or paddled (but not as handily as a regular canoe) or powered with outboards up to 9½-hp. Traveling speed is good with the 5-hp motor I selected for its compactness, fuel economy and light weight. The boat is excellent for float-tripping rivers and fishing small lakes—and adequate for large lake and reservoir fishing, except in very rough weather. I have not yet had it in salt water. One man alone can unload it from the luggage rack.

My dream outfit also includes the following equipment, hopefully to cope with any outdoor situation a writer or other vagabond is likely to encounter: a light tent and light sleeping bags with foam mattresses for "spike" camps; mountain pack boards; axe and shovel; a supply of rope; three-burner gasoline stove and two-burner gas lantern; camp heater, a broad selection of fishing tackle, including waders and landing net; spare fuel cans; water jug; a plug-in (to the cigarette lighter), spotlight; all necessary cooking and dining gear;

This is the Concord, Coleman's trailer designed to be pulled by a compact car for real gas savings. When the trailer is unhitched the car can make side trips without pulling unnecessary weight.

lifesaver boat cushions; whatever guns and ammo are required for the specific trip; bow saw; a portable grill; flashlight; aluminum folding chairs; first-aid kit plus extra medicines; tool kit; clothing for various weather conditions; emergency food supplies; and a small library containing maps, birds, rock and plant guides, etc. Other vagabonds with special interests might wish to add or subtract certain items from the list. For example, a screened patio attachment to the trailer, a portable shower, and toilet would add considerable comfort to any camp. Either a manually operated or power take-off winch could prove valuable. And playthings for very small children could come in handy. On the other hand, some campers might have no desire to take fishing tackle or firearms along.

Last fall my dream outfit became a mobile hunting camp for my friends and me. At first I suffered some doubts about the outfit's value in *really* cold weather, but I need not have given it a second thought. All winter long it was the headquarters for weekend grouse hunts in the southern Ohio hills and on one raw evening in December, while fresh venison liver fried in the skillet, Lew Saner described (over and over) how he had outwitted the big buck whitetail which hung from a white oak.

That deer hunt could have ended in deep trouble—or rather mired in deep snow—without the 4-wheel drive and low range power of the Jeep. We had set up camp near the end of a thin fire trail to escape as far as possible from other hunters. We also delayed striking camp when a wet snow began to fall because the whole adventure was proving so much fun. All at once the snow was more than a foot deep.

"What the devil," Lew had laughed, "who cares if we get snowed in?"

Nobody. Being snowed in is exactly what happened to many other hunters who had camped in the woods, and they had headaches aplenty. But we plowed out very neatly, camper trailer and all and spent a good part of one afternoon in helping other hunters out of slightly snowy predicaments. At that particular time I wouldn't have traded my dream outfit for a working gold mine.

Does it have drawbacks? Deficiencies? Well, there are a few and of course in these recent days of fuel shortages and the high cost of gasoline, the mileage I get is not what it should be. I may look around for a vehicle which will pull my camper-trailer safely and still be a fuel miser. At the same time I will examine maps carefully to go from place to place over the shortest route and avoid the temptation to drive from one place to another when remaining at the original destination will do.

Another drawback is that the boat is a bit small for turbulent water. It would increase my working range to have a larger craft with more power. But that would mean more horsepower to pull it and that I couldn't load and unload alone. All in all what I have seems the best choice.

Everything considered, once I manage the fuel situation better, I figure I've got the ideal camping outfit.

Tips and Checklists for Enjoyable Safe Camping

Tire Tips for the RV Owner

FOR MAXIMUM towing ease, tire life and trailering safety:

1. Make certain tires are inflated to the recommended pressure as indicated on the vehicle I.D. plate.
2. Wheel lugs should be securely tightened. Check them from time to time, especially after rough road usage.
3. Visually inspect tire tread and walls for wear and tear before each trip.

Loading Tips for Camping Trailers

1. Extra care taken when loading a fold-down camping trailer will pay off in reduced strain on the engine and springs of the tow car.
2. There are two basic rules: Keep your trailer as light as possible and distribute the weight evenly.
3. Place heavy objects as near the trailer's axle as possible.
4. Do not load heavy items such as motor bikes or storage bins on the rear bumper.
5. When in doubt check the gross vehicle loaded weight (GVWR) on the trailer's certification label. This figure represents the maximum loaded weight and should not be exceeded.

Know the Model Number of Your RV

How long has it been since you reviewed the contents of the owner's manual that came with your recreational vehicle? A careful run-through at the start of the camping season and another when the rig goes in storage for the winter should be minimal, according to a customer service representative of the Coleman Company. All too frequently owners spend time and money on calls and letters which ask questions that are clearly answered in the owner's manual. If a call or letter is necessary, the owner should first jot down the model number and the month and year of purchase. It is a good idea to take down the serial number also. The owner's manual also may have a safety check list. Following it carefully will prevent costly and sometimes serious problems sure to mar otherwise pleasant excursions into the outdoors.

Camping Trailer Doubles as a Guest Room

When company arrives unexpectedly, lucky indeed is the family with a modern recreational vehicle parked in the drive. While grown-ups may welcome the comfort of innerspring mattresses and other conventional comforts, kids will likely cheer at the prospect of bunking in the host's RV. The idea is even more inviting if the RV is a camping trailer with canvas sides and large screened windows that keep the bugs out but let the breezes in.

Safety Rules for Small Camp Stoves

Every season far too many trips are plagued with cooking stove accidents, all of which can be avoided by following a few simple rules.

1. Read the instructions and thoroughly familiarize yourself with any new stove before starting out.
2. Always handle any fuel with caution, keeping it away from heat. Store and carry white gas in a metal container.
3. Never light a stove in a tent or indoors.
4. Keep your head to the side of the burner when lighting any stove.

212

As an emergency fire starter look for a dry abandoned bird's nest. A single match gives a bright, hot blaze.

5. Never remove the fuel or filler cap when the stove is still hot. Also never try to fill or refuel a stove which is still hot.
6. Many stoves have safety valves with the release pressure set at the factory. Do not tamper with these.
7. Do not leave a burning stove unattended. It is a waste of fuel and dangerous besides.

New Uses for Old Items When Camping

Large Plastic Garbage Bags
1. Good for collecting litter — your own and that left by others.
2. Use as a bath tub. Excavate a bag-size hole, line with bag, fill with luke warm water and enjoy a refreshing bath. Be sure to refill the hole, later.
3. Use as a solar water heater. Using a dark color bag, fill it about half full of cold water, secure the opening near the top and allow the bag to spread out on the ground in a sunny place. By late afternoon there will be enough warm water for a sponge bath or two. A real energy saver.
4. Use as a refrigerator. Place perishable foods or canned soda pop in a bag, secure the opening and anchor well letting the sack dangle in the cold waters of a stream or river.

Small Plastic Bags (Zip-Locks are needed for some of these uses)
1. Use to protect cameras, binoculars and other items from water spray and/or dust.
2. When cooking, mix ingredients in a bag to save washing a bowl; knead with fingers to save the spoon.
3. Mix Jello gelatin and allow to set in the same bag.
4. Make a small pillow by inflating a Zip-Lock bag and closing securely.
5. Remove inner cardboard core from a roll of toilet paper and start the roll from the center. Place the paper and a flash light in a plastic bag. Paper is kept clean and dry and light is at hand for after dark use.

A Square of Tarp
1. Use as a ground cloth under a sleeping bag or as a removable rug in a tent which can be shaken out to clean.
2. Use as a cooking area.
3. Use as a windbreak or lean-to.
4. Can be used as a protective cover for exposed gear either outside or in the vehicle.

Aluminum Foil
1. Use as a griddle.
2. To make a ladle, straighten a wire coat hanger making a fist sized loop at one end. Form a cup with foil and crimp the edges over the loop.
3. Use as a lid for pots and pans.
4. Use as a wrap for cooking fish, potatoes, apples, etc. on coals.
5. Use to form a drinking cup.

Choosing a Campsite

In an organized campground look for a well-drained area that provides sunlight and shade, breeze and nearby water. Avoid parking or pitching camp too near a camp's service or swimming area. Comings and goings are frequent and noisy.

In the backcountry:
1. Find a place where adequate drinking water is handy.
2. Pitch a good distance from well-traveled roads.
3. Try to assure shade during the afternoon and early evening hours.
4. Choose a flat area so you won't be sleeping on a slope.
5. Stay "high and dry." Campsites on knolls and hilltops are warmer at night, provide natural drain-off in case of rain and are often breezy during the warmer hours of the day.
6. Never pitch the tent under a dead tree or one with large dead limbs which may choose just your night to fall.
7. Plan your campsite to give yourself room for cooking, eating and sleeping. Pitch the tent away from the campfire and upwind from it.
8. Staying at one campsite for several days is much more relaxing than frequent moves.

Potatoes wrapped in heavy-duty aluminum foil bake to hot goodness. Also note that the grate here is not an old refrigerator shelf which could be dangerous.

A Checklist for Tent Care

Before camping:
1. Set tent up in back yard (for practice).
2. Wet tent thoroughly for maximum waterproofing and permanence of shape.
3. Let dry thoroughly.
4. Never pack a wet tent since mildew thrives in wet canvas and rots fabric.

In Camp:
1. Keep floor clean and unpunctured.
2. Air it frequently.
3. Don't let anything or anyone touch walls or roof during rain, otherwise fabric will lose its surface tension and could leak.
4. In striking tent, pull out stakes with a stick or another stake, don't pull on the canvas.
5. Don't pack poles/stakes in tent, keep them separate.

After Camping:
1. Clean out tent thoroughly.
2. Wash off dirty areas with water and a scrub brush.
3. Patch any leaks with waterproof dressing by paint brush or spray can.
4. For other repairs see a canvas supply house.
5. Store when completely dry in a dry place.

How to Accurately Predict the Size Cooler Your Family Will Need

To determine size in quart capacity for 2 days (one night) in camp, allow 20 quarts for a 25-pound block of ice, 8 quarts for a 10-pound block. For each adult allow 8 quarts, for each child allow 6 quarts. Combine ice allowances with human allowances and add 4-8 quarts for extras. Total should give you minimum capacity requirement for your cooler.

Camp Freezer

Take along an extra cooler and use it as a freezer. Special care must be taken for this:
1. Wrap pieces of dry ice in newspaper since it can burn on contact.
2. Insulate cooler with thick layer of folded newspaper and place wrapped dry ice next to it. *Note:* Dry ice can damage cooler liner with direct contact so take necessary precautions.
3. Place frozen products in cardboard boxes small enough to fit within insulation and place in cooler next to dry ice.
4. For best, most long lasting results, open only once daily and quickly reseal.

Tips for Easier Outdoor Cooking

1. When buying new utensils choose the Teflon lined items since they are easiest to clean, a point which is especially important when fewer kitchen helpers are at hand.
2. Do not use a shelf from an old refrigerator as a grill. Many were cadmium plated and heat under cadmium produces a chemical change that is poisonous.
3. Save the drippings from your skillet in a coffee can.

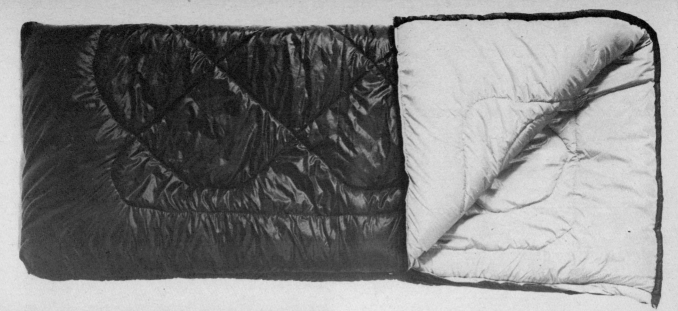

(Above) A rectangular sleeping bag most resembles at-home slumber conditions. Coleman's Peak 1 series are all completely machine washable which is comforting knowledge when traveling with children.

Cooking utensils coated with Teflon like this griddle make clean up time faster and easier.

Besides being useful for future cooking, the hardened fat can be scooped on leaves, sticks, etc. to make an excellent campfire starter.

4. To save space, take pans and bowls that nest together.
5. If you camp in the mountains allow 10 to 20 percent more cooking time for each 1,000 feet of altitude.
6. If cooking over an open wood fire, squirt the bottom of the cooking utensil with dishwashing liquid first and the accumulated soot will rinse off with almost no effort later.
7. To make any pan deeper, make a collar with aluminum foil.

Kitchen Equipment Checklist

camp stove
funnel for fueling appliances
folding stands for stoves, cooler
folding grill and charcoal
kitchen matches in waterproof case
fire starter
fry pan
saucepan (more than one should nest)
coffeepot
heavy-duty aluminum foil
pot holders or asbestos gloves
mixing and serving spoon
cooking fork and tongs
spatula
kitchen knives with sheaves
can/bottle opener
storage containers
plastic bags/film wrap

215

This folding oven goes over the stove and turns out delicious things for the camper's picnic table meals.

cooler
ice pick
insulated jug
water container
folding table and chairs
extra fuel in approved container
table cloth, napkins, plates
mugs, glasses
table knives, forks, spoons
dishpan
detergent in plastic bottle
pot scrubbers
sponge
plastic garbage bags
paper towels
whisk broom
fire extinguisher
plastic bags for leftovers

Super Tip for Starting Campfires Easily

Before leaving on the camping trip save lint from the trap in the clothes dryer and pack it in the compartments of a cardboard egg carton. When full, melt parafin and carefully pour over all and allow to solidify. To use, break off a single section of the carton and light. It will burn for about 10 minutes igniting the most stubborn fire material.

Mosquitos and Other Pests

1. Spray clothing and inside of tent with repellent and apply liquid to exposed areas of the body.
2. Check yourself and others for ticks. To encourage the imbedded tick to retreat to the surface apply a hot cigarette end and then pluck it off with tweezers. They can also be killed by suffocating them with a thick layer of petroleum jelly for several hours. Do not just pull them out as the head may be left behind to infect the victim.
3. Chiggers can be killed by sealing them with a drop of clear nail polish. There are many soothing anti-itch products on the market today, most superior to the old calamine lotion.

Tips for Water Safety

1. When swimming, use the buddy system. Never swim alone.
2. Do not dive in unknown areas.
3. Have an adult present when children are in the water.
4. Whether swimming or boating, get out of the water whenever a thunderstorm is gathering.
5. After eating, wait a while before swimming—about 45 minutes for a moderate meal.

In Case You Get Lost

1. Don't panic; people will be looking for you.
2. If you find a road or man-made trail, follow it. It will usually lead to some point of civilization.
3. Do not travel after dark. Stop in time to have an hour of daylight to make yourself comfortable for the night (with a windbreak and sleeping place).
4. Be careful of fires, especially in areas where fires present the even greater danger of injuring you. It's far better to be just plain lost than lost and injured.

5. Three means distress. A series of three whistles, shouts, shots, flashing lights, etc., mean distress; but use them only in an emergency.

A Few Last Words

1. Wear shoes around the campsite.
2. Watch the weather for early warning of storms. If caught in the open during a lightning storm, get into a ditch or other low area. Stay away from tall trees and out of creek beds.
3. Keep a flashlight available in a convenient place.
4. Make sure the water you drink is pure. Carry purification tablets and use them in case you are unsure of the source.
5. Include a first-aid booklet in your first-aid kit.
6. Do not bring your dog. They often become ill, are not allowed on most trails and no fellow camper wants to contend with a dog's barking and inevitable mess. Remember, what's acceptable to you is usually abhorant to your neighbors. When you plan camping costs be sure to include the cost of kenneling the dog.

Dinnertime on the deserts of Baja California is no time to discover you've forgotten something vital. Using checklists can avoid problems.

CRY OF THE WILD

by ERWIN A. BAUER

ONE DAY long ago my friend, Don Miller, was floating free on the dead-calm surface of a northern Ontario lake. It was August, and dog days had fallen on the north country—and on the fishing. Nothing stirred; so Don lazily baited with a large minnow, pitched it far out from the boat and settled back for a nap in the sun.

He had been dozing, for some time probably, when his reel whined abruptly and his rod was torn from his hand. Dazed, he managed to catch it on its way overboard, but he lost the skin on half his knuckles before he got the reel even partway under control. If this isn't the largest pike in the province, he thought, it's mighty close. That's when a "pike" like no pike he'd ever seen before lurched out of the water and tumbled back in again. It had wings. It was, in fact, a loon.

In camp that evening, Miller described the incident: "I've caught some big fish hereabouts—muskies, lakers and pike—but none of them ever battled like that bird. It was fast and powerful. And when I got it in the boat, my troubles really began. I practically had to sit on it while I extracted the hook. But I did release the bird unharmed. I hope I don't have to go through that again." Miller still carries souvenirs of the encounter—a couple of deep punctures in the fleshy part of his hand.

It isn't even once in a lifetime that the average angler in the north woods actually hooks a loon. It's a rare outdoorsman, though, who goes camping in the vast evergreen country from Maine to Alaska without meeting one of the region's most fascinating citizens. The common loon, or great northern diver, is a bird, but one that almost defies classification. It's the critter that, more than any other, puts the genuine stamp of "wilderness" or "remoteness" on any lake in which a wandering sportsman finds it.

Loons are no ordinary residents of the north woods—or of anywhere else. They can swim more easily than they can fly for example, and few fish are a match for them under water. But the weirdest thing about the loon is its cry—probably the loneliest voice on earth.

Depending mostly on your state of mind, a loon's call can be thrilling, maniacal, haunting, nostalgic or terrifying. It has been mistaken for many things. Once on a canoe trip in the Timagami region, Dan Marsh and I met another party of anglers on their way back to base camp. Newcomers to the northland, they were utterly terrified. They said they had been driven from a camp on a rocky peninsula the night before by wolves howling and prowling all around them. They hadn't heard wolves at all, of course, they'd heard loons. These weren't the first men to be fooled. At other times in other places, crying loons have been mistaken for everything from men in pain to evil spirits.

The Crees of another generation believed that the loon's cry was really that of a warrior denied admittance to the happy hunting ground. Even today the Crees regard the birds as supernatural. The Chippewayans considered them supernatural too, but in a different way. Since a loon's cry can be anything, really, from a wail to a yodel or a distinctive eerie tremolo, they took its calls as a sort of prophetic code. One kind of cry signified that fishing would be good the next day; another that someone in the tribe would die soon.

On occasion loons have actually helped mounted policemen and game rangers patrolling deep in the bush by blowing the whistle on illegal trappers in springtime with a sudden cry that has been described as crazy and as laughter. To most listeners, though, the loon's call is lonely rather than like laughter, and sorrowful rather than crazy.

An adult loon is a handsome bird roughly the shape and size of a small goose. That would be about 8 or 9 pounds in weight and from 28 to 36 inches long. It has webbed feet so far astern that walking on land is virtually impossible. The bill is dark, pointed and sharp. Adult plumage is never complete until the third year, and then it becomes a striking pattern of black and white for both sexes. The neck is shining greenish black with either white or black-striped white throat patches. From a distance the body color seems black, but actually, it's a unique checkered pattern of white squares and dots on a black background.

Draw a line from Maine to Oregon, and the breeding range of the common loon is generally north of it as far as Baffin Island. The loon is a migratory bird; its water range includes open water along both seaboards, the Great Lakes and the Gulf coast.

(Opposite page) There are few birds as sleek in outline and distinctive in summer plumage as the loon. But more than appearance makes this bird a symbol of northern wild areas; its haunting cry echoing through slender spruce tips and over mirrored ponds sends shivers down the backs of wilderness campers. (Below) With its legs attached far to the rear of the body, the loon is far more at home in the water than while clumsily waddling on land. It only leaves the water to nest. (Photos courtesy of Karl Maslowski)

Laying eggs on dry land is one qualification for being a bird. In this, the loon just barely makes the grade. The average nest is not elaborate and is usually located just a couple of feet above high water and as close to the edge as possible, to save walking. Islands are preferred nesting sites. Precisely the same spots are used year after year. Only one or two olive-drab eggs are laid, in early summer. Both males and females incubate. They never renest if a first attempt fails, as many other birds do. If all goes well though, the young ones are off the nest when the first big invasion of fishermen reaches the north country. It's then that most anglers see them.

It isn't difficult to find a loon's nest in late June or early July. Just paddle along the shore of a northern lake far enough, and eventually a female loon will catapault off the bank, shrieking as if a bobcat were close behind. From there she'll volplane across the surface, for a mile if necessary, trying to lure you into following. Look around where the bird first appeared, and you'll find a nest.

Some Alaskan Eskimos living along tundra lakes make long detours deliberately not to find nests. They credit loons with many extraordinary powers, and firmly believe that a female, if frightened, will dive beneath a kayak and puncture it from below.

Al Staffan and I once had an unhappy encounter with a loon family on Reed Lake, deep in the Manitoba wilderness. While camped beside a bay that seemed alive with northern pike we flushed a female and a single baby from the vegetation close to shore. The female fled toward the open lake. About 150 feet away she began to scream, flutter and demonstrate wildly. Meanwhile the baby, which probably had just left the nest followed close in the shadow of our canoe, paying no attention to its frantic mother.

We shot several pictures of the sooty little ball of fluff and then leaned hard into the paddles to get away and leave the young one to its parent. We weren't more than a couple of canoe-lengths away when there was a heavy boil on the surface and the little one vanished—calories for a pike. In some lakes, pike must account for many of them. On the other hand, loons certainly account for many small pike.

The eggs of a loon are hatched in about 3 weeks, and the young ones hit the water immediately. Although the adults feed them for a month or more, a training course in swimming and diving begins right away. At first just getting under water is a chore for the small birds, but by late summer catching a submarine meal is no problem at all.

When a loon sights a school of forage fish, it simply crashdives, outdistances them, and swallows them underwater. It dives by compressing its body and feathers enough to drastically reduce buoyancy, and it can go deep—loons have been found trapped in the nets of fishermen 200 feet down. There is much disagreement on how long loons can stay down, because

any loon can return to the surface completely undetected—with only the bill exposed—if there is the slightest ripple on the water. Some ornithologists believe a loon can stay down, if necessary, for 10 or 15 minutes.

The common loon is a true trencherman, but of fish almost exclusively. With a stomach completely filled, one loon was captured with 15 flounders from 4 to 6 inches in its gullet. Finding a loon with an empty gullet is virtually unknown.

A loon swims gracefully and effortlessly, rather like an otter, cavorting under water. There is disagreement on how he does it, but he probably employs his feet alone for propulsion. The wings, small for the bird's size, are partially folded and used only to maneuver.

Flying is no easy matter, but once a loon is aloft it's a strong, swift flyer that has been clocked at around 60 miles an hour. The actual process of becoming airborne is a dramatic, major effort, not unlike getting an overloaded aircraft off a runway. The loon has one of the smallest ratios of wing area to body weight of any bird anywhere. Depending on wind and how well filled its stomach is, it needs from 50 feet to ¼-mile to "taxi." For that distance, the bird half runs and half flies across the surface in a truly wonderful demonstration of wings beating on water. Loons rarely exceed 200 or 300 feet in altitude, even during migration. They never fly at less than top speed—probably because it's impossible.

Landing is equally spectacular. After a couple of tight circles to lose altitude the bird slides in belly-first, like an amphibious airplane, rather than feet first like a duck or a goose.

The difficulty in attaining flight has been the undoing of many a loon. Often they've been attracted by the abundant living at a fish hatchery, but once down they have to stay. Invariably they're unable to leave because of the short "runway" or "flight deck" in most rearing ponds. Their appetite for smelt and alewives has entrapped them wholesale in seines, gill nets and trotlines. One lake-trout fisherman in Lake Superior once hooked 48 loons during a migration on a 200-hook trotline baited with herring. The sudden freezing of a northern pond or marsh has been fatal to many a loon too.

Nowhere in North America are loons very numerous. Instead they're evenly distributed over a wide range. Nor are they gregarious like ducks or doves; rather they stay apart in nothing larger than family groups. The only attempt at sociability between them seems to be long-range gossip from one hidden cove to another. One calls, a neighbor answers, and more join in to form a mournful chorus. These spontaneous concerts can happen either in daylight or after dark. On an otherwise silent night, to hear one break out can be a chilling experience for a traveler alone in camp far from his home base.

Many wild creatures are so shy that humans seldom see them. The loon seems to enjoy showing off, lolling

Some northern natives believe that if a female loon is disturbed at her nest she will take revenge by diving beneath a boat and rising to stab a hole in its bottom with her beak.

in the water and preening in full view of watchers. One habit, a rolling preen, is almost comical. The bird rolls over on one side and while waving the upper leg leisurely in the breeze, something like an ape, preens its breast vigorously. Next it does the other side. After that it may rise upright on the water, flapping both wings noisily. But if a canoe comes too close, it suddenly slips from sight.

Four species of loons live on this continent. The common loon is much more plentiful than all its cousins—the yellow-billed, black-throated (or arctic) and red-throated species—put together. The range of the last three extends into Asia and Europe. All are very similar in habit and diet.

From time to time the loon has been described as a nuisance by anglers and commercial fishermen, but it's hardly a true indictment. There aren't nearly enough of them to make a difference anywhere. On the other hand, their wild, weird calling contributes much in atmosphere to what wilderness we have. A single encounter with them can make a trip more memorable.

Once, when a still, damp February day broke over a Louisiana marsh, I heard the haunting half laugh, half cry of a loon. It sounded out of place there. It reminded me of a cold, clear lake I knew in Canada 2,000 miles away.

Cutlery for Campers

by ANTHONY J. ACERRANO

MY UNCLE GUS watched me soberly, shaking his head now and then, while I fruitlessly tried to whittle a stick into a tent peg. My knife was as dull as a political speech, and the blade skipped and jumped over the stick. When I applied more muscle, the edge bit into the wood and jammed there. It took an almost violent push to tear it free.

Uncle Gus, a woodsman of great skill and vintage, regarded me with his flat blue eyes. "Hold it, son," he said, "before you do some damage—and I don't mean to the stick. Let's see that blade."

The old man inspected the knife's edge, running it gently over his thumbnail. He shook his head almost sadly. "Son," he said, "this thing's so dull it couldn't break the skin on a banana."

He rummaged in his pack for a moment and came up with a sharpening stone. He worked the knife over the

stone for a few minutes, then handed it back to me. I was amazed to find that I now could whittle easily. The shavings came off the stick evenly and cleanly.

"Remember, boy," Uncle Gus said. "A sharp knife is one of the most important tools a woodsman owns. But a dull knife is one of the most worthless. A good blade will cut you an apple, clean a fish, or carve out a tent peg. A dull knife is as useless as a car without brakes—and almost as dangerous."

I was 12 when I heard those words, and I've never forgotten them. No great philosopher ever uttered a more immutably true piece of wisdom. For, as any camper of experience will attest, cutting-tools, properly cared for, are essential to any camping venture. Two high-quality, well-honed knives and a good ax should be part of every camper's paraphernalia.

Cutlery is a sorely overlooked aspect of the camper's

Knives come in many sizes and shapes, but the guidelines for choosing are simple. The knife at bottom is too large and heavy to be of great practical value. The center knife sports a 4-inch blade—ample enough to perform nearly any camp task.

craft. I recall a young woman in Glacier Park, swinging an ax so improperly I feared for her continued use of both feet. Or the fellow in Wisconsin who assaulted a can of baked beans with a dull and oversized Bowie, and who nearly lost a finger in the process. Not unlike my Uncle Gus, I stood back, shaking my head. But there's hope. If I learned how to sharpen and handle a knife—and later an ax—I suspect that nearly anyone can.

Of course, it's true that you can dig as deeply into the lore of cutlery as you like. The subject can be endlessly complicated when you delve into the intricacies of steel composition, specialized shapes, and so on. But the practical camper has no need to bother with these esoteric avenues of lore. Choosing, maintaining and safely using the necessary camping cutlery is a straightforward matter. The basic guidelines are not at all complicated.

To start, every camper needs at least two knives—a high-quality folding knife that fits easily in pocket or pack and a well-made sheath knife of reasonable proportion. Claims that folding knives are inferior to straight blades are nonsense. There is one, and only one, difference: A folding knife will be slightly weaker at the junction of blade and handle. But, as my knifemaker friend Carl Bodek puts it, "Unless you try to jack up your car with the knife blade, you'll never be aware of the strength difference."

Choosing these knives is not difficult. You'll want a blade forged from high-carbon *stainless* steel. Despite myths to the contrary, a stainless blade will not dull quickly, or refuse to take an edge. A stainless knife, on the other hand, *will* resist pitting and corrosion better than any other.

The problem of steels becomes no problem at all if you simply purchase only brand name knives—such as Gerber, Buck, Browning, Track, and so on. All of these reputable knife makers use the finest steels. Conversely, beware of "cheapo" knives—the kind you buy at discount stores for reduced prices. Rarely will these blades hold an edge well since most are stamped from inferior steels. Again, stay with brand names and you can't go wrong. For, say, $15 or $20, you can purchase a fine knife that will last for years and years if you allot it a modicum of proper care.

Within the realm of name-brand knives there are a seemingly infinite array of sizes and shapes. The best blade design for general use is the standard hunting-knife shape—a straight or slightly sweeping back (false-edge) that flows to a pronounced point. The edge itself should lead straight from the hilt, sweeping slightly as it nears the point.

Size of the blade is important, and here's where many a novice woodsman goes astray, tending to choose overally cumbersome weapons that look deadly but are nearly useless in the woods. A folding knife should sport a blade of 3½ to 4 inches maximum. Straight-knife blades should be, almost without exception for general use, 4 inches long. No more. Nor should the blade be unnecessarily thick. The so-called "survival" knives one sees now and then—those baring ¼-inch serrated backs and 2-inch wide blades—are gimmick products aimed at unknowledgeable and perhaps overally romantic customers.

Handles are another important consideration, though they're more open to subjective preference. It's usually best to avoid handles with exaggerated finger grooves since they restrict the ways you can grip the knife.

223

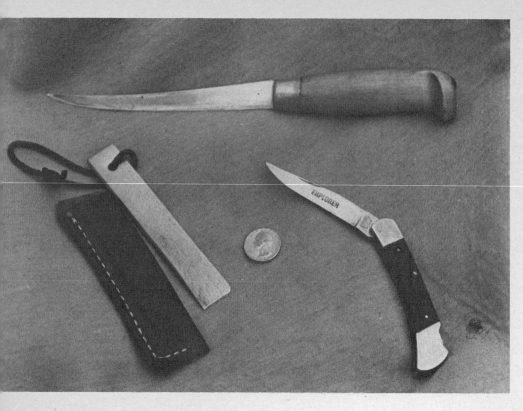

The knife at top has a long, thin blade conducive to filleting fish, while the folding knife serves well for field dressing. All knife owners should possess a "steel," pictured left, for easy maintenance of the best possible blade edge.

Slight grooves are less implacable, and can in fact be an aid to a steady handhold. Also helpful is a "choil," a pronounced inward curve in the handle right above the blade. A choil makes it possible to grip the handle firmly above the blade, which in turn makes delicate or forceful cutting easier. All straight-blade camp knives should have a hilt that extends far enough from the handle to serve as a guard, one which prevents your fingers from slipping onto the honed edge.

Most good knives come with a well-sharpened edge. But all, of course, must be resharpened with use. Rumors of steels and knives that never need to be resharpened are fiction. No such steel exists—and it is unlikely that any ever will.

The sharpening process is not difficult. In fact, once you acquire the knack of it, the act of sharpening your knives becomes a relaxing exercise in camp craft. As with most aspects of knives, there is a whirling body of mythology and bias inherent to the subject of sharpening. And also as before, the camper interested in practical results need not bother with any of it.

First you need a whetstone. You'll want a two-sided stone, one rough side, one finish side. This can either be a natural Washita/Arkansas material, or a man-made facsimile. More important is that the stone be slightly longer than the longest knife you'll use on it. This is necessary to produce the proper sharpening stroke.

Never sharpen on a dry stone. If you do, bits of metal will rub into the stone, clogging and eventually glazing it—ruining it as a sharpening instrument. Instead, spread an ample amount of honing oil or mineral oil on the stone. (Do not use oils containing molybdenum disulfide or graphite; these substances will cause clogging and glazing.) The oil's task is to float the particles of metal to the surface, where eventually they can be wiped away.

Now for the sharpening process. Anchor the stone either by clamping it to a table or by placing it on a high-friction surface, such as on a rubber mat. Hold the handle of the knife with both hands, placing the heel of the blade against the stone. Raise the back of the blade about 10-15 degrees (Gauge this by stacking two pennies under the raised blade.) Push down hard on the blade and draw it across the stone, away from you, as if you were shaving hairs from it. The motion begins with the heel of the knife, curving with the stroke to end at the tip of the blade. It's very important to maintain an even angle as you draw the knife over stone.

After the first stroke, reverse the knife and stroke in the opposite direction, this time drawing the blade toward you. The angle should be the same as on the previous stroke.

Repeat this process for perhaps 15 strokes. Then flip the stone over to the smooth side and perform the same technique. Then strop the blade by drawing it backwards over your hand or pant-leg to set the edge.

How to test for sharpness? Rest the heel of the edge on your thumbnail. Without applying any pressure, drag the knife across. A sharp blade bites steadily into the nail; you can feel the slight resistance as you pull. Another test is to shave a few hairs off the back of your arm. Yet another, to hold a piece of paper by one corner while slicing into the other. A sharp knife will cut the paper without crinkling or tearing it.

A knife is sharpened by stroking it across a whetstone with the back of the blade raised about 10-15 degrees. It's important to push down firmly against the stone, and to maintain an even angle throughout the stroke.

All campers should carry a "steel." This is used to clean up the edge from time to time after mild use. Steels don't technically sharpen a blade; rather, they help realign the microscopic teeth of the edge that are flayed with use. Oftentimes a recently-honed knife that appears to be dulling need only be stroked over the steel a few times. This saves wear on the blade, and is quick and easy. (The strokes for using a steel are identical to those on the stone.)

To get the most mileage out of a sharpened edge, take care not to needlessly abuse the blade. For instance, never stick a knife into the ground (as is often done by television mountain men), since this dulls the blade severely. Nor should you use a knife to cut metal or open cans. There are other tools designed for this purpose that work far more effectively. Avoid the temptation to throw knives at trees or targets. Unless a knife is made for throwing, the continued shock of impact will soon shatter even the best blade. And don't attempt to chop wood with a knife; that's a job for an ax.

An ax is another important piece of camping cutlery, and thus deserves some mention. A good all-around ax for general camp use is the popular Hudson Bay model. It's light, equipped with a handle long enough to use

A good ax, well kept and safely used, should be part of every camper's gear.

(Left and right) Use of an ax does not require violent strength. An easy, sure stroke gets the job done.

(Below) An ax is sharpened by stroking a whetstone over the blade in a circular motion.

knot or tough spot of wood. A sharp edge, on the other hand, is more likely to sink in and bite where you aim it. Dull axes can be slicked into shape with a file and whetstone; the file smooths out the rough edge; the whetstone is rotated in a circular motion across the blade to add the finishing touches.

Always exercise great care when handling an ax. Before you start swinging, check the full arc of your swing for obstacles that may catch or deflect the blade while in midstroke—for example, overhanging branches, tent guys, clotheslines, children and dogs. Clear them away or shift to a safer position. If you're chopping down a standing dead tree, look carefully for dead branches that may jar loose from the impact of your ax. A falling branch can cause serious injury.

Next comes proper stance. Your feet should be spread wide and your body should be limber and relaxed. If you're chopping logs or splitting kindling, the wide stance makes it less likely for a deflected ax to hit your foot or leg. Logs are stood on end if possible, and on a chopping block. Uneven wood should be leaned upright against another log on the side opposite you. Never follow the greenhorn practice of holding the target log in place with your boot. There are few better ways to loose your toes. Similarly, never hold a log in place with one hand while swinging the ax with the other. If you need to slice off sections from a thin piece of wood, lay it horizontally on the chopping block or

with both hands but short enough to swing with one, and sports a single blade. Single-blade axes are safer than double-bits, and for most campers, far easier to wield.

When buying a new ax, inspect the grain pattern of the handle to make sure it flows evenly along the sides. Severe curves and twists in the grain normally indicate weak spots. Never buy an ax with a completely painted handle. Not only does the paint hide the telltale grain, it also causes hand blisters.

As with knives, a dull ax is more dangerous than a sharp one. A blunt edge will bounce or deflect from a

(Left) Never hold a piece of wood while chopping it. If you need to slice off a thin section, sink the ax in far enough to catch the wood. Raise both wood and ax off the chopping block, and (right) bring both down against the block firmly.

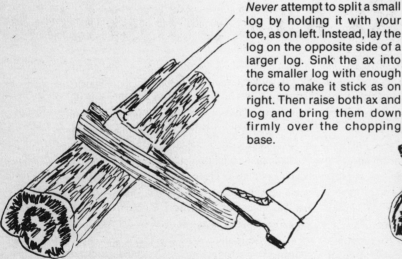

Never attempt to split a small log by holding it with your toe, as on left. Instead, lay the log on the opposite side of a larger log. Sink the ax into the smaller log with enough force to make it stick as on right. Then raise both ax and log and bring them down firmly over the chopping base.

lean it on the far side of a log and strike with just enough force to sink in the ax. Lift the ax—with wood still attached—and bring down both together against the block or log, splitting the wood completely.

If your ax head is loose on the handle, coat the blade with petroleum jelly and immerse it in water overnight. However, during cold weather, be sure to warm the blade before using it. A very cold blade can shatter when driven into hard wood.

Lastly, keep all cutlery sheathed when not in use. Knives left open in boxes or on tables invite accidents, axes left on the ground or leaning against the tent or camper are easily tripped over or fallen upon—especially when children are about. Sink an ax deeply into a chopping block or log, or sheath it completely. Knives should also be sheathed when not in use. But be sure to wipe them dry and clean before encasement—else rust and corrosion will attack the blade—even if it's made from the finest stainless steel.

That's a rundown on camp cutlery. Not at all complicated, but of utmost importance. The care, keeping and safe use of cutlery requires a mild outlay of cash, a small bit of time, and a modicum of precaution. The reward is safer and more pleasurable camping.

This shoreline is typical of the beauty seen from the coastal highway. The surf breaks on rocks which were once part of Heceta Head lighthouse promontory.

Guaranteed Rx for Spring Fever:

MY FRIEND, Denny Hannah, of Lakeside, Oregon, is a busy professional fishing guide. He rarely misses a day on the water and, depending on the time of the year, may be in hot pursuit of everything from salmon and shad to steelheads or the giant sturgeon which are abundant thereabouts. But all other fishing ends in March or April when, on a cool and misty morning, he finds schools of striped bass fresh from the sea migrating up his favorite Umpqua River.

"It's high time then," Denny assured me, "to take the best cure I've ever found for spring fever."

Perhaps it should be established here that neither Denny nor striped bass are Oregon natives. The guide is an expatriate of southern Ohio, which was getting too crowded for his tastes. The bass were introduced from the Atlantic seaboard a half century ago when their survival in Chesapeake Bay and the Hudson River was threatened by pollution. Since then stripers have so prospered from San Francisco Bay northward to the Columbia River that the species is becoming as popular with sports fishermen as are native salmon. That is doubly true in the Umpqua, a magnificent waterway of the Northwest which empties into the Pacific at Winchester Bay.

Because of a typically long winter in Wyoming, where we live, my wife and I were easily persuaded to test Denny's theory. Our own fishing water was still frozen solid and *any* kind of fishing action would work wonders. Still we weren't prepared for such a remarkable experience on the Umpqua.

Launching at Reedsport's public dock, Denny aimed his specially designed (for *both* bay *and* river cruising) boat upstream. He didn't pause until reaching a point well above tidewater where the Umpqua races over rocky cascades between steep and dark fir forests. Here an anchor was pitched overboard. All the wilderness scene lacked was a grizzly bear or a trout angler wading waist deep in the cold green current.

"This is striper water?" I asked in disbelief.

"Cast across that deep pool and see for yourself," Denny answered, handing me a wooden surface plug as big as a foot-long hot dog.

What happened next is no longer clear and maybe it never was. On light tackle I tossed the lure as directed and began to retrieve it erractically to imitate a stricken bait fish. Immediately, not one but several fish charged it and one struck; all at once I had both hands full just trying to catch reel handles spinning out of control. Meanwhile a mad striped bass noted its mistake and headed back toward the ocean, peeling more line from

Visitors to Shore Acres State Park get a grandstand view of waves breaking on the tilted 40-foot high sandstone coastal rocks. The 683-acre park was once an estate noted for its unusual botanical gardens.

Camp Oregon's Coast by ERWIN A. BAUER

the reel. Peggy cast out and also had a strike. I just held on. There was nothing else to do.

To keep the account brief, much later we somehow managed to net both of those stripers. One weighed 19 pounds and the other 22. But they were only for starters. We had similar action throughout the day, releasing most of the fish unharmed, until eventually it became more fun to forget the fishing in favor of watching a glorious day go by and of cooking a shore dinner. Too few angling trips wind up that way. And seldom is a serious case of spring fever cured so completely. But we soon discovered that striper fishing alone is not the only medicine a winter-weary traveler can find in springtime along the Oregon coastline.

From Astoria southward to Coos Bay and beyond to the California border, no shoreline of any state remains so largely undeveloped and so wild. Nor is such a large percentage of the beaches elsewhere in public ownership.

Scenically, Oregon's coast would also rate high with any in North America. Just inland from sand beaches, and rocky headlands, evergreen forests slant upward to form the Coast Range and this snowcapped mountain range is drained by rivers such as the Smith, the Alsea, the Nestucca and the famous Rogue—to name only the

largest. So there is ample raw material for an outdoor holiday where springtime does arrive a little earlier than it does inland. It also arrives well ahead of the great invasion of summertime tourists, which is another dividend.

Obviously it would take a series of springtimes back to back to explore and sample everything—the whole coast. But consider some scattered opportunities which Peggy and I discovered at random last spring. Fishing would have to head the list. Check over any map of coastal Oregon, and you will note a series (it may seem to be a chain) of lakes located just a short distance from the Pacific and along U.S. 101, the main (and in fact the only) north-south artery. Some notable examples are Devils Lake near Lincoln City, Siltcoos just south of Florence, Tahkenitch north of Reedsport, Clear, Eel and Tenmile Lakes near Lakeside. No great skill or elaborate tackle is necessary to fish any of these. If you trail or cartop-carry your own boat, catching bass, bluegills, rainbow trout or crappies costs only as much as the price of a fishing license. Or small boats can be rented near any of a whole series of lakeside campgrounds in state parks. We spent several days sampling the lake fishing, and it was surprisingly good.

From border to border the Oregon coast is punc-

229

tuated by 69 different parks. Most are state-operated but there are a good many federal, county and even timber company campgrounds. Overnight rates are $1 for primitive sites (toilets and water only), $2 for tent sites (stove, water, access to showers and laundry) and $4 for trailer and camper sites with all hookups. A free folder *(Oregon Camping)* which lists every type of recreational facility in much detail is available from the Travel Information Section, Oregon Department of Transportation, 101 Transportation Building, Salem, Oregon 97310.

As early as 1778 when the United States was still a new experiment, Capt. James Cook brushed close to the central Oregon coast en route northward in search of a new sea passage to Europe. Sailing by one particularly forbidding point of land, the English explorer named it Cape Perpetua in memory of a Christian martyr who died in Carthage on the same date in 203 A.D. Except for a tidy U.S. Forest Service visitor center (where a movie, *Forces of Nature,* is shown daily) and a network of nature trails, Cape Perpetua is the same primeval place which Cook saw, only from the sea. Now it is a favorite place of hikers and campers. And that is no wonder. A self-guiding auto tour (leaflets available) winds for 22 miles along the Cape to and from U.S. 101 near Yachats.

Hikers and picnickers can collect driftwood and glass floats in a sheltered sandy cove which is called Cape Cove Beach. One morning we found starfish, sea urchins, anemones and a hermit crab left temporarily exposed in tide pools by receding water. Not far away ocean swells foamed and roared inside Devil's Churn. At another spot—Spouting Horns—water is forced up through small vents in the rocks to resemble the vapor spouts of giant whales. Elsewhere around Cape Perpetua, there is shore fishing for perch, rock fishes and greenling.

A short drive south of Newport, and near Florence, is a wildlife spectacle that compares with any in this country. Sea Lion Caves is the site of the only mainland sea lion colony on this continent and an important sea bird rookery as well. Completely without hokum or gimmicks, on a normal springtime day a traveler can watch (or photograph) the mating and tribal antics of several hundred sea lions just beneath a vast cormorant rookery. Access to an awesome sea level cave where the surf pounds inside is possible via an elevator shaft almost 1,000 feet straight down through solid granite from cliff top on U.S. 101.

While browsing in Florence on a sunny afternoon we were invited on a kind of pre-dawn adventure which attracts more Oregonians to their coast than anything else. An extremely low (or minus) tide was scheduled to occur shortly after daybreak and that meant being on the vast mudflats in the bay just outside of town before sun-up. To participate, we would need a shovel and a bucket apiece.

"If you decide to go clamming," Denny Hannah had warned us earlier, "wear hip boots and your oldest, dirtiest clothes."

We took the advice and never had a better, more mud-spattered time. The exact clamming area was easy to find because of the many cars already parked there and of other shovel-armed citizens gathered nearby.

Miles of sandy beaches and Pacific Ocean surf can be seen from the summit of Neahkanie Mountain on Oregon's northern coast.

Private sports craft and commercial fishing boats sail in and out this narrow inlet to Depoe Bay. Landbound anglers fish from the rocky shoreline. Charter trollers take fishermen out from several Oregon ports in search of Chinook and silver salmon.

(Left) Digging for clams at a minus tide is an activity everyone engages in. The locals can be told from the tourists by their appropriately old clothing and their quick successes. It took us twice as long as the experienced clammers to fill our buckets.

(Below) This may look more like moving day than camping, but to avoid the intrusion of motor vehicles into the camping area, gear is wheeled for ¼-mile to the tent sites. Oswald West State Park on Oregon's northern coast is one of the state's most popular.

We simply followed the leaders out across the knee-deep muck to where tiny bubbles betrayed the presence of mud clams just below us. That's where we started digging, at times successfully enough to acquire the legal limit of 10 apiece. Peggy noted that we needed twice as much time to do so as the more experienced clammers. At the end we probably were also more mud-encrusted. But no matter, because we also enjoyed the clam chowder we made from our catch at least twice as much as any others who shared the mudflat that morning. Clamming can be contagious.

Florence isn't the only area for clam hunting; in fact the entire Oregon coast is justifiably well-known for it. One or more of six highly edible species inhabit every tidal flat. All, including the most desirable razor and gaper (or empire) clams, are abundant around Coos Bay, which is a sort of promised land for clammers almost the year around. No license is necessary to dig them in Oregon. But daily limits must be observed.

However, it isn't necessary to wallow in muck or even to rig up any fishing tackle along Oregon's seacoast to enjoy the seafood bounty. Every crossroads town along U.S. 101 large enough to have its own post office also has at least one open-air drive-in seafood shop. Here a passerby is tempted by everything from cooked crabs and uncooked shrimp to smoked salmon or rockfish, plus home-made piquant sauces and pickled kelp to go along. All of it is irresistible. On our last day in Oregon, we stopped at one roadside stand in picturesque Yachats just in time to see trays of dark red salmon come out of a blackened, fragrant, brick smoker. Then and there we bought enough to last for all of our noontime picnics during the long drive home. And then some.

So Denny Hannah was absolutely correct. Fishing and exploring Oregon's coast had completely cured two severe cases of springtime fever. "I only hope," Peggy commented, "that we get the dread disease again."

Wheelbarrows are provided at Oswald West State Park for campers to move their equipment the last ¼-mile to primitive sites. This coastal area also offers sandy beaches and fishing waters. Agate caves and hiking trails lure explorers to this 2,509 acre park.

Be sure to bring plenty of food since camping Oregon's cool green coast makes for hearty appetites.

Treetop Tough Guy: Camper's Friend or Enemy?

by ROGER ERSKINE

A lucky thing it is that red squirrels are no bigger than they are. With their tenacity, aggressiveness and wit they might just rule the world. (Photo courtesy of Karl Maslowski)

HAVING CAMPED widely across North America for many years, I recall many strange and wonderful wilderness experiences. But none matches the incident involving one tiny animal that demolished a whole hunting camp and practically drove the occupants out of the woods.

They were deer hunters from Pennsylvania, and their camp was located on a lonely blue lake in good deer country. They had hunted hard for almost a week without seeing the hide or the horns of a trophy buck. Then, late one evening, one of the hunters scored. They toiled far into the rainy night to dress, quarter, and carry the carcass into camp, where they hung the quarters beneath a canvas fly and just above a collapsible table that held all their foodstuffs under cover. With the meat hanging in the only dry place available, they fell exhausted into sleeping bags.

It was a short slumber, though, because at daybreak all hell broke loose. A hundred pounds of venison came crashing down onto the table, smashing cartons, breaking bottles, mixing vinegar with pancake flour, marmalade with dill pickles, and even spilling the con-tents of the hunters' last fifth of bonded on the spongy ground. Fifteen feet away the culprit, a red squirrel, raced up and down a tree trunk, barking and screaming at the mess he'd made by gnawing through a new manila rope.

But that was only the beginning. Until the outfitter returned by float plane to pick the hunters up, the squirrel practically moved in with them, like an unwel-come and obnoxious nephew. With a friend—a girl friend, presumably—he raced and wrestled along the full length of the tent every night, all night long. Nothing frightened him away. He ate the rubber shoulder pad on a rifle and eluded all the traps set to catch him. He virtually drove the hunters crazy.

This was no isolated performance. Red squirrels have been giving some campers headaches ever since the days of Dan Boone and Ethan Allen. Boone almost lost his scalp one day when a red squirrel betrayed his treetop hideaway to a band of Indians below. Under-standably, he never liked either red squirrels or Red-skins after that. And many a serious sportsman today will share the first half of his sentiments.

233

A red squirrel will eat most anything: berries, nuts, mushrooms—and strawberry jam if he can get it.

"Pineys," and old guide once remarked, "make me think of wanted-dead-or-alive posters."

The red squirrel—or pine squirrel or chickaree or piney—is something of a woodland delinquent, one of the meanest little critters in the forest. He's noisy, and he's probably the world's worst example of wasted energy—a tough hide being all that keeps him from exploding. But give the devil his due; he's handsome and he's the most exciting citizen of any forest he inhabits. This range includes nearly all of the fir, spruce, or pine forests of northern United States and Canada, plus a few deciduous woodlots coast to coast.

It would be hard, maybe impossible, to find a beast anywhere in the world with so much energy concentrated into so small a package. Wide-eyed, measuring only a foot long—and half of that a bushy tail—a full-grown red weighs no more than ½-pound. Actually a red squirrel would be the most formidable creature on the face of the earth if it reached the size, say of a lion. Its color runs from tawny or red-brown on top to white underneath. Usually a blackish line along each flank separates the two colors. The tail is a solid reddish brown, but all colors are likely to be paler in winter.

Spring is the busiest time of all for red squirrels, because it's then that females born the year before are raising rowdy families, usually two litters in succession. The nest may be a natural cavity, a woodpecker's hole, a repossessed crow's nest with a canopy added, or even a burrow in the ground. The first litter of four or five is born in late springtime; the second, 6 to 7 weeks later. At birth the young are completely blind, completely naked and, for the only time in their lives, completely quiet. Each one weighs only ¼-ounce. Hair begins to grow on day 9, eyes open on day 17 and weaning is completed in less than 5 weeks.

A mother red squirrel is violently protective of young in the nest. If danger of any kind appears, she either fights or quickly carries the young to another nest or hiding place. Once I watched a female move an entire litter. She seemed to do it by grabbing the young by the belly or neck with her teeth. The little one would then hang on with four feet while the mother hot-footed at high speed through the foliage.

About the time the young squirrels are full-grown there's plenty of action around the old homestead. First thing they do is to drive their mother away. But shed no tears; she can take care of herself. Besides, she's probably happy to be rid of them.

It was an early October morning on Michigan's Upper Peninsula, and I was bowhunting for deer. Unfortunately the stand I selected along a runway was beneath the nest tree of a late litter of red squirrels. It was a nerve-wracking but enlightening experience. First, they drove away a spike buck before he came in arrow range. Then, between bouts among themselves, they tormented me. When I moved, they followed me. Not one of the five pineys present ever relaxed for as long as a split second. I doubt if they ever slept because I've known them to be active all hours of the night.

These Michigan pineys had a most explosive vocabulary. Besides the chattering *tcher-r-r,* which is a trademark and which every woodsland hunter knows, they grunted, growled, barked, gargled and whistled—always with much twitching of body and tail.

Any red squirrel is completely incompatible with his family and other forest dwellers. Put two brothers in a cage overnight and by morning one will be dead. And reds have been known to attack—even to kill—much larger gray and fox squirrels that share the woods in some parts of their range. But the oft-repeated myth about reds castrating their larger cousins just isn't true.

Pineys are pure, unaltered murder on birds nesting nearby. It's doubtful if any other wildlife eats more eggs. And when the birds are hatched, the reds eat the babies. Sometimes they just bite their skull and push them out of the nest, while the parent birds scream nearby. The size of the parent doesn't make much difference either, because pineys have even been observed destroying crow's nests.

Red squirrels have their share of natural enemies. The most deadly, particularly in northern latitudes, is the pine marten, which can catch them with ease on the ground or treetops. Hawks and owls also take a toll.

Once on Ontario's Yesterday River a pair of pineys practically haunted our camp, tipping over anything they could move and even prying into a large can of strawberry preserves by using their incisor teeth like a can opener. Then, late one evening, I noticed an owl watching silently from the crown of a spruce. Two days later only one squirrel was haunting our camp, and I assume the owl ate the other one. I never saw it again.

It seems to me that a piney's diet consists of anything that contains calories or vitamins—or neither. They eat mushrooms, nuts, seeds, fruits, and berries. I also happen to know that they will gnaw on such items as fly rods, window sashes, and panchromatic film. A northwoods guide I knew had a "pet" (actually there's no such thing as a genuinely tame pet red squirrel) that enjoyed drinking ale.

Since red squirrels do not hibernate in winter, they spend much time in autumn hoarding anything from pine cones to lichens. Sometimes whole hollow logs, tree trunks, or similar dry places are completely filled, perhaps with more than a bushel of food. Even though squirrels seldom consume all they collect, a fierce fight begins the second a strange piney approaches a food cache. It's a noisy no-holds-barred fight that can be heard for an incredible distance on an otherwise pleasant autumn day. Fighting—that's the story of the red squirrel's life.

The woods—any woods—would be quieter and more peaceful without the piney, the original Little Cuss. But it would also be a less exciting place for a camper to spend his leisure moments.

A PIONEER CAMPING PROFILE

the Sidelingers
of Kamishak Bay Alaska

by ERWIN A. BAUER

ALTHOUGH SHE lives in a lonely, primitive wilderness, Cindy Sidelinger wasn't prepared for the sudden terror she faced one morning early last summer. Breakfast was finished, the dishes washed. It was raining. From habit, she pushed through the tent flaps to hang up a dish towel outside on the clothesline. Turning around, she stood toe-to-toe with a brown bear almost 10 times her size.

Its shaggy coat dripping, the bruin stood half erect and regarded her through myopic red-rimmed eyes. Its odor was rank, and it seemed to sway uncertainly. Time passed in slow motion. Cindy wanted to faint, but didn't. Finally, the bear woofed softly, dropped to all fours, and shuffled away into the dense overcast which enveloped the camp.

Back inside the tent, Cindy collapsed onto her bed. "I was so liquid in the knees," she recalls, "I could have stirred them with a spoon."

Close encounters with bears are a fact of Cindy and her husband Kevin's lives from June through August. Brown bears are their only neighbors, and usually can be spotted anytime they look through the screened tent window. Cindy and Kevin live in a lonely camp on one of the wildest coasts left in Alaska or anywhere else on the face of the earth.

From Cold Bay at the tip of the Alaska Peninsula, northeastward past Kodiak, through treacherous Shelikof Strait and Kamishak Bay far up into Cook Inlet, the Alaskan coast is literally a no man's land, uninhabited and still virtually unexplored. Foul

Kevin Sidelinger shows off a sockeye salmon, one of thousands in migrating up Chenik Creek. An alert, hungry person can catch one by hand with a little practice.

The brown bears also are the reason Kevin and Cindy happen to live on Kamishak Bay.

Since 1974, young Mike and Dianne McBride have opened their attractive home on China Poot Bay to a few special summer tourists seeking a bush experience in Alaska. They built the place from scratch, largely with natural materials and immense ingenuity, just a short boat run from Homer on the Kenai Peninsula. It is called Kachemak Bay Wilderness Lodge. But as Homer becomes busier and more popular during Alaska's current boom, the McBrides sense some encroachment. Being a restless soul anyway, Mike began to search for an outpost camp where he wouldn't get that closed-in feeling. Late one fall day guiding waterfowlers, he discovered Chenik Lagoon.

On a typical day, Chenik is a stark, narrow inlet on the extreme western end of Kamishak Bay that contains water deep enough for boat anchorage only during the high tides. As bays go along this wild coast, it might be considered sheltered. Several sweet rivers including the Chenik empty into the ocean nearby. On his first visit Mike saw many bears, including two that were digging clams on the beach. Checking his map, he also noted that the mouth of the famous McNeil River (and McNeil Cove) is only about 15 miles away and thus accessible from Chenik by boat. Toward the tag end of July when the dog salmon are running, it is not unusual to count 30 brown bears in a single day's vigil at the falls of the McNeil. Just a little farther south is the boundary of Katmai National Monument. When McBride explored Chenik Lagoon the second time, Kevin Sidelinger (who worked for him then at Kachemak) was along.

"How would you like to build a summer bear watching camp right here with me?" McBride asked bluntly. "You operate the camp, and we're partners."

Sidelinger can't recall hesitating. "Why not?" he answered.

Now 26, Kevin Sidelinger was born and raised in rural Maine, where he spent "too much time behind a pack of beagle hounds chasing bears, bobcats, and cottontails in the balsam swamps. "I quit only when deer season was open." He worked one summer on a white-fenced horse farm in Virginia's Blue Ridge, but felt himself getting "soft" there so began vagabonding northwestward toward where the trees are evergreen and it's cool in summer. His trail ended with a handyman job at Kachemak Bay where Cindy, 25 but already a widow, was also working.

Cindy is, or was, a city girl from Oregon whose parents regarded bush Alaska as nowhere at all for sensible, civilized humans. But she was hooked on it and married a man who was just getting started in the outfitting business. Then a tragedy abruptly changed that idyll. In September, Cindy's husband was guiding a German moose hunter. From their camp one evening, he saw his boat drifting away in a brisk wind. Attempt-

weather is endemic. The coast is lashed continually by gales, which, with the surge of massive tides, make navigation dangerous. In places the coast is a barrier of cliffs, fjord-like with windblown waterfalls plunging directly into saltwater. Elsewhere, gravel and quicksand flats extend for miles into the sea at low tide. Inland, steam and smoke still belch from active volcanoes. The whole region remains a pure and fantastic wilderness.

One other factor distinguishes this remote southwest area of Alaska: Here thrives the largest concentration of bears in the world. These are the Peninsula brown, *Ursus arctos,* which may reach more than ½-ton in weight. The bruins, probably more than anything else, have attracted a few humans to this coast, at first to hunt, but more and more nowadays just to see them.

ing to swim for it, he drowned in the icy water.

For a long while Cindy would not or could not communicate with anyone, including Kevin. She worked hard and ignored people. One evening Kevin spoke to her while she was dressing salmon near camp. When she barely grunted in reply, Kevin picked up a whole fish and cracked her across the fanny with it.

"I was furious," she remembers, "but he got my attention. In a minute I had to laugh. We've been buddies and I've been laughing ever since. Maybe Kevin saved my life."

For their first summer together the Sidelingers returned to Maine where they farmed Kevin's homeplace and roamed in the nearest woods. But Maine simply wasn't home. For one thing it seemed to swarm with traffic and noisy tourists from eastern cities they couldn't understand. When autumn began to blend into winter, they drove northwestward.

Building even the most primitive camp at Chenik quickly tested the new partners' determination, ingenuity, and logistical planning. The first hurdle was to transport everything for a whole summer's operation from Kachemak Bay 160 miles across turbulent Cook Inlet to Kamishak Bay. The cost of flying it by floatplane, the quickest, easiest way, was totally prohibitive. The alternative was to charter an ancient, rusting barge in Homer and then to load it with three tents, provisions for 3 months, plenty of tools and spares, a small amount of fuel, one Franklin and two oil-drum stoves, a kitchen stove, a Boston Whaler and outboard, and some finished lumber. They figured they could salvage much of the camp's construction materials from the driftwood accumulated on Chenik beaches and in this they proved correct. The beaches also yielded an almost unlimited, although damp, supply of firewood.

"The thing that scared me most," Kevin admits, "was making that voyage across the Inlet. We had to estimate the required time, cross our fingers in hopes for at least moderate weather, and we absolutely had to time our trip to reach Chenik Lagoon during a high tide. Any small miscalculation could have cost us the whole damn thing, including our lives. Cindy and I prayed."

That must have worked because they got all their gear into Chenik and unloaded it without incident. Then the serious work began. McBride stayed briefly to help get the project underway. The first job was to build wooden platforms above the tundra on which to erect the three wall tents. One larger tent would be for Cindy and Kevin and would include a kitchen and a warm, dry, sit-down area for visiting bear watchers. The other two would be two-person guest sleeping tents.

By the time my wife Peggy and I arrived in mid-July, what they'd accomplished amazed us. A supply storehouse had been established beneath the deck of the main tent. A one-hole toilet was finished and a "Sourdough Trip South"—a surprisingly efficient

Cindy and Kevin assume a traditional pose.

sod-roofed sauna—was ready for its first steambathers. Although it may be hard to visualize three lime-green canvas tents blending well into a bleak Alaskan coast, the Kamishak Bay Brown Bear Camp seemed to be almost a thing of beauty in a very lonely, lovely land. In August the green grass was knee-deep, and speckled with purple lupine, cow parsnip, lousewort, and other wildflowers.

For the first time the Sidelingers had a chance to seriously explore beyond their immediate vicinity. The mouth of Chenik Creek at high tide seethed with sockeye salmon—silvery fresh from the ocean—trying to negotiate a steep cascade to spawn farther upstream. It was easy enough to obtain breakfast or dinner right here in Chenik Creek simply by grabbing a salmon by hand. Bears were taking advantage of the salmon bonanza too, but whenever we approached, they would vanish into the dense surrounding Arctic willows. Signs of their presence were everywhere. By following bear trails for an hour or so upstream, we came to Chenik Lake. Probably few humans had ever walked around its

Cindy, foreground, dips fresh water from the end of the lagoon. This is a high tide; 6 hours later ½-mile of mud flats will separate the tent from the water.

shore. Although we couldn't catch the lake trout here by hand, it was easy enough with flies and spinners.

And then there was McNeil Cove. We had to wait our chance to explore it. McNeil is now greatly restricted by a lottery-permit system to avoid bear-human problems there. Only 10 persons are allowed to hike to McNeil Falls on any one day.

The golden glow that came from seeing 15 magnificent bears fishing for salmon at one time followed me on the long hike from McNeil Falls back to the coast. I was still warmed by it during the 2-mile hike across a windswept tidal mud flat, in one place coming uncomfortably close to a female bear with triplet cubs. Kevin, meanwhile, had retreated to wait for me with the boat. It was grounded when I returned at low tide, and we had to wait in gathering twilight for the first surge of a fresh flood tide. Finally we aimed out of the cove toward Chenik Lagoon. Then the wild ride back began— almost 3 hours against wind and heaving swells, against whitecaps which drenched us repeatedly, to cover the 15 miles mostly in darkness. Sidelinger, I found, is as good a man with a small boat as he is hacking out a camp on a wilderness shore. That evening, with too much hot, fresh pastry and baked red salmon under my belt, I wondered aloud why two young people would want to stay in a situation most others would consider a dreary exile. Their answer was immediate and unequivocal.

"We get along," Cindy said. "I've never felt less pressure in my life." Kevin said, "Anyone honestly willing to work—to show up every day, sober—can get a good money-making job in Alaska today. But I guarantee you I'd rather make much less right here."

Sidelinger is mildly sensitive to weather. "I start feeling a little glum when the weather stays too dismal for too long. The rain begins to get to me. But the sunny days are absolutely indescribable. They make you fly. I sit and watch the flowers and foxes and bears for hours at a time. The bears like it too; once I saw a ½-ton sow rolling in the flowers like a puppy dog. On sunny days I hope that summer will last forever and that I never have to leave this place."

So the Sidelingers get along at Chenik Lagoon. They own a cat, but do not plan to have children. Work appears to be divided in traditional ways; mostly Kevin does the heavy chores—the building, the boat running, the wood gathering. Cindy, who barely stands 5 feet in two pairs of woolen socks, does the cooking, but never hesitates to swing an axe if it's necessary.

Garbage disposal is a headache, especially with the ever-present bears and the family of red foxes which dug an underground apartment nearby to raise four kits. (Strangely, the foxes seemed afraid of the Sidelinger's cat.) Normally biodegradable and flammable items must be burned. Glass and cans leave with guests.

"Whenever we leave this place for the last time," Kevin said, "there will be nothing left behind to interest the anthropologists." Or the bears.

by MARV LINDBERG

WHY STRUGGLE with ropes and knots (especially when they get wet or freeze) when it is a "snap" to do many of the same jobs with rubber bands cut from old innertubes?

Although it might seem the tubeless tire has made innertubes obsolete, there are still a lot of them in use and they are subject to punctures or other misadventures that make them unusable. You may have to do a bit of scrounging at service stations, tire shops, motorcycle shops or farm implement dealerships to obtain a few in various sizes. Or, you might ask them to save some for you. They have always given them to me free of charge instead of throwing them away.

As to sizes, tubes from motorcycles will furnish bands about 4 to 5 inches long, passenger cars about 7 to 9 inches long, and trucks from 10 to 15 inches long. In very rare instances, you might pick up a tube from a farm combine that will provide bands about 24 inches long. Of course, the circumference of the band is double this length.

Such sizes are important only if the size of any of them happens to fit your needs. For example, to snap one over each end of a rolled sleeping bag to eliminate using tie cords or to keep tent frame poles in a neat bundle. Otherwise, you can tie an overhand knot in a band that is too long. This also provides a "handle" to grasp when removing the band.

For use as tie-down tension cords, you will need "S" hooks of a size suitable to your needs. Often, as on motorcycles and snowmobiles, you can fasten one end of a band to a part of the frame by passing one end of the band around a frame part and looping the band through itself. The other end of the band will require the use of an "S" hook to attach it to another part of the frame or to pass through another part of the frame and secure the "S" hook back over the same band. Two bands, each looped through itself on opposite sides of the frame can meet in the middle connected by an "S" hook. To make a longer tension cord, pass one end of a band through another band, then through itself. As many as neeeded can be so looped to make a cord of any length.

You can make your own cartop carrier "spider web" holddown by using a large steel ring for the centerpiece and looping 6 or 8 bands to the ring and adding the required number of bands to each to obtain the lengths needed.

Use Rubber Bands to

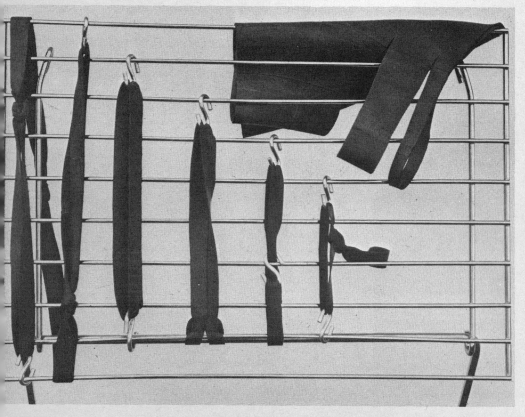

Variations on an innertube band. From left to right: several bands looped together to make one long band; a single band with two "S" hooks; a band looped over a frame part plus one "S" hook; a band with one end passed around a frame part and the "S" hook secured to the same band; and varying with width of bands to produce greater or less tension (the wider the band, the greater the tension).

Backpacks, sleeping bags, etc. are easily secured to a snowmobile or motorcycle with the use of innertube bands and "S" hooks.

Make Camping a Snap

For extra long bands, you can make one or more by cutting them along the outside circumference or tread of the innertube. A tube from a 15-inch wheel will give you bands about 40 inches long. If you make one cut across such a band you will have a single strip 80 inches long. You can tie an "S" hook to each end of the strip. Tying a knot in a rubber band is tricky because it stretches. Two half-hitches work best but you must work the first snug against the "S" hook before you add the second. Leave about an inch of the end of the band protruding from the knot.

"S" hooks can be used on roof-mount carriers as described for motorcycles. If you need to protect the frame of a cycle, snowmobile or cartop carrier from being marred by the "S" hooks, shop around for rubber tubing that will fit the hook. Auto parts stores have a variety of sizes. If you have a wooden box for a carrier, fasten single-hole electrical conduit straps to the sides or bottom of the box. The cast iron kind are best, but the

To make a sheath for your axe, use a piece of old garden hose, split lengthwise, over the blade and secure it in place with two small rubber bands or one long one stretched twice over the axe head and hose.

stamped variety will do. You will find them at electric supply shops in a variety of sizes. No "S" hooks are needed, simply secure the end of the bands over the conduit straps. To make an "S" hook a permanent part of a band, close one half of the hook against itself so the band cannot slip off.

The distinct advantage of using bands cut from innertubes instead of purchased tension ("shock") cords is in being able to adjust to whatever degree of tension and length is required. To achieve greater tension, simply cut wider bands.

The hunting camper can certainly use a rifle rack to keep the arms safely out of the way in camp. A simple, effective rack can be made by bolting spring clips (broom holders) to a length of sash chain and using a band with two "S" hooks to secure the setup to a tree. With the rifle butts resting on the ground, the spring clips anchor the barrels, keeping the guns accessible. Strips of felt, cemented to the spring clips will prevent damage to the bluing on the barrels and a covering sheet of plastic or tarp will allow the guns to remain clean and dry.

A small rectangle of pegboard attached to a tree can keep gear handy yet out from underfoot. With trusty "S" hooks they neatly hold a lantern, axe or cooking utensils and can do so without harm to the bark of the tree.

Whatever size board you choose, bolt the mid-point of a length of sash chain (at least 6 feet long) to the backside of the pegboard spacing the two bolts about 3 inches each way from the centerline of the board. After wrapping one end of the chain as far as possible around the tree, use an innertube band and "S" hook to cover the remaining distance. Select hooks, spring clips for broom or tools and spring-loaded clothes pins as needed

A rifle rack from sash chain and innertube bands.

for the items you plan to hang. A sheet of plastic, clipped to the top and sides of the pegboard with clothes pins, will protect camping gear from dust and rain.

In cutting the bands from the tube you will quickly discover you must cut a wedge-shaped piece out of the tube to keep the bands straight. Don't throw this away; cut it into narrow strips and use it for tinder to start a fire.

Avoid nicks when cutting your bands. They tend to cause the band to tear in two. A sharp pair of tin snips will cut a double thickness. Please don't use sewing shears or we will both be in trouble. With a bit of thought you are sure to think of many other ways to "snap into it" using innertube bands.

Kitchen utensils, tools and camp gear can be stored handily on this "hanging tree." The pegboard is reusable anytime.

walk—or willing to get that way. You have to live in a tent which may be smaller than a cupboard back home. You might have to sleep with a rolled up sweater for a pillow and cook your own dinner on a tiny stove. At day's end you will be thoroughly, bittersweet weary to the bones. But if all these "hardships" do not bother you, you may be missing a lot because backpacking was never better than it is today.

Age makes no difference. I am 59 and last summer met plenty of backpackers who were much older. And it matters very little where you live. There is good backpacking country laced with trails within a day's drive of absolutely anywhere. And just one word— *terrific*—describes the splendid backpacking equipment which is now available. But exactly what does that mean? What equipment *does* a backpacker need? How does a total novice get started?

One mistake must be avoided from the start. Too many beginning backpackers carry too much too far, and the first adventure becomes an ordeal instead of a pleasure. So let's avoid that. In mid-summer when the weather is warmest everywhere, we can walk with a minimum of gear. And the first trail hike or two should be kept short, very short. Would you believe that today you can go backpack camping for a whole weekend with only 20 pounds? Or maybe even less? Take my word that you can.

Backpacks come in two general types—with or without exterior (usually aluminum tube) frames. Modern frame packs are the most popular for toting the modest weight (about 20 pounds) we're talking about and that load is carried on the packer's hips, rather than his shoulders, via a wide waist band or hip belt. Some years ago a packer had to carry everything on his shoulders alone. Most men and women of average build and

The Coleman Peak 1 backpack with top pocket removed shows the lightweight single piece frame with slots for carrying the bag at just the right place for the individual packer.

Let's Try a 20-Pound Weekend
by ERWIN A. BAUER

OF ALL kinds of camping, none have become more attractive, more popular, especially with younger sportsmen, recently than backpacking, and it isn't any wonder. What better, cheaper way exists to enjoy the American wilderness? How else do you reach the great fishing which waits just beyond the beaten tracks?

Let's admit here and now that backpacking is not for absolutely everyone. It can be hard work, and it can be demanding. You must be in good enough shape to

strength find it far more comfortable to carry weight on the hips and legs. In fact they are surprised how easy it is.

So the best advice is to start with a pack with a hip belt, which would weigh about 3 pounds or so, and which has a rated capacity of 2,000 to 2,500 square inches. That's as big as you need for summertime and short trips.

Nowadays backpacks are sold everywhere, even in drug stores, but for a better selection, go to a bona fide

Today's freeze-dried foods combined with water in a small pot can provide delicious meals even deep in the wilderness.

(Above) A versatile backpack is Coleman's Peak 1. The top pocket can be removed and used instead as a fanny pack for short day trips. The lower duffle bag holds a sleeping bag and is also removable. Long side pockets hold pack fishing rods and other tall items most other backpacks cannot accommodate.

(Right) This Great Pyramid Tent by REI, Seattle, is perfect for winter camping. Four can crowd in. The shape allows snow to slip off and the fiberglass rods are easy to handle in the cold and are identical for quick assembly. Of course, this is an admirable tent in less severe conditions, too.

mountain or sporting goods store where backpacking is fluently spoken. If possible (to save money) rent your first pack and ask to have the rental applied to the cost if you decide to buy it. That's a common practice, at least in the West.

Nobody can enjoy camping overnight without a good night's sleep and next to his carrier, every backpacker needs a sleeping bag. Again the object is to keep it light. For summertime use in all above-freezing temperatures, there are down-filled, mummy-shaped bags which weigh 2½ pounds or less. These can be stuffed into a package no bigger than a loaf of bread. Synthetic-filled bags can also be used, are cheaper, but will be slightly heavier and more bulky. But our total weight so far is still only about 6 pounds for pack and sleeping bag. Add another pound for a mattress which can either be a hip-to-shoulder length foam pad or a light air-inflatable.

If you are backpacking in an extremely dry region, say the Southwest, or where you can take advantage of overnight huts or lean-tos (as along some major hiking trails), you can forget about carrying a tent altogether. Instead, a space blanket or ground cloth will suffice—something to lay flat under your sleeping bag and then fold as a sandwich over the top of it. But the odds are you should carry a tent, to use alone or to share with one or two companions. The smaller the capacity, the lighter it will be.

There are many tents on the market suitable for one-

All the ingredients for a 20-pound weekend are pictured here. **1.** Flexpack with vest, anorak, and miscellaneous small items **2.** Tin cup **3.** Cloth canteen **4.** Fishing lines **5.** Stove **6.** Packaged concentrated foods **7.** Pack rod and reel **8.** Cooking pot **9.** Air mattress **10.** Tent **11.** Sleeping bag.

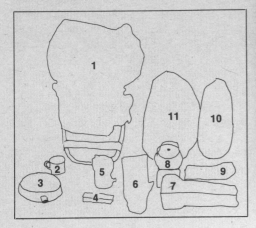

Checklist of Gear for 20-Pound Weekend

Alpine Designs Flexpack	3 lbs., 10 oz.
Early Winters Light	
Dimension tent	3 lbs., 8 oz.
Camp 7 Pioneer sleeping bag	2 lbs., 5 oz.
Airlift inflatable mattress	1 lb., 3 oz.
Coleman Peak 1 stove with fuel	2 lbs., 6 oz.
Pan, tin cup, spoon	6 oz.
Anorak from Country Ways kit	1 lb., 2 oz.
Olam insulated vest	9 oz.
Change of woolen socks	5 oz.
Matches, twine, water purification	
tablets, biodegradable soap,	
toothbrush, pocket knife	8 oz.
Bob Hinman Guzzler canteen	6 oz.
Concentrated high energy food	3 lbs., 0 oz.
Diawa Mini-Cast pack	
rod and reel	15 oz.
Fishing lures, flies	10 oz.
Total	**20 lbs., 13 oz.**

person use in summer, which weigh as little as 3 pounds. For the past 2 years, Peggy and I have used a roomy, easy to erect two-person tent which weighs only 3¾ pounds, stakes, poles and all. But most two- and three-person tents will weigh 5 pounds or so, a carrying weight which can be split among those using it. Figuring a maximum of 3 pounds of tentage per person, our total weight is now up to only 10 pounds. For a 20-pound weekend, we still have 10 pounds to use for food, clothing and anything else.

During normal summertime weather once more, not much clothing beyond what you wear is really necessary. You should carry a sweater or warm vest for evening and probably a very light plastic foul weather suit. I prefer a waterproof Gore-Tex anorak and carry rain pants only during late season. A packer should also have a change of socks.

Cooking hot meals on short, summer (say no longer than a weekend) trips may be far more bother than it's worth. Many times I have got along very well on just such foods as dried fruit, nuts, jerky, cereals, gorp, raisins and chocolate candy. All of these are concentrated and light in weight for the nutrition and energy provided. Figure that you can survive very well on 1½ to 2½ pounds total per day.

But if you need something more elaborate, you are still in luck. Packaged camp meals of bewildering variety are available today. You can carry along everything from creole shrimp and lasagna to beef stroganoff and Mexican ranch-style omelet, all freeze-dried in meal-size packages for light weight and convenience. They're sold everywhere. But with these menus you also need a backpack stove with fuel (figure 1¼-2½ pounds), a pan, a cup and spoon (per person). There are aluminum backpack cook kits in which the stove fits inside the cooker. Plastic "throwaway" cups, spoons, forks, even plates are as good and as light as anything for backpacking. Never carry such heavy, bulky items as fresh fruits and vegetables, canned goods or juices, although dry juice mixes are fine.

In much of the mountain West, a canteen really isn't necessary because water is available and pure, but elsewhere an aluminum, plastic or cloth container of at

(Above) Tiny, lightweight tents of Gore-Tex provide snug sleeping space for two beside a mountain tarn high above timberline.

(Left) Backpackers can reach magnificent alpine scenery like this in the Tetons in Wyoming, and set up a comfortable camp in some of the most spectacular landscapes in North America. New equipment makes backpacking possible for those who may have thought themselves too out-of-shape or old for such activities.

least 1-quart capacity is necessary. Also carry iodine water purification tablets. A list of other items in every backpack would include waterproof matches, a knife, toothbrush, a tube of all-purpose biodegradable soap. With all of the above, food for 3 days and 2 nights on a trail, your total pack load should not exceed 20 pounds and should be well under it. That means you can carry a pack fishing rod and camera.

A good, strong hiker can easily carry 20 pounds for 10 or 12 miles a day. But a first-time backpacker is wise to proceed more slowly, limiting himself to half that distance. If it seems too easy, he can extend himself. But even before starting out, he should be familiar with *all* his camping gear. Spend a night outside at home in the tent and bag. Cook on the camp stove. Try living for a day or so on trail foods. Determine exactly how much you really need and then why burden yourself with carrying any more? If possible, try to pick predicted good weather for starting a first trip.

Given half a chance, backpacking is a game which grows on you. With a little experience you quickly learn a lot about gear, how to pack it, how to tote it most comfortably. Pretty soon it becomes the greatest, most rewarding experience in the outdoors. You can add cameras, flyrods, map, a compass and field guides to your load—and never even notice the extra weight. Summed up briefly—you're hooked.

Want to Know More About Backpacking? Here's a List of Good Books on the Subject

Backpacking One Step at a Time, by Harvey Manning, The REI Press, Box 22088, Seattle WA 98188.

The Best About Backpacking, Edited by Denise Van Lear, Sierra Club Totebooks, 1050 Mills Tower, San Francisco CA 94104.

The Complete Walker, by Colin Fletcher, Alfred A. Knopf, Publisher, New York.

America's Backpacking Book, by Raymond Bridge, Charles Scribner's Sons, New York.

Wilderness Areas of North America, by Ann and Myron Sutton, Funk and Wagnalls, New York.

The Backpacker's Budget Food Book, by Fred Powledge, David McKay Co., 750 Third Ave., New York.

Lightweight Camping Equipment and How to Make It, by Gerry Cunningham and Margaret Hansson, Charles Scribner's Sons, New York.

Wildlife Country: How to Enjoy It, National Wildlife Federation, 1412 16th St. NW, Washington D.C. 20036.

North Cascades National Parks Area in Washington State

by MARV LINDBERG

Scenic vistas like this make the northwest part of our country a favorite area for camping. Pull outs are frequent so drivers can appreciate the view.

WHEN MOTHER EARTH flexes her muscles, the result is sometimes a devastating disaster such as an earthquake. More often, especially when she takes her time, the result is one of scenic splendor. Such is the case with that portion of the Cascade Mountain Range in northwestern Washington state.

Created some 15 million years ago, this area contains some of the most spectacular mountains in the conterminous 48 states. Fortunately, you can now drive across this area on a highway that was completed in the fall of 1972. Camping areas along Highway 20 are many. It took 77 years to complete State Highway 20, with most of the construction done since 1959. That gives some indication of the rugged terrain it traverses through what is now the North Cascades National Park and the Ross Lake National Recreation Area.

The park is surrounded, clockwise from the Canadian border, by the Pasaytan Wilderness, Okanogan National Forest, Lake Chelan National Recreation Area, Glacier Peak Wilderness, Wenatchee National Forest, Snoqualmie National Forest and Mount Baker National Forest.

Snowcapped peaks overlook cirque lakes and deep valleys. Over 40 percent of the glacier-covered area in the lower 48 states lies within this area. Vegetation varies from the tender alpine plants on the peaks to dense forests in the valleys. Many of the naked rock formations remain unchanged since the last ice age 10,000 years ago.

An added bonus is the three climate zones you pass as you travel along the highway. On the eastern slopes, after the mountains have drained the moisture from the westerly winds, you will encounter ponderosa pine, mixed conifer and open grassland. On the mountains you find alpine meadows, timberline spruce, glaciers and barren rock. On the moisture-laden western slopes, rain forest conditions produce large stands of Douglas fir and at the lower elevations a mixture of deciduous trees.

If yours is a one-way trip across the North Cascades, you will miss half the scenic vistas unless you stop often and look back. Each view is different. It's only 90 miles between Winthrop on the east and Marblemount on the west, so you can make a round trip in one day. Such a trip is best started from the east entrance so you have the sun at your back both ways. Mountains are best photographed under these conditions. Backlighting, created when traveling facing the sun, produces dull photos with little detail.

Several highways across eastern Washington lead to the town of Winthrop at the eastern end of the North Cascades area. En route you may pass through the Colville Indian reservation, via Grand Coulee Dam or via Wenatchee, "The Apple Capital of the World."

You won't be able to resist a stop at Winthrop. All the buildings have been recently renovated with false fronts to resemble an Old West town of the late 1800s. The residents have adopted the hospitality that goes with the atmosphere. Regular events include '49er Days in mid-May, Memorial Day Rodeo, River Rat Races on July 4th, Labor Day Rodeo and an Antique Auto Rally in early September. A smoke-jumper base is also located at Winthrop. Check your gas gauge before you start across the pass. It's 90 miles to the next filling station.

Except for the winter of 1976, when it was kept open

You expect Liberty Bell Mountain to ring out loud and clear as the sun casts its shadow over the valley at eventide.

all year, the road has been closed due to the heavy snows as early as November 21 in 1973 and as late as December 15 in 1978. The earliest opening date in the spring was April 10 in 1979; the latest opening was June 14 in 1974. The North Cascades Highway is closed to vehicular traffic between Winthrop and Newhalem during the winter.

As you travel west from Winthrop toward the newly constructed portion of the highway near Mazama the highway is old and narrow. From Mazama to Diablo Lake the wide blacktop highway has gently sloping shoulders that permit frequent stops along the roadway.

At Mazama, a 20-mile side trip is worthwhile if you are not concerned about driving on narrow mountain roads and have a good set of tires to cope with the graveled roadbed. The road served the 1890 gold miners whose mines and old buildings still survive. A 3-mile hike to the top of Slate Peak, elevation 7,500 feet, will afford a full-circle view of several hundred square miles of rugged mountain scenery.

About 18 miles west of Mazama be sure to stop at Washington Pass Overlook on a short spur off the highway. A towering granite peak known as Liberty Bell stands watch. From this viewpoint you can see Kangaroo Ridge, Early Winter Spires (7,807 feet) and, 1,000 feet below, the valley through which you just drove. Incidentally, the grade of the entire highway is driveable in high gear.

The next viewpoint is Whistler Mountain. This will be your only close look at alpine meadows. It will survive as such only if viewers refrain from hiking off the road, and trampling the fragile vegetation.

Rainy Pass offers you a chance to hike a portion of the Pacific Crest National Scenic Trail. A 1.4-mile hike leads to Lake Ann, one of the few lakes close to the highway.

About 55 miles west of Winthrop, you will enter the Ross Lake National Recreation Area. Ross Lake is an impoundment behind one of three dams on the Skagit River. The 24-mile lake extends into Canada. Access to the dam is by foot, horseback or by boat to the foot of the dam. The private owners of Ross Lake Resort will haul your own small boat up to the lake itself, where they have cabins that float on logs, and boats of their own to rent. The only other access by road is at the north end of the lake in Canada. Ten small campgrounds are located on Ross Lake with access by boat only.

The next viewpoint will be Diablo Dam, where the glacier-fed streams, loaded with rock-flour from the action of the glaciers, turn the water green. Privately owned Diablo Lake Resort is located below the dam. The 389-foot dam when completed in 1930 was the highest arch dam in the world. The hanging glaciers of Colonial and Pyramid Peaks can be seen from here.

At Diablo you will no doubt be intrigued by the unusual inclined railway originally used to transport

Mt. Shuksan challenges the hiker to become a mountaineer. (A National Park Service photo.)

material 600 feet up the mountainside during construction of the dams. Tourists can now take a ride up this inclined railway. Farther west, the Gorge powerhouse is open to the public. Nearby Ladder Creek Falls Trail displays a beautiful nature garden. Seattle City Light has guided tours of the three-dam complex. Reservations are required, and they are often sold out a year in advance. For those without reservations a mini-tour is available. A fee is charged for each tour.

As you travel farther west, you will enter Mt. Baker National Forest. Interestingly, unless you have already taken off on one of the numerous hiking trails leading from the highway, you can't say you have yet set foot in the North Cascades National Park. The park is in two units, north and south, divided by the Ross Lake N.R.A., which lies on both sides of the highway.

An enjoyable side trip most tourists miss due to lack of publicity is the road up the Cascade River out of Marblemount. A graveled road that twists and turns, with single-lane traffic in many places, covers 25 miles of beautiful country. Heavy timber abounds. At the end of the road, you will be within shouting distance of the glacier on Mt. Johannesburg.

A goodly number of you people who read this article

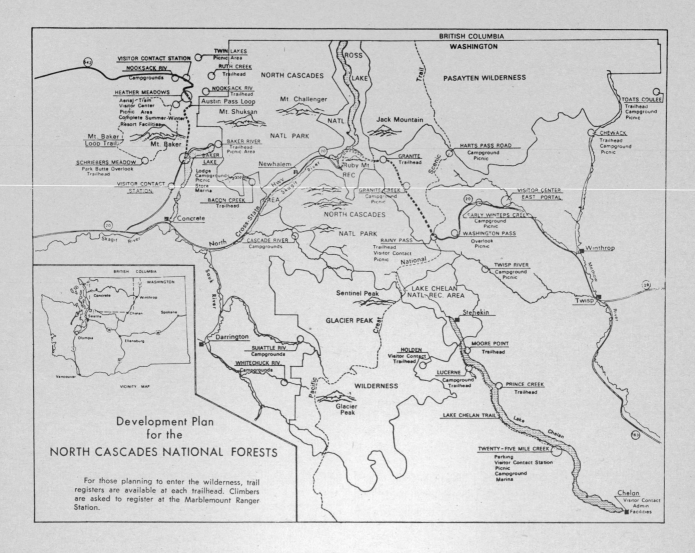

Development Plan
for the
NORTH CASCADES NATIONAL FORESTS

For those planning to enter the wilderness, trail registers are available at each trailhead. Climbers are asked to register at the Marblemount Ranger Station.

are going to have interests other than merely driving through the Cascades National Park, or you wouldn't be buying this book. Many will be campers with tents, trailers, motorhomes or fifth wheelers. Many of you will be hikers, backpackers, fishermen, snowmobilers, skiers or just outdoor people who enjoy what nature has to offer. Some of you will be traveling with no definite itinerary and, because you find this area so intriguing, you will need a place to stop overnight. Suppose we explore these potentials in further detail. At the end of this article we will list places to write for further information. In some instances you will need reservations.

Campers will find numerous campgrounds in the area, but due to the popularity of this new addition to scenic travel, you may find space at a premium. The Okanogan National Forest on the eastern end has a number of campgrounds, but many have limited space. Within roughly 30 miles of Winthrop there are about 25 national forest campgrounds with anywhere from a single campsite to about 30. About half of them have trailer sites, but connections for electricity, sewage and water are usually not available. Many are on streams and a few are on lakes. Some have piped water, some have wells and in others you use stream water. Only one, Lost Lake, has flush toilets.

Near Winthrop, Pearrygin State Park, 4 miles out, has 88 campsites of which 30 have hookups. No reservation is required, but a 7-day limit is imposed. It has modern restroom facilities and a boat launch. There are at least five private resorts and a KOA (Kampgrounds of America) with campgrounds.

In the Ross Lake N.R.A. itself, there are only two campgrounds: Colonial Creek at Diablo Lake and Goodell Creek near Newhalem. Colonial has 164 sites, most of which will accommodate either tents or trailers. It has flush toilets, piped water, a dumping station, but no hookups. Goodell has 26 sites, water and pit toilets.

Within and beyond the Ross Lake area along Highway 20 at or near the towns of Newhalem, Marblemount, Rockport and Concrete, private resorts or campgrounds, including a KOA near Concrete, offer overnight facilities.

There are two Mt. Baker National Forest campgrounds up the Cascade River on Forest Road No. 3528, out of Marblemount. The first is Marble Creek with 28 well-spaced sites for tents or small trailers (about 22-footers) and vault toilets. Mineral Park farther up the road, has 22 sites and four vault toilets.

In spite of the row of today's vehicles, the remodeled old-time buildings in Winthrop promise the imminent arrival of a stage coach, ladies in belled skirts and grimy cowhands. At the eastern edge of the park, Winthrop is a popular stop.

Both are located on streams for water amid a rain forest setting due to the abundant moisture deposited west of the mountains.

Going west about 12 miles farther, you will come to the Baker River Ranger Station. Here you can obtain information about the eight auto-access campgrounds about 18 to 23 miles up the Grandy Creek road. All are located on or near Baker Lake. Campsites number from two to 27, but only five campgrounds have trailer sites. Horseshoe Cove has modern facilities; the others all have pit or vault toilets. There are several boat launching facilities on Baker Lake.

Other attractions in this area include Dillard Point Lookout for a view of the surrounding mountains from an elevation of 2,500 feet, Shadow of the Sentinels Nature Trail, Rainbow Falls, Baker Hot Springs and the Upper Baker salmon rearing ponds. On a clear day, wisps of steam may be seen coming from Mt. Baker. If you want to rough it, ask about the undeveloped road-access campsites in the Baker River District. These are primitive areas with few or no facilities.

If hiking and backpacking interests you, this entire area is interlaced with trails in the national park, all the surrounding national forests, recreation areas and the wilderness areas. There are too many trails to go into detail here. You should write for information and determine which kind of trails interest you. Some are relatively short and easy; others may be quite difficult for those not in shape for rough terrain. Many trails are restricted to hikers only; the use of horses is permitted on others, and a few national forest trails are even open to motorcycles. You will want to avoid these. Due to the popularity of some trails and the limits set for traffic

on them, a permit may be required. It would be wise to write in advance.

The Pasayten Wilderness offers over 500 miles of trails, including 27 miles of the Pacific Crest Trail, through alpine meadows amid the towering granite peaks and glacier-fed streams. Horses are permitted, but motorized vehicles are not. This area is administered by the Okanogan National Forest.

Glacier Peak Wilderness offers much the same experience and beauty including 98.7 miles of the Pacific Crest Trail. The western portion including Glacier Peak itself is administered by the Mt. Baker N. F. The eastern portion is administered by the Wenatchee N. F. Commercial packers and outfitters are available in both wilderness areas.

Many of you will want to try the fishing in the streams or lakes. The Skagit and Sauk Rivers are noted for steelhead fishing. Most lakes provide good fishing, including rainbow, Dolly Varden, silvers, cutthroat, eastern brook, Mackinaw, whitefish and Kokanee. The rivers and streams, in addition to some of the above, offer five kinds of Pacific salmon and sea-run cutthroat. The Washington State Game Department stocks many of the high lakes. The Puget Power and Light Company stocks Baker Lake with rainbow. A Washington State fishing license is required everywhere.

When snow closes the highway and winter takes over, you can avail yourself of the area's potential for ski-touring, downhill skiing, snowshoeing and snowmobiling. A ski lift is located near Twisp in the Okanogan N. F., and four lifts are at Mt. Baker N. F. You will have to make local inquiry for location of touring trails for skiing, snowshoeing and snowmobiling. Generally,

The view from Washington Pass Overlook shows not only the great beauty of the landscape but also the easy grade of the road rising from the valley.

snowmobiling is restricted to snow-closed roads in the national forests and the national recreational areas. None is permitted in the park itself.

For the most enjoyment from your trip, plan for any kind of weather. Summer temperatures may climb into the 90s on the hottest days or produce goose pimples on chilly nights. East of the mountains you will encounter drier weather. On the west side, count on rain. Precipitation ranges from 65 inches annually at Concrete to over 200 inches at higher elevations. By April 1, the snow is usually gone below 2,500-foot elevations. By July 1, it usually recedes to about the 4,000-foot level. Warm clothing, rain gear and emergency survival equipment should be included in your campgear.

We have been able to provide only a teaser to acquaint you with the North Cascades National Park and its surrounding area. Any camper will enjoy exploring this silver and green area for himself.

Following is a list of places to write for further information. Be specific as to what information you need. When you get there, stop in at any of the national park or forest ranger stations and get details firsthand. You'll find them all most helpful. There is a small charge for some maps.

North Cascades National Park
Skagit District Office
Marblemount, WA 98267

Winthrop District Ranger
Okanogen National Forest
Winthrop, WA 98862

Forest Supervisor
Wenatchee National Forest
P.O. Box 811
Wenatchee, WA 98801

Forest Supervisor
Snoqualmie National Forest
919 2nd Ave.
Seattle, WA 98104

Baker River District Ranger
Mt. Baker National Forest
Concrete, WA 98237

State Parks & Recreation Commission
7150 Cleanwater Lane KY-11
Olympia, WA 98504

Seattle City Light
1015 Third Ave.
Seattle, WA 98104

You can also write to the Chamber of Commerces of the following cities:

Winthrop, WA 98862
Newhalem, WA 98267
Marblemount, WA 98267
Rockport, WA 98267
Concrete, WA 98237

Camping This Winter?

Here's How to Really Have Warm Feet and Stay Warm All Over

Bama Sokkets are often the magic ingredient for keeping feet warm and dry. They are layered to bring moisture from the feet to the outer layer. Rubber pacs like these prevent water from entering from the outside, but also preclude evaporation from the inside. The Sokkets are the solution.

by ERWIN A. BAUER

AS STRANGE as it may seem, one of the best ways to keep yourself and your feet warm in winter is to wear a warm hat. Cold feet are more than just uncomfortable, they are a sure sign that you are losing too much body heat too fast. Although you may be otherwise adequately dressed, trying to keep feet warm while hatless is like trying to heat up your camp with the door flaps and windows open. Your feet will get cold even before your face. So cover up that part of your body where the most heat always escapes.

But please read on because the matter of keeping feet warm in cold weather is a little more complicated than that. You must maintain body heat by eating enough nutritious food, by muscular exercise, or by some combination of the two. Of course you must also insulate your feet against the cold. And as much as possible, you must keep your feet dry, which means wearing proper socks and shoes.

Let's consider socks first. Socks provide both a cushion and insulation for your feet and lower legs.

They also wick off or absorb sweat. Your foot comfort and warmth depend entirely on how well a pair of socks—or more than one pair—does these three jobs for you.

It is important to have a good pair of thick, fairly soft socks next to your skin for a comfortable "feel." If the day is warm and you are constantly active, that may be all you need. But layering is the factor which provides sufficient warmth when the temperature drops or when you are standing around rather than walking. Then you add an extra or second pair of socks and in some instances maybe a third. Besides the extra insulation, you also have an additional air space between the two to trap heat.

There are a good many theories and formulae for selecting winter socks, but for the typical camper or hunter the best and most unfailing is also the simplest; wear two pairs of woolen socks inside boots large enough to accommodate them. Socks too tightly packed inside any boot will lose insulation value (by

253

being compressed too much), will cut off circulation and perhaps blister your feet. I emphasize woolen socks, which is the best covering you can have on your feet, for several reasons. First, wool gives excellent insulation, the natural crimp and structure of its curly fibers trap air in the sock and form a barrier against cold. There is also a natural springiness—or resilience—in wool which absorbs shock and, incidentally, also protects a foot against abrasion. But no doubt the most important and exclusive advantage of wool is its ability to absorb perspiration. A woolen sock can absorb as much as a third of its own weight in moisture—perspiration—before feeling clammy or damp on your foot. Synthetic fibers, by comparison, have much lower absorption and feel wet on the foot much sooner. And the wetter the foot, the colder it is bound to be.

Of course two pairs of woolen socks must fit comfortably and smoothly over each other without wrinkles or folds. Most wrinkling can be avoided by pulling the socks on carefully, smoothing them out before slipping into boots. If you feel socks bunched up inside your boots, take them off and start all over again.

Keep in mind that your feet are certain to sweat constantly, more if you are very active, less if you stand motionless, so moisture is always a consideration. I repeat that high quality woolen socks will absorb more moisture than any other kind without losing insulation. The socks will then wick this perspiration from the foot part of the sock upward into the ankle and above the boot top where it can begin to evaporate.

In many socks nowadays, nylon is blended with wool and as a reinforcement, this has advantages. Nylon improves the fit, reduces wear and makes the socks a little easier to wash. Pure woolen socks are susceptible to shrinking when carelessly laundered but the presence of nylon in a wool blend sock will reduce this shrinkage. But be careful anyway. It is very important to wear clean socks all the time, but emphatically so during cold weather. Dirty woolen socks do not insulate as well as clean ones and absorb less sweat. They also are rougher and less comfortable against cold feet.

Recently tube socks, socks without heels and stretchable to fit several sizes of feet, have suddenly appeared on the market. But they do not fit snugly, have a tendency to bunch up inside boots and should not be

One of these five types of boot will be best for a particular need. The Danner Mountain Trail Boot (far left) is the best all-'round hiking boot for dry trails and also comes in womens' sizes. Second from left is an all leather breathable boot for moderate hiking through brush in dry weather. The light boot in the center is Timberland's insulated, waterproof leather boot which can't be beat for damp, soggy conditions in brush. The rubber pac (second from right) is also insulated and good for walking through shallow water. It is best worn with a Bama Sokket. Far right is L.L. Bean's perennial favorite, combining a waterproof bottom with a breathable leather top. It is good for a variety of situations but has little support for steep climbing.

used during winter if anytime at all.

So-called insulated and/or thermal socks also have become fairly popular. Some of these are ribbed and others feature a heavy terry stitch on the inside to give thickness—padding comfort—and to trap air for insulation. These socks work fairly well and are best of all when worn with one pair of pure woolen socks.

Within the last year or so, another new and very effective low cut "sock" has appeared on the market. Sold as Bama Booties or Bama Sokkets, these are instep-high thick, and fit over a pair of wool socks. They are manufactured of layers of fibers which allow moisture to pass through while wool socks underneath keep feet dry and warm. I have found these Bama Sokkets to be especially effective when a good bit of vigorous walking is necessary.

But being outdoors in late fall and winter doesn't necessarily mean all walking. You may spend a lot of time standing around a cold camp or waiting motionless on a deer stand or duck blind while a cold wind blows. That increases the chances of cold feet because your body is generating less heat and your socks remain compressed inside your boots (between foot and sole) decreasing their insulation value. Circulation in your toes decreases and the cold penetrates upward through the soles of your boots. The best answer here is an insole, or inner sole or boot liner.

An insole is shaped to slide in and fit right on top of the regular sole of your boot. Insoles have been made in a variety of materials from cork to closed-cell foam, but one of the most effective is felt about ¼-inch thick. It resists compression from standing, transfers sweat away from your feet and keeps them warm. Insoles should be used with woolen socks, not instead of them, and it is a good idea to carry spares for frequent changing as the insoles soak up moisture. I do not advise felt insoles when walking long distances.

Recently the Danner Shoe people have come out with their new model #7730 (Pacific Crest) which has a ⅜-inch innersole of carpet padding with a glove leather top which absorbs foot moisture and is removable for speedy drying at the end of the day.

Keeping feet warm depends equally on proper outer footwear—your boots—as on what you wear inside them. And the very narrow choice today, as for a long time in the past, is between leather and rubber. By comparison, leather is porous, allowing your feet to "breathe" and moisture to escape. But the same porosity allows rain and melting snow to penetrate from the outside, eventually resulting in soaked socks and cold feet. Rubber boots will keep the water out, but will also trap sweat inside. No matter which material you choose, you have to make a compromise. So the final choice will depend on where you live, whether you are outdoors in mostly dry or wet conditions. In northern and mid-America your best bet may be to own both leather and rubber boots, or some combination of the

Danner's new Pacific Crest Boot (#7730) is superior for rocky trails since it protects the foot and supports it at the same time. It has a removable 3/8-inch innersole of carpet padding topped with comfortable glove leather.

If, in spite of all precautions, you return to camp with damp, cold feet, the best way to warm them quickly is to put on a pair of clean dry socks and a pair of down booties. These from Outdoor Products (530 So. Main St., Los Angeles, CA 90013) are especially good because they include not only down, but also a layer of 3/8-inch closed cell foam as an innersole and have a non-skid sole and wall of waterproof pack cloth nylon. An elastic band across the instep and around the ankle keep out cold drafts.

two materials in one boot, rubber-bottom, leather-top as in a pac.

For a fairly busy, active day outdoors in a dry environment it is difficult to match a pair of leather hiking boots, or leather bird shooting boots with Vibram soles. With two pairs of woolen socks, these can keep a camper or hunter warm in temperatures to freezing and below, as long as he is also otherwise adequately dressed.

If the ground and ground cover are really, thoroughly

Selecting the proper boot in the right size is the first step toward keeping feet warm and dry.

wet, there is no alternative except a calf-high rubber boot or leather boot which has been impregnated by the manufacturer to be waterproof. There are a good many such fine leather boots on the market today, but we've learned that not all remain waterproof after a lot of hard use. For much mid-winter wear, especially under thawing conditions or with a light snow on the ground, boot pacs just may be ideal down to freezing and below.

Both rubber and leather footwear come "insulated." Usually closed cell foam is sandwiched between outer and inner layers of leather or rubber, but some insulated boots depend on fleece linings or removable felt insoles. Although insulated boots can indeed keep feet warmer in sub-freezing temperatures if the wearer is fairly inactive, they have the disadvantage of being heavier than uninsulated boots. So the very active outdoorsman should try to keep his feet warm with proper heavy woolen socks instead.

It is possible to waterproof for short-time use boots at home or in camp. Applications must be made frequently on completely dry leather boots. As a rule of thumb, chrome-tanned leathers are best treated with silicone or wax waterproofing such as Kiwi Mink Oil or Sno-Seal. Other leathers can be treated with oil or grease compounds such as Kiwi Dubbin or Wet Pruf. If you do not know whether your boots are chrome-tanned or not, check with the manufacturer, on the box or in the store where you bought them.

At the end of every winter day, try to dry both boots and socks in camp, absolutely avoiding the urge to do so quickly by placing them close to a hot stove. Too many valuable boots have been ruined forever that way. Instead, stuff the boots loosely with crumpled dry newspapers or paper towels and place them in a warm, dry spot. Change the stuffing several times. If the camp has electricity, you can suck air out of boots (or blow dry air in) with the nozzle of a vacuum cleaner.

Wring as much water out of wet socks as you can with your hands. If it happens to be dry outside, hang the socks in the open sun. If really very cold, let the wet socks freeze solidly and then beat the ice crystals out by crumpling or cracking the socks together and complete the drying inside. But the best way is to hang them on a line rigged in your camp, well above the stove, not near enough to singe the fibers or cause shrinking.

Having warm feet all winter long is very much a matter of having dry feet. Keep them that way, wear woolen socks and keep a warm hat on your head.

Six Capsule Commandments for Warm Feet in Winter

1. Cover your feet well with thick woolen socks inside comfortable boots. Change to clean, dry socks as often as is practical. Change insoles, too, if you're using them.

2. Wear warm clothing with emphasis on a warm hat and gloves. Cold feet are only the first signal that you are losing body heat somewhere else.

3. Use every means possible to keep dry from head to toes, especially your feet. Regulate your exertion so as not to sweat excessively.

4. Not surprisingly, a healthy body in good physical condition, well rested and on a good nutritious diet goes a long way to keeping feet warm during winter.

5. Avoid smoking and drinking alcohol. The latter increases heat loss by dilating capillaries. Tobacco smoking reduces blood flow to the extremities, especially to the feet. But do drink plenty of water. Inhaling cold dry air dehydrates your body and therefore also restricts circulation to your feet.

6. Do not wear clothing or (especially) footwear which is too tight. Shoes should fit well over whatever layers of socks are underneath. The boots should also be broken in for prolonged cold weather use.